THE BALLPARK SOURCEBOOK: DIAMOND DIAGRAMS

2ND EDITION--REVISED, UPDATED & EXPANDED

BY OSCAR A. PALACIOS

WITH
ERIC ROBIN,
GRANT BLAIR, ETHAN COOPERSON, DAN FORD,
TONY NISTLER & MAT OLKIN

Programming Assistance by Dave Carlson

Edited by Don Zminda

Published by STATS Publishing
A Division of Sports Team Analysis & Tracking Systems, Inc.
8131 Monticello Avenue, Skokie, IL 60076-3300
Second Edition October, 1998

DEDICATED TO MY WIFE, SARAH E. STEWART,
MY DAUGHTER, ELENA SOFÌA PALACIOS,
MY SON, CHRISTOPHER GABRIEL PALACIOS,
AND MY AUNT, NORMA PAGUAGA

May we continue as a family to enjoy, celebrate and create beauty together.

Cover by Michael Parapetti

Cover photo of Jacobs Field by Scott J. Levy

Second Edition: October, 1998

Second Printing: January 2000

Printed in the United States of America

ISBN 1-884064-65-5

CONTENTS

BALLPARKS
BY CITY

FOREWORD

BY BILL JAMES

Sometimes the best books are created from the things you love. The role that Oscar Palacios plays at STATS is more or less that of a Shaman, a wise man. I don't mean that that's his job title or anything--in fact, I don't think I know what his actual duties are. Something to do with customer service in the game department, as best I understand it.

I speak more of his role at the company in a theater-of-life sense, in the sense that Scott Adams intends when he says that there are six basic roles in a business meeting--Master of the Obvious, Droner, etc. If companies were wise enough to actually hire a Shaman, why then of course they would be wise enough that they wouldn't need one. You hire people to bring you programming, management skills, fiduciary expertise and editorial experience. You never think to hire somebody who will bring to the table a powerful, leveling common sense. Oscar Palacios has an ability, faced with the most formidable smokescreen of highly pertinent and hotly contested trivia, to keep his focus on what is genuinely important.

And by simply doing that, in an odd way, he reminds us to care about one another. I don't mean that Oscar is the Leo Buscaglia of STATS, tossing out little pleasantry bouquets whether appropriate or not. He's certainly not; what makes Oscar special is not superficial pleasantry, but a genuine affection for the good things and good people around him.

And that's why this is an appropriate book for Oscar: because ballparks are an element of the game that we love, but we forget to love. We forget to celebrate them. Maybe we need a National Baseball Holiday: Ballparks Day. Ballparks Day will be celebrated every May 11, let us say. Whoever is broadcasting the game that day will be reminded to talk about the old ballpark over on the corner of 7th and Quincy. If he doesn't know anything about the old park, he can have Oscar on as a guest.

We get a lot of questions about the old ballparks. We are happy to cite the references--Green Cathedrals, Total Baseball, etc.--but it has become obvious, from this, that there is a reference book missing, a book that gives the facts about ballparks, but which also embraces them. Nobody could be better to write that book than Oscar Palacios, and we're glad that he stepped forward and made the effort. Hope you enjoy it.

CREDITS

All stadium diagrams and other computer graphics were created by Oscar Palacios, except for the diagram of Crosley Field I, which was created by Dan Ford, and the Rosenblatt Stadium, which was created by Eric Robin.

The statistic of Areas of Fair Territory was created by Oscar Palacios and calculated with the assistance of Jordan Levine, Seth Horwitz and Charles Schoenfeld.

Additional editorial assistance by Sarah E. Stewart.

Additional photos from the private collections of Mat Olkin and Oscar Palacios.

Photos of current major league parks obtained by Grant Blair and Kacey Schueler-Poulos.

Photos of minor league parks obtained by Eric Robin.

Logos of minor league teams obtained by Eric Robin & Seth Horwitz. Thanks to all the minor league teams for allowing us to use their logos. Thanks to the minor leagues for providing their league logos.

Turner Field, "Aerial from RF" by J. Stoll. Courtesy of Dena Hamby of the Atlanta Braves and the Atlanta Braves Baseball Club. Turner Field, "Pitt at Atl Braves" by Kathy Davison Photos. Courtesy of Dena Hamby of the Atlanta Braves and the Atlanta Braves Baseball Club.

Astrodome photo courtesy of Sandy Beck, Houston Astros Media Relations, and the Houston Astros Baseball Club.

Three Rivers Stadium photos, "Inside Stadium," "Inside Stadium '96," "Aerial Photo of Three Rivers Stadium," "Outside Stadium '97," all by David Arrigo. Photos courtesy of Jim Trdinich, Director of Media Relations, and the Pittsburgh Pirates.

Three Rivers Stadium, "Outside Stadium '96" by B. Hubert. Photo courtesy of Jim Trdinich, Director of Media Relations, and the Pittsburgh Pirates.

Anaheim Stadium , "Stadium '89" by V.J. Lovero. Courtesy of the Anaheim Angels.

Anaheim Stadium, "Anahein Stadium," courtesy of the Anaheim Angels.

Fountains of Edison International Field courtesy of Angel pitcher Mike Holtz.

The Ballpark in Arlington, cover photo "The Ballpark in Arlington July 11, 1995" by Glenn Patterson/SkyCam. Photo courtesy of Lydia Martin, Assistant Director, Public Relations, and the Texas Rangers.

The Ballpark in Arlington, "The Ballpark in Arlington '95." Photo courtesy of Lydia Martin, Assistant Director, Public Relations, and the Texas Rangers.

SkyDome photos courtesy of the Toronto Blue Jays.

3Com Park photos courtesy of the San Francisco Giants.

Kauffman Stadium photos courtesy of the Kansas City Royals.

Yankee Stadium photos courtesy of the New York Yankees.

Hubert H, Humphrey Metrodome photos courtesy of the Minnesota Twins.

Olympic Stadium photo courtesy of Peter Loyello, Media Relations Director, and the Montreal Expos.

County Stadium photo courtesy of the Milwaukee Brewers.

Miller Park model photo courtesy of the Milwaukee Brewers.

Bank One Ballpark model photos courtesy of the Arizona Diamondbacks.

Photos of Wrigley Field, Comiskey Park, Minnie Miñoso, Sheridan's statue, Wrigley ivy by Oscar Palacios.

Photos of Fenway Park by Mat Olkin.

Photos of the 1972 Managua earthquake by Noé Palacios U.

Photo of Roberto Clemente Jr: Associated Press FILE

Canal Park photos courtesy of James Carpenter, Manager of Media Relations, and the Akron Aeros.

Albuquerque Sports Stadium photos courtesy of the Albuquerque Dukes.

North AmeriCare Park photo courtesy Matt Herring, Public Relations Assistant, and the Buffalo Bison.

Joseph P. Riley Stadium photos courtesy of Norman LoRusso, Jeffery Gold and the Charleston Riverdogs.

Cooper Stadium photos courtesy of the Columbus Clippers.

Cohen Stadium photos courtesy of RQ Productions, Roger Quiñones, Burke McKinney and the El Paso Diablos.

Sec Taylor Stadium photos courtesy of Karen Sisson and the Iowa Cubs.

AAA All-Star Game photos courtesy of Dick Evans and the Iowa Cubs.

Oldsmobile Park photos courtesy of David Prout and the Lansing Lugnuts.

Zephyr Field photos courtesy of the New Orleans Zephyrs.

Linquist Field photos courtesy of Robert Paul, Director of Media Relations, and the Ogden Raptors.

McCoy Stadium photos courtesy of the Pawtucket Red Sox.

Hadlock Field photos courtesy of John Kameisha, Assistant General Manager, and the Portland Sea Dogs.

Epicenter photos courtesy of the Rancho Cucamonga Quakes.

Frontier Field photos courtesy of Barbara Jean Germano and the Rochester Red Wings.

The Ranch photos courtesy of Lorrie Payne and the San Bernardino Stampede.

Municipal Stadium photos courtesy of Bernard André, David Moudry, Director of Public Relations, and the San Jose Giants.

Lackawanna County Stadium photos courtesy of the Scranton/Wilkes-Barre Red Barons.

Ned Skeldon Stadium photos courtesy of the Toledo Mud Hens.

Old Kent Park photos courtesy of Aerial Impact Photography, Lori Clark, Media Relations & Merchandising Manager, and the West Michigan Whitecaps.

Judy Johnson Field at Daniel S. Frawley Stadium photos courtesy of Bradford L. Glazier, Mark Nesser, Director of Broadcasting & Media Relations and the Wilmington Blue Rocks.

Engel Stadium photos courtesy of the Chattanooga Lookouts.

Jerry Uht Park photos courtesy of Art Becker Photography Kale Beers, Director of Broadcasting and Media Relations and the Erie SeaWolves.

C.O. Brown Stadium photos courtesy of Danielle Disch, Media Relations Director, and the Michigan Battle Cats.

Johnny Rosenblatt Stadium photo courtesy of Mike Mashanic, Director of Media Relations, and the Omaha Royals.

The Diamond's photos courtesy of Todd Fagens and the Richmond Braves.

Soviet satellite photos courtesy of SPIN-2, a SOVINFORM-SPUTNIK and Central Trading Systems Inc. joint venture.

Additional satellite photos courtesy of the United States Geological Survey.

Additional photos courtesy of the Library of Congress.

Other photos from the STATS Photo Library.

For individual photo information, please check the captions on each photo.

Dimensions of Bank One Ballpark provided by the Arizona Diamondback's Bob Crawford.

ACKNOWLEDGEMENTS

The *Diamond Diagrams* project began as a supplement to the Bill James Classic Game computer simulation game. I am an avid player of this game, which requires you to choose a home park for your team. Back in 1993, I began to research the historical ballparks no longer with us. Although there was much written about when ballparks were built, what they were built with and even what their capacity was, I really wished I could see the actual playing fields. *Total Baseball* was the only modern publication that attempted to display historical ballpark diagrams. Unfortunately, several of these diagrams were inaccurate. For example, Parc Jarry in Montreal and Colt Stadium in Houston were shown with rounded fences, when in fact, their outfield walls were comprised of three straight fences. Another issue with *Total Baseball* is that it did not indicate the time period each diagram represents. Ballparks are constantly changing, and not being able to know which version of a ballpark a diagram depicted made their drawings unreliable. An example of why the years are necessary is Braves Field. Please check pp. 17-19 to see how the park changed through the years.

Total Baseball deserves credit for publishing the diagrams of historical parks. However, the latest edition did not include any diagrams at all, so now I'm really happy that STATS has published *The Ballpark Sourcebook: Diamond Diagrams*, so that people like me can visualize the playing fields of these gems and appreciate how much ballparks have changed. Please don't interpret this as a putdown of *Total Baseball*. I find it an honor to be able to build on *Total Baseball*'s diagrams--they were my inspiration.

Another book that greatly changed my perception of ballparks was *Green Cathedrals*. Phillip J. Lowry's work will always remain an essential authority on the subject.

There are three other books that influenced my work heavily: The Sporting News' *Take me out to the Ball Park* by Amadee Wohlschlaeger and Lowell Reidenbaugh; *Diamonds: The Evolution of the Ballpark* by Michael Gershman; and *Ballparks of North America* by Michael Benson.

OK, back to *The Ballpark Sourcebook*. My first ballpark hand-drawn diagram looked like a cave painting, so I had no choice but to learn graphic design. I thought it was terribly important to eliminate any possible miscommunication between researcher and artist. It took me over six months to be able to draw the diagrams accurately. I wanted diagrams that were to scale and could be used as possible research tools. The scale of the diagrams is: one inch equals 60 feet. If you get your hands on an engineer's triangle ruler, use the side that goes up to 72. Each one of those divisions equals one foot in the ballpark diagrams. Please note that some distortion does occur in the printing process.

It is amazing how many people are involved in the production of a book. If you don't mind, I'd like to thank each of them. First, I'd like to thank my family for having played without me while I was writing. I'd like to thank my father, Noé Palacios U., for sending me his collection of old newspapers and personal photos of the Managua earthquake and Roberto Clemente.

I'd like to thank the Evanston Library, the Morton Grove Library, the Northwestern University Library, the Skokie Library, the National Baseball Hall of Fame Library, the Library of Congress and the United States Geological Survey.

I'd like to thank Peterlin & Associates for their support: Donald F. Peterlin, Cyrus Piraka, Drew Sedrel, Brigid A. Hughes, Micha Dillge, Nadja Millaire, Tim Barber, and Lisa Clingan and crew out in Phoenix.

I'd like to thank STATS CEO, John Dewan, and STATS Vice-president of Publications, Don Zminda, for trusting me with this project.

During my research, I wished I could go back and record the past myself. Then I realized that I indeed could do that. Except that my piece of the past was my present. Many historians have done a lousy job recording their present time, and so have hurt future students. In order to do a better job recording the present, I asked for Eric Robin's help in writing a minor league section. Eric, thank you for your contributions. I hope we'll be able to build on your work.

I'd like to thank Mat Olkin for assisting with the editing of this book as well as contributing an essay and photos of Fenway Park. I'd like to extend my warmest thanks to Tony Nistler, who edited this book along with Mat Olkin. I'd like to thank Grant Blair, Dan Ford and Ethan Cooperson for contributing key essays.

I'd like to thank Dave Carlson for providing programming support for this book. Without his work, *Diamond Diagrams* would be a cacophony of unsupported opinions. With his number-crunching, it is a little more scientific.

I'd like to thank future Hall-of-Fame writer Bill James for giving his blessing to the Diamond Diagram project. In addition, I'd like to thank him for having created Bill James Classic Baseball. Without this game, this book would not exist. I'd also like to thank all the Classic Game players. They were the patrons of the first edition of this book.

I'd like to thank the remaining members of the STATS, Inc. team: Doug Abel; Art Ashley; Andrew Bernstein and his magic monkey pen holder; IVR-guru Derek Boyle; my boss, Stephen Byrd, who put up with my writing this book despite the distractions it created to my normal assignments; Jim Callis; the great ringleader of all STATS programmers: Michael Canter; Jim Capuano; Jeff Chernow; Brian Cousins; Sue Dewan; Steve Drago; Marc Elman; Scott Enslen; Drew Faust; Kevin "Can't-Dribble-to-his-Right" Fullam; Mike "Stink!" Hammer; Jim Henzler; Sherlinda Johnson; the leader of our book order operation: Antoinette Kelly; the voice of STATS: Jason Kinsey; "Gambling" Greg Kirkorsky; data collection rookies: Ryan Ellis and Robert Klein; STATS' perennial Employee of the Year: Stefan Kretschmann; Kenneth "Chef" Li; Tracy Lickton; Barton Lilje; Walter "Da Coach" Lis; Jennifer Manicki; Bob Meyerhoff; Chuck Miller; Betty Moy; Jim Musso; Ozzy (A.K.A. Jim Osborne); Mary Owen; Doug Palm; STATS' East Coast presence: Dave Pinto; Michael Parapetti; Dean Peterson and his Boy Wonder Jim Ethington; out in Tucson, Arizona: Pat Quinn; Corey Roberts; John Sasman; out in Colorado: Carol Savier; Jeff Schinski at STATS West; Taasha Schroeder; Matt Senter; Leena Sheth; Allan Spear; Scott Spencer; Nick Stamm; Bill Stephens; Devin Tuffy and Susan Zamechek. Also the phone operator crew of Sean Bush, Christopher Chocol, Seth Horwitz, Jordan Levine, Marc Moeller, Carlos Panizo, Alex Sicner, Todd Skelton, Fern Verceles, Emmet Welch & Mike Wenz. I'd like to thank the dynamic duo of Mike Sarkis and Mike Janosi, as well as their tremendous aide, Mike O'Donnell. Nothing but Mikes in the mailroom. Thank you for the quality work.

A good ballpark and a good person to date are very much alike. They must:

1. Inspire you
2. Energize you
3. Entertain you
4. Provide you with memories
5. Provide you with comfort when your team loses
6. Look attractive to you
7. Let you know when you're home

The 1960s were the dark ages of stadium construction. All the ballparks were built identical, hence their nickname: "cookie-cutter" stadiums. You could be dropped in one of these stadiums and not know the city you're in, failing rule number seven above. The cookie-cutter stadiums failed most of the seven requirements above.

Watching a ball rattle around in the corner while the winning run is about to score can be a magical moment that occurs with much less frequency at ballparks with rounded walls. Seeing Wrigley Field for the first time on a sunny day is an awe-inspiring experience. The noise at the Metrodome can be exhilarating. You have no doubt about what city you're in when you see the Green Monster. You can't help but feel bathed in the beauty of Jacobs Field. As for getting comfort when your team loses, get a date for that one. Back to the ballparks...

The Ballpark Sourcebook: Diamond Diagrams contains some information that may be obvious to weathered baseball fans, but we must not discriminate against any young readers. I will now explain some obvious things. If I insult your intelligence, please pat yourself on the back and move on to the first park.

Ballparks can affect a baseball game as much as any of the players on the field. Generally, more home runs are hit in smaller parks, and fewer home runs in larger parks. Some parks favor hitters tremendously, while others favor pitchers. The single most important factor in how a park will affect games is the size of the playing field. The second most important factor is the ballpark's elevation above sea level. The higher the park, the faster and farther a baseball will travel. The third and fourth most important are the height and shape of the fences. The fifth most important is how weather affects games. The sixth most important is the size of foul territory (pop fouls turn into outs with more frequency in certain parks). The seventh most important is the quality of the playing field (for example, the park's ability to foster bad-hop singles). The eighth most important is the hitting background (you can't spot a ball well with a background of white shirts).

There are five standard dimensions which are commonly used to gauge the size of the park: the two distances from home plate to the foul poles, the distance from home plate to center field, and the distances from home plate to the points halfway between the each foul pole and center field (the alleys). These points are referred to as left-center and right-center, and are 22.5 degrees away from each pole toward center field.

These five measurements, LF (left field), L-C (left-center), CF (center field), R-C (right-center) and RF (right field) alone are not sufficient to gauge the true size of the park. That's why these diagrams were created. On paper, two parks may look identical if you read the following measurements: LF, 325 feet; L-C, 375 feet; CF, 405 feet, R-C, 375 feet; and RF, 325 feet. Yet in reality, they could be as different as the two ballparks below:

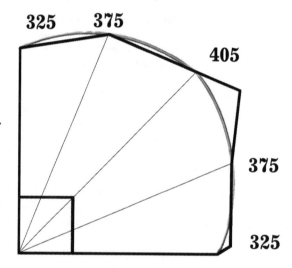

As you can see, ballparks can have identical dimensions in LF, L-C, CF, R-C and RF, yet in reality be very different. That's why the diagrams in *The Ballpark Sourcebook: Diamond Diagrams* are crucial to understanding a park. For this reason, I have also created a new statistic: The Area of Fair Territory (AFT). AFT is not meant to be the defining statistic of a ballpark; instead it is one more tool in understanding ballparks. Next to every diagram you will see a box listing the AFT of the park.

In addition to AFT, each box next to the diagram contains the name of the park and the years that the diagram represents. The years do not mean when the ballpark opened or when it closed. The years tell us what stage of the ballpark is depicted. Below those years is the date the park opened for major league baseball (many ballparks opened for minor league baseball before a major league team used it). Also included are the fence height and the seating capacity, when available.

All the diagrams were drawn to the scale of one inch equals 60 feet. If you own an engineer's triangle ruler, use the side that goes up to 72. On that side, you will see 720 divisions. Each one of those divisions equals one foot.

All the major league articles were written by Oscar Palacios, unless stated otherwise. Eric Robin wrote all the minor league articles, unless stated otherwise. You can better tell who wrote what by the initials at the end of each essay:

 Oscar Palacios

 Eric Robin

 Grant Blair

 Ethan Cooperson

DF Dan Ford

MO Mat Olkin

Thank you very much, and enjoy.

Oscar Palacios
October 14, 1998

60   0   2   4   6   8   10   12   14   16   18   20   22   24   26   28   30   32   34   36   38   40   42

Each one of these tiny lines equals one foot. The scale is 60 feet per inch. Using the scale, the ruler above measures 425 feet

---

"Where are the monuments? Where are the monuments?" people asked in the stands of Yankee Stadium. The champagne flowed. The politicians grinned from ear to ear. But the monuments were no longer allowed to play. The souls of great men were now fenced behind the shadows. The fans of the game had lost access to some of baseball's power.

When Eurocentric art scholars first studied sub-Saharan African art, they were perplexed by how "dirty" it was. In order to study the quality of the works, they cleaned away layers of dried slime and dark sediments. Then the artifacts were polished to a shining finish. The scholars, happy with their restoration, proceeded to study the craftsmanship of the artwork.

Unfortunately, the well-intentioned scholars had no clue how to study this art. To the creators of the idols, it was not the craftsmanship that determined the importance of the piece. What mattered was the power in these idols. Beautiful art pieces were empowered in rituals. The slimy layers were the result of pouring over the artifact the blood of relatives, enemies or powerful animals. Alcohol, feathers, hair and sacred soils were often sprinkled on them as well. The more layers, the more powerful the art. So the dirtiest piece was in fact the most powerful.

When Yankee Stadium was renovated in 1973 and 1974, many fans were sad to see that the monuments of Babe Ruth, Lou Gehrig and Miller Huggins were no longer in play and hidden from the view of most people. The well-intentioned renovators had no clue as to what empowered a baseball park. Yankee Stadium was polished to a shining finish, but it was less powerful. Old-time Yankee manager Casey Stengel once saw a drive get past his center fielder. With his hand slapped against his jaw he waited for the outfielder to pick up the ball. He finally gave up on the stumbling outfielder and started yelling, "Ruth, Gehrig, Huggins, someone throw that *@! ball in here!" A story like this is less likely to happen in a cookie-cutter stadium.

Baseball is empowered by history. Ballparks are not baseball itself. They are like idols representing a god. Our ballparks are covered with one more layer of power every time a game is played. Every time a seat is dented by a home run a park is empowered. This book is about the appreciation of the history that empowers our stadiums. This book is about preventing people from "cleansing" our ballparks and hiding their monuments.

Just like a holy idol is a gate to a powerful being, baseball is a gate to the American Experience. Our written history is filled with the accounts of the rich, powerful and extravagant, while the voices of average Americans often go unheard. Yet, the history of average Americans is more important. Baseball history has been richly kept for over 150 years, and for the most part, baseball history archived the thoughts of average thinkers. One hundred years from today, a classroom may find the racial views of Jackie Robinson or Ty Cobb more enlightening than those of Franklin Roosevelt. They may find the life of Bugs Raymond more educational than the life of Al Capone, and the accounts of John McGraw more informative on the Irish struggle than those of John F. Kennedy.

Art historians study their subject to learn what people thought. Studying baseball history has the same scholarly merit. Anthropologists study pottery shards and even feces to understand their subjects. Baseball history is a richer source of knowledge than either of those subjects.

This book is not about preventing new stadiums from being carved on our lands. It is about how to build better ones. And it's about reminding baseball park builders: The day we will accept a green carpet instead of grass is the day all homes in America have Astroturf on their lawns.

So let's study baseball in the pages that follow by considering the temples of our game: our ballparks. Just as art history classes spend time on brush strokes and techniques, we will discuss the art of throwing a curve ball in Colorado. However, I hope that when you take a few steps back from this book and look at the big picture, a clearer view of our ballparks and America will appear.

When people talk about turf wars in Los Angeles, the last thing that comes to mind is baseball, but a turf war is exactly what has been going on for a long time between the Angels and the Dodgers. When the Dodgers came to Los Angeles in 1958, they marched into town uncontested. They first played in the Memorial Coliseum, which was not the best place for baseball, but the Dodgers got away with it because they were a richly talented team. They did struggle in 1958, finishing 12 games under .500 after having a decent season in 1957, but they rectified matters in 1959 by winning the World Series. Dodger fever was a full-blown epidemic going into the '60s.

In 1961, the Angels stumbled into LA. Winning a lottery a second time is not as exciting as winning it the first time. LA was happy to have a second team, but from their first day in town, the Angels were second bananas to the Dodgers. As an expansion team, the Angels didn't have the Dodgers' talent, but they were good. Their winning percentage for an expansion team has stood as the best since 1961. At the time of this writing, it looks like the expansion class of 1998 will not surpass this mark.

The Angels decided to play their inaugural season in Wrigley Field (a carbon copy of Chicago's Wrigley Field, only smaller). Wrigley Field was a gorgeous stadium, but it was not suited for the major leagues. It was too small (see page 7), with a capacity of 20,457, which the Angels found unacceptable. The Angels had to leave the LA Wrigley after one season.

The Angels shared Dodger Stadium from 1962 to 1965 with the Dodgers. In 1962, the Dodgers won 102 games, but blew their chance to make the postseason in dramatic fashion. The same year, the Angels finished 10 games over .500--a remarkable feat for a second-year team. Nonetheless, the Angels were overshadowed by the Dodgers' 102 wins. From 1963 to 1965, the Angels won 227 games and lost 258 games. In the same period of time, the Dodgers won two World Series. Los Angeles had been carved up. The Dodgers got all breast and the Angels got the wings. In 1966, the Angels moved to their new stadium

Anaheim Stadium--courtesy of the Anaheim Angels

30 miles from Dodger Stadium--as far away as you could get from the Dodgers, and still be considered an LA-area team.

Anaheim Stadium opened in 1966. The crowds flocked to the new park, setting a franchise record of 1,400,321 that would not be surpassed for a decade. Despite a shining new stadium, the Angels still played second fiddle to the Dodgers, who made it to the World Series and drew 2,617,029 in 1966. Through 1997, the Dodgers led the Angels in attendance every single year. The Angels have made significant strides, though, drawing over two million people four times in the '90s. But the Dodgers have always stayed ahead of the Angels, drawing over three million people five times in the '90s. The battle for Los Angeles has not been close; the Dodgers are the undisputed champions. This has soured the relationship between the teams. The last major trade between the teams was March 21, 1976. Since the Angels came into existence, they have made three major trades with the Dodgers. Meanwhile, the Angels have made 145 major trades with other franchises. ESPN reported after the 1998 trade of All-Star catcher Mike Piazza to the Florida Marlins that the Angels thought the Dodgers made the trade to steal media headlines from the front-running Angels.

Perhaps the Angels have fallen behind in this war for LA because of Anaheim Stadium. The "Big A," as the ballpark is often referred to, opened in 1966 with a capacity of 43,204. In 1981, the stadium was completely enclosed, adding outfield seats in order to make room for the Los Angeles Rams. The capacity was increased to 65,158. A new state-of-the-art video scoreboard was added. When the Walt Disney Co. purchased a large stake of the Angels, the first thing the new owners decided to do was get rid of the name "Anaheim Stadium" (the second was change the team logo to match the logo for the Disney remake of the movie "Angels in the Outfield"). The new management changed the name from California Angels to Anaheim

	Dodgers	Angels
1962	2,755,184	1,144,063
1963	2,538,602	821,015
1964	2,228,751	760,439
1965	2,553,577	566,727

From 1962 to 1965, the Angels and the Dodgers shared Dodger Stadium. This is their respective home attendance figures for those years:

Source: The Anaheim Angels 1998 Media Guide and Los Angeles Dodgers 1998 Media Guide.

Angels for the 1997 season. It was the dawn of a new era. The Dodgers could no longer kick the Angels any time they felt like it. The Angels had acquired an awesome partner. Disney is not only one of the most powerful companies in the world, it may be the best marketer ever.

The renovations of Anaheim Stadium began October 1, 1996. On September 15, 1997, the stadium's name was changed to **Edison International Field of Anaheim**, after the energy company agreed to pay $2.5 million per year for 20 years for the name. The money was needed because the total costs of the renovations exceeded $117 million. Much of the renovation took place during the 1997 regular season. The Angels played the 1997 season at Anaheim Stadium, but the park's capacity was cut to 33,851 during the construction.

When the stadium reopened in 1998, it had a capacity of 45,050. The shape of the outfield

"Stadium '89" by J. Lovero

fences was changed, and an 18-foot wall was added in right field. Not only was the appearance of the stadium changed, but so, too, were the playing conditions. The 1998 version of the stadium has to be considered a completely different stadium from the 1996 version. Edison International is not completely enclosed. Rock formations and a green background decorate center field. Taking down the outfield seats allowed fans to view the mountains in the distance. The new ballpark isn't required to accommodate football, since the Rams left Los Angeles long ago. The new ballpark feels like a true baseball venue and hopefully will mark better times for the Angels.

How the Ballpark Affects Baseball Games

It is too early to predict how the renovations will affect scoring, but we can clearly state that before 1998 Anaheim Stadium was a home run stadium. The lack of foul territory down the lines, specifically down the right field line, resulted in far fewer triples than normal. In fact, hits and doubles were also less frequent than normal. In 1997, one of every 6.4 runs allowed by Angel pitchers was scored by a hitter driving himself in with a home run, while on the road, one of every 9.1 runs they allowed were scored by a hitter driving himself in. Because of the lower number of hits, doubles and triples, home runs play a greater offensive role in Anaheim Stadium.

An interesting feature of Anaheim Stadium is the four-foot, nine-inch fence that runs from each of the foul poles to each bullpen. The low height allows fielders to go into the stands and catch would-be homers over the fence. However, fielders enter the stands at their own risk. It is perfectly legal for a fan to take the ball from a fielder in the stands, and the player must return to the field with the ball to record the putout.

Renaming the Angels

Year	Name
1961-1965	Los Angeles Angels
1966-1996	California Angels
1997-	Anaheim Angels

Ballparks of the Angels

1961	L.A. Wrigley
1962-1965	Dodger Stadium
1966-1997	Anaheim Stadium
1998-	Edison International Field

Park Factors

Year	Avg	R	H	2B	3B	HR	L-Avg	R-Avg	L-HR	R-HR
1992	103	109	105	92	84	90	95	108	67	97
1993	101	110	103	90	68	122	98	116	133	116
1994	98	106	101	93	67	130	103	96	127	131
1995	95	96	94	90	64	106	103	88	117	97
1996	97	95	97	89	35	121	96	97	117	124
1997	100	112	101	108	64	136	104	97	139	134

**EDISON INTERNATIONAL FIELD
ANAHEIM ANGELS
(1998)**

Opened for MLB in 1998
Fences:	Left field to right-center: 8 feet
	Right-center to right field: 18 feet
Altitude:	160 feet
Capacity:	45,050
Area of fair territory:	110,000 sq. ft.
Foul territory:	Average

CF Fountains

Chuck Finley pitching with the center field fountains behind him.
--Photo by Mike Holtz, Anaheim Angel pitcher & photography aficionado

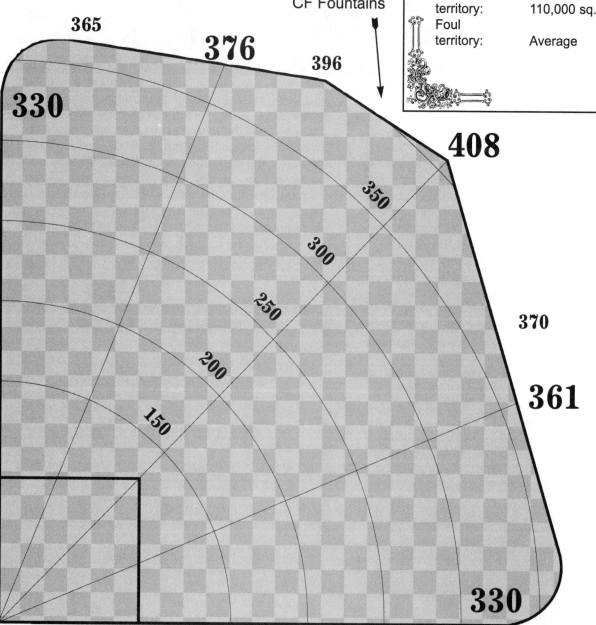

365

376

396

330

408

350

300

250

370

200

361

150

330

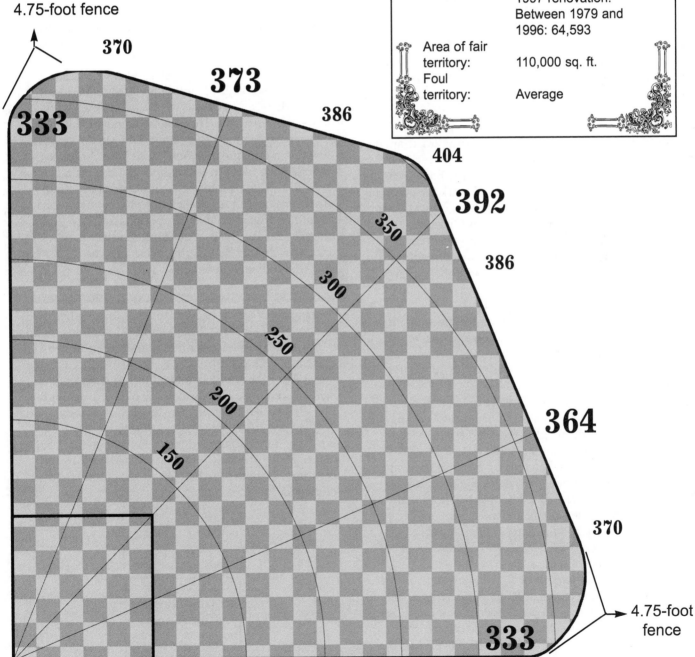

4.75-foot fence

370

373

386

333

404

392

386

364

350

300

250

200

150

370

333

4.75-foot fence

WRIGLEY FIELD (LOS ANGELES)
HOME OF LOS ANGELES ANGELS

Many people think that this ballpark was named after the Wrigley Field in Chicago, but in reality this park was named Wrigley Field one year before the Chicago park changed names from Weeghman Park. Finished in 1925, this park was named after William Wrigley, owner of both the Chicago Cubs and the minor league Los Angeles Angels. In addition to housing the Angels between 1925 to 1957, it was also home to the minor league Hollywood Stars from 1926 to 1936, and in 1938.

In 1957, architects had the idea that they could enclose the park for the Dodgers. But the Dodgers shelved the idea and played in the Coliseum instead. The park didn't have to wait long before becoming a major league venue. In 1961, the American League expansion Los Angeles Angels made the park their home for one year.

Originally, both Wrigleys were identical except that the LA Wrigley was smaller. Knowing the size of the Chicago Wrigley, you'd be correct to assume that the L.A. version was a bandbox. The Angels and their opponents connected for 248 homers in one season. No other park in the majors has ever been the site of so many "quadrangular." The "power" alleys in the L.A. Wrigley were 345 feet from home plate. There were twice as many home runs in this park in 1961 than in the average AL park for that year.

Unlike the Chicago Wrigley, whose capacity was increased by building permanent outfield bleachers, the LA Wrigley had nowhere to go to increase its capacity of 20,457. The Angels found this number unacceptable and moved to Dodger Stadium, sharing it with the Dodgers until Anaheim Stadium was built.

Built at a cost of $9.2 million (in 1997 dollars), L.A. Wrigley may have been the best minor league stadium of all time. It had a gorgeous white facade and was roofed with red tiles. It had a 10-story tower with a charming clock on top. The neighborhood was visible from every seat in the park.

In order to move his Dodgers to Los Angeles, Walter O'Malley had to buy the minor league Los Angeles Angels and their park, Wrigley Field, in 1957. O'Malley was entrenched in negotiations with Los Angeles for the site of Dodger Stadium when the city proposed a swap: the land in Chavez Ravine for Wrigley Field. Both sides threw in a little more to make the trade balanced and shook on it. LA Wrigley changed hands, and the City of Los Angeles demolished the park in 1966. A public park, a recreation center, a mental health center and a senior citizens' center now occupy the site.

The previous tenants of LA Wrigley were one of the best minor league teams of all time. LA Wrigley helped the Angels win 14 Pacific Coast League championships. Minor league hero Steve Bilko won three consecutive home run crowns from 1955 to 1957. The Angels had the

By Dan Ford

Wrigley Field was the site for television's "Home Run Derby," filmed in 1959 and 1960. The show, featuring one-on-one matchups between the top sluggers of the time, has been rerunning on the Classic Sports Network. Basically, the contest entailed batting practice pitchers feeding the contestants a steady diet of hanging curves and (not-so-) fastballs while the hitters launched their assault on the dinger-friendly fences for nine "innings." Any single strike or batted ball that did not clear the outfield wall was considered an out; the hitters were allowed three outs per inning.

One of the earlier contests pitted Mickey Mantle against Ernie Banks. Mantle previously had defeated Willie Mays, and after his first licks, took a seat next to the commentator. The announcer noted something different in Mantle's gear, and asked Mick if he was wearing a golf glove on one hand. "Yeah," replied Mantle off-handedly, "sometimes it gives me a better grip on the bat." Batting gloves were not in regular use in major league baseball until Ken Harrelson, a one-time professional golfer, popularized them in the late 1960s. But Mantle's use of a glove on "Home Run Derby" appears to be one of the first recorded.

right chemistry and power for the park, which helped them go undefeated in 21 games in 1941 (20 wins and one tie). No Angel had a longer tenure with the club than Jigger Statz -- 18 years.

After the Dodgers moved to Los Angeles, the Angels were forced to relocate to Spokane, Washington.

The other minor league tenants, the Hollywood Stars, had left LA Wrigley before the Dodgers came to town. The Stars had moved into a brand new park called Gilmore Field. The new park was located back in Salt Lake City, the town they had left in 1926 to move to Hollywood.

L.A. Wrigley Major League Park Factors		
Year	R	HR
1961	127	199

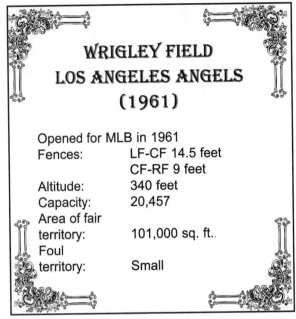

WRIGLEY FIELD
LOS ANGELES ANGELS
(1961)

Opened for MLB in 1961
Fences: LF-CF 14.5 feet
                 CF-RF 9 feet
Altitude: 340 feet
Capacity: 20,457
Area of fair
territory: 101,000 sq. ft..
Foul
territory: Small

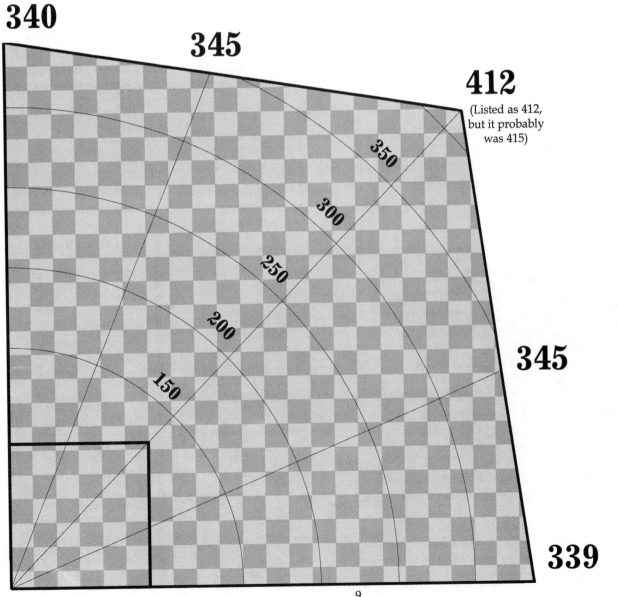

340

345

412

(Listed as 412,
but it probably
was 415)

350

300

250

200

150

345

339

BANK ONE BALLPARK
HOME OF THE ARIZONA DIAMONDBACKS

Bank One Ballpark is being heralded as a break-through in ballpark design. It has a retractable roof, air conditioning and natural grass. The first two are terribly important in the desert climate of Phoenix. The most important contribution of the stadium is demonstrating that natural grass can survive under a retractable roof. The University of California at Riverside developed a new strain of grass that could be kept in the shade for long periods of time especially for this park.

The goal of the stadium's architects was to provide the best baseball ambiance along with modern conveniences. Having natural grass allowed Bank One Ballpark to bring back the dirt corridor between the pitchers' mound and home plate. That corridor is a great reminder of long-gone historical parks. The quirky angles by the foul lines as well as the towering wall in center field are other touches, aiming to cash in on the classic ballpark nostalgia.

The "BOB," as the ballpark is often referred to, also features a swimming pool behind the right field wall. It is not the first ballpark to have a pool; nevertheless, replays of bikini-clad women celebrating after a home run are sure to make the evening sports highlights quite often.

The BOB has been welcomed with open arms by baseball enthusiasts, but in reality, BOB looks like an overgrown basketball arena. Little of Phoenix is visible from the stands of the park. The ballpark makes a great television studio, but its reputation will be tested when San Francisco's new ballpark opens. The hoopla surrounding the BOB is similar to that which greeted the New Comiskey Park. The moment Oriole Park at Camden Yards opened, New Comiskey fell from favor. In the not-so-distant future, the BOB may be one of a half-dozen similar parks. What, if anything, will distinguish BOB from the others? Well, favoring offense would go a long way toward making this park a memorable one.

I designed this x-ray of Bank One Ballpark for the Diamondbacks in the spring of 1998. They used it on their official Web site.

The preliminary park factors show the BOB to be hitter-friendly. Please remember that park factors based on only one year's worth of data can be very deceiving. The park seems to boost batting average and runs. Despite many predictions saying that the park would favor home runs, in 1998 BOB had a home run park factor in the 90s. But we won't know for sure whether BOB is or isn't a home run park for another year or two. The monster wall in center field makes sure there are no cheap homers to dead center. To review the unofficial home run park factors for 1998, please turn to pages 186 and 187.

BOB in a Box

As of 1998, Bank One Ballpark is the only sports facility in the world featuring a retractable roof, air conditioning and a natural turf playing field. Ground was broken on November 16, 1995, for a construction project that cost $354 million and took 28 months to finish. BOB was designed by Ellerbe Becket, with architect Bill Johnson as the design principal.

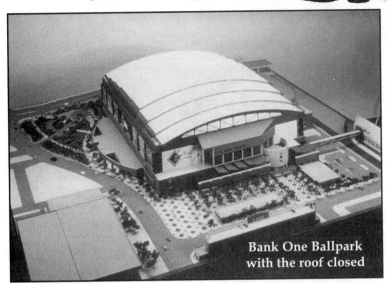

Bank One Ballpark
with the roof closed

BANK ONE BALLPARK
ARIZONA DIAMONDBACKS
(1998)

Opened for MLB in 1998
Fences: LF corner 8'6" to 10'
                      LF 7'6"
                      CF 25 feet
                      RF 7'6"
                      RF corner 8'8" to 9'6"
Altitude: 1,090 feet
Capacity: 48,700
Area of fair
territory: 113,000 sq. ft.
Foul
territory: Below average

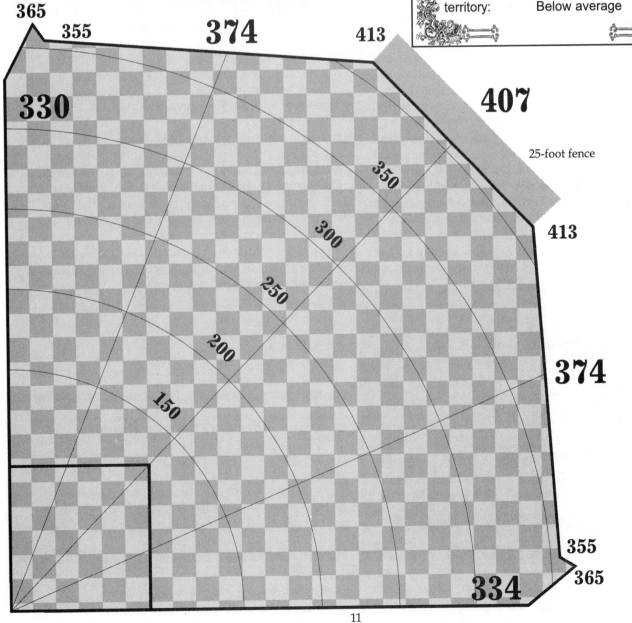

365
355
374
413

330

407

25-foot fence

413

350

300

250

200

374

150

355

334

365

TURNER FIELD
HOME OF THE ATLANTA BRAVES

After seven months of arduous remodeling, Turner Field was converted into a baseball stadium. Ground was broken for the new stadium in 1993. It was first used for the 1996 Summer Olympics, and opened for baseball in April of 1997.

This is the same stadium where Muhammad Ali made a surprising and triumphant appearance to light the Olympic flame, marking the beginning of the games. This is also the field where Michael Johnson set the sprinting world on fire with his gold medal performances. Now that the stadium has been remodeled for baseball, it bears little resemblance to Olympic Stadium, except for the number of ways in which people can spend money at the new park.

In the East and West Pavilions people can buy food or have their likeness stamped onto a baseball card. There is a museum at the park, which features anything from the B&O Railroad cars that used to haul the Braves players in the 1940s, to Hank Aaron's 715th homer bat and ball, to the knee brace Sid Bream wore while sliding home to score the run that clinched the 1992 NLCS pennant.

Make no mistake about it, the park was designed to be a cash cow. The ushers took to enforcing some money-making rules too far in 1997, however. Fans were not allowed to bring food into the park, and the ushers cracked down on violators with the zeal of the guards at the Berlin Wall. They went so far as to confiscate the special candy bars of a diabetic. An embarrassed Braves' owner Ted Turner, after whom the park was named, later apologized and commented that food at the park was overpriced.

Not everything is expensive at Turner Field. They do offer upper deck seats for $1 each. The view is removed

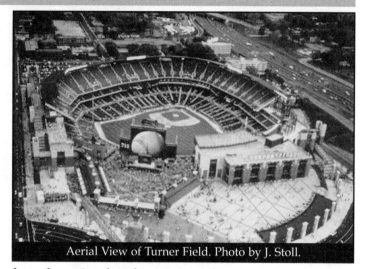

Aerial View of Turner Field. Photo by J. Stoll.

from the action, but the price is right.

Turner Field has generous dimensions for pitchers. Not surprisingly, Chipper Jones told reporters that the stadium should be burned down. Ryan Klesko hit a team-high 24 home runs in 1997, after leading the team the previous year with 34. The Braves slugged .417 at home in 1997 after slugging .460 at the old Launching Pad, Atlanta-Fulton County Stadium, in 1996. Turner Field was a pitchers' park in 1997. Single-season ballpark stats can be deceiving sometimes. For example, the new Comiskey Park seemed to be a much better hitters' park at first, but after a couple more years, it became clear that it is a pitchers' park. Nevertheless, Turner Field looks like it will remain a pitchers' haven due to its generous dimensions. Its pitcher-friendliness has continued in 1998. With a couple more years of similar data, we may safely conclude that Turner Field is indeed a pitchers' park.

Turner Field is a larger park than the previous Braves' field, Atlanta-Fulton County Stadium. Photo by Kathy Davison.

Ballparks of the Braves

1871-1914	South End Grounds, Boston
1915-1953	Braves Field, Boston
1954-1965	County Stadium, Milwaukee
1966-1996	Atlanta-Fulton County Stadium
1997-	Turner Field

Park Factors

Year	Avg	R	H	2B	3B	HR	L-Avg	R-Avg	L-HR	R-HR
1997	100	97	100	90	125	84	100	100	79	88

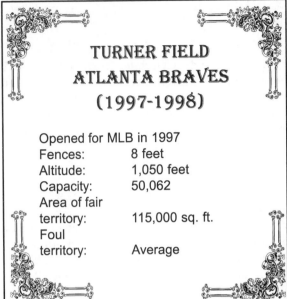

TURNER FIELD
ATLANTA BRAVES
(1997-1998)

Opened for MLB in 1997
Fences: 8 feet
Altitude: 1,050 feet
Capacity: 50,062
Area of fair
territory: 115,000 sq. ft.
Foul
territory: Average

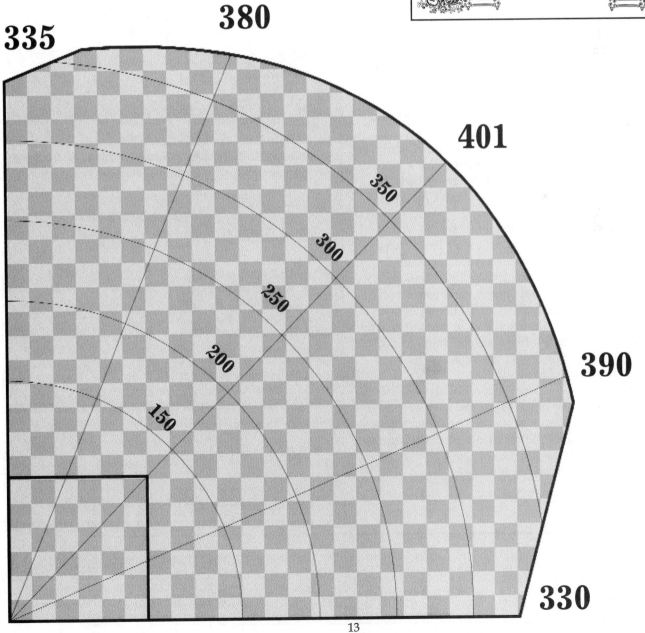

335

380

401

350

300

250

200

150

390

330

ATLANTA-FULTON COUNTY STADIUM
HOME OF THE ATLANTA BRAVES

Before the Colorado Rockies joined the circuit, the Atlanta Braves played their home games at the highest altitude in the majors. The lighter air resulted in many home runs, earning Atlanta-Fulton County Stadium the nickname the "Launching Pad." Lefthanded pull hitters were 25 percent more likely to homer than righthanded pull hitters. Unlike Coors Field, which favors most offensive categories, this park favored only home runs and singles. The number of doubles and triples hit here were below what would be expected at an average park.

Toward the end of its life, fewer errors than normal were being committed at this park--quite an accomplishment for a park that did not have a full-time groundskeeper until 1989. When manager Bobby Cox and General Manager John Schuerholz arrived that year, they went to work to stop the Braves from continuing to be the laughingstock of the league. One of their first steps was to remove the old infield and resod the entire field. The playing conditions futher improved when the Atlanta Falcons, and their grass shredding cleats, moved to the Georgia Dome after their 1991 season.

Even after the Braves gained respectability in the 1990s, the stadium was still an eyesore. As one of the "cookie-cutter," multi-purpose stadiums, Fulton-County Stadium looked more like a smoke detector than a place of recreation. Ultimately, the stadium was demolished, and a parking lot for the new Braves' park, Turner Field, now lies on its site.

Atlanta-Fulton County Stadium had the second-shortest life span of any ballpark built after 1960. It was the first cookie-cutter stadium to go. Atlanta-Fulton County's brief lifespan ran from 1965 to 1997. The only other stadium built in the 1960s that is no longer standing is Arlington Stadium (also built in 1965, but as a minor league stadium). Colt Stadium and Parc Jarry, the last temporary stadiums built in the 1960s, are still standing. Montreal's Parc Jarry now hosts pro tennis matches, and Colt Stadium was moved to Mexico.

The short lifespan of Atlanta-Fulton County Stadium is a testament to the failure of its design. We are currently going through another boom in stadium building, following the slow decade of the 1980s when only two stadiums were built. The current boom probably will mark the end of the "cookie-cutter" stadium design.

Atlanta-Fulton County Stadium, Jan. 27, 1993.
Satellite photo by the United States Geological Survey

Only two parks built after 1960 have been demolished:

Arlington Stadium--Built in 1965
Demolished in 1994
Atlanta-Fulton County Stadium--Built in 1965
Demolished in 1997

3Com Park--Built 1960
R.F.K. Stadium#--Built in 1961
Colt Stadium*#--Built in 1962
Dodger Stadium--Built in 1962
Shea Stadium--Built in 1964
The Astrodome--Built in 1965
Busch Stadium--Built in 1966
Anaheim Stadium$--Built 1966
Oakland-Alameda County Coliseum$--Built in 1966
Qualcomm Park at Jack Murphy Field--Built in 1967
Parc Jarry*#--Upgraded to major league standards in 1969

* Temporary stadiums
# No longer in use in Major League Baseball
$ Renovated extensively

15 ML parks built from 1970 to 1998; none demolished.

Park Factors										
Year	Avg	R	H	2B	3B	HR	L-Avg	R-Avg	L-HR	R-HR
1992	103	102	101	97	57	109	104	103	116	103
1993	102	98	103	104	84	92	109	97	124	69
1994	101	93	100	90	91	92	98	103	87	95
1995	102	109	102	99	76	140	105	100	174	115
1996	100	107	100	95	119	119	101	99	101	106

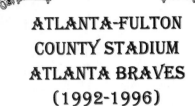
330   **385**

402

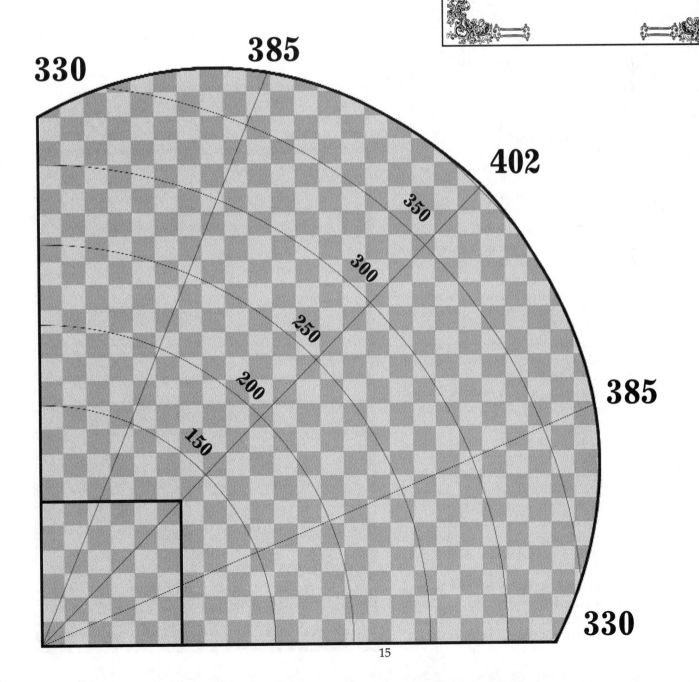

350

300

250

200

150

385

330

BRAVES FIELD
HOME OF THE BOSTON BRAVES

"Cavernous" is a fairly accurate description of Braves Field. When the stadium was being converted from a golf course into a baseball field, 12 horses and mules were buried alive during a cave-in. Legend has it that the workers were unable to rescue them and left the animals buried underneath what later became third base. During one game, the area settled, sinking about eight inches in the shortstop area. Braves shortstop Rabbit Maranville freaked out over the incident and did not want to return to the field.

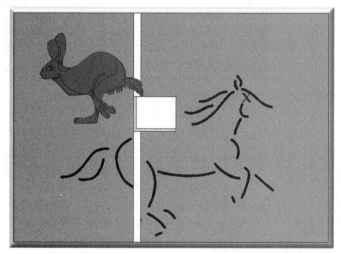

The early Braves Field was far different from the bandbox the Braves later played in before they moved to Milwaukee. For example, in 1916 the distance just to the right of center field was 550 feet, compared to 390 feet from 1949 to 1952. The original Braves Field dimensions all but eliminated conventional home runs; not a single ball cleared the fences until 1925. There were 187 homers in its first 10 years, but they were all of the inside-the-park variety. In 1923, the opposition legged out 27 homers against the Braves. By that time, the inside-the-park homer was becoming much less frequent, at least in other ballparks. In the 1920s, Braves Field was the only park where those types of homers were being hit with regularity.

Please note that as the size of the playing field increases, the number of runs scored there doesn't necessarily drop. For example, there's really no difference between a center field that is 600 feet deep and one that is 700 feet deep. While it's true that an increase in the size of the field usually will reduce runs, enlarging the size of the field beyond a certain point actually may begin to increase the number of runs scored. Balls that would be stopped as doubles by a fence would become triples or homers because they would just keep on rolling. In order to prevent these hits from rolling all the way out to the Charles River, outfielders in Braves Field had to play a little deeper, and more singles fell between them. The 1916-1920

Braves Field did favor pitchers, but only slightly. About five percent fewer runs were scored here than at an average park. What the park took away in homers, it gave back in singles, doubles and triples.

The Boston Braves were known for poor marketing and poor attendance. One example of bad customer service was the re-painting of Braves Field in 1946. Fans were allowed into a section that had not fully dried. The team ended up shelling out $6,000 to 5,000 people with cleaning bills.

Despite the paint job and other minor cosmetic changes to the park, fans still did not flock to the games. In 1952, the Braves' attendance was a paltry 281,000. The next season, the Braves became the first team to change cities in half a century. At first, the Milwaukee Braves set attendance records, but once again -- perhaps due to the team's lack of marketing savvy -- the fans stopped coming to see the Braves. So, they moved again to Atlanta, where the story repeated itself -- until Ted Turner bought the team.

Home cities and names of the Braves:

The first professional team (independent):
Cincinnati Red Stockings, 1869-1870
National Association:
Boston Red Stockings, 1871-1875
National League:
Boston Red Stockings, 1876 - (circa) 1888
Boston Beaneaters, (circa) 1889 - (circa) 1906
Boston Braves, (circa) 1907-1953

Milwaukee Braves, 1954-1965

Atlanta Braves, 1966

The Cincinnati Red Stockings of 1869 were the first openly professional baseball team, as well as the ancestors of the Braves.

Braves Field Park Factors		
Year	R	HR
1916	85	31
1917	87	63
1918	88	48
1919	100	65
1920	97	38

BRAVES FIELD
BOSTON BRAVES
(1916-1920)

Opened for MLB in 1915
Fences: 10 feet
Altitude: 21 feet
Capacity: 40,000
Area of fair
territory: 128,000 sq. ft.
Foul
territory: Large

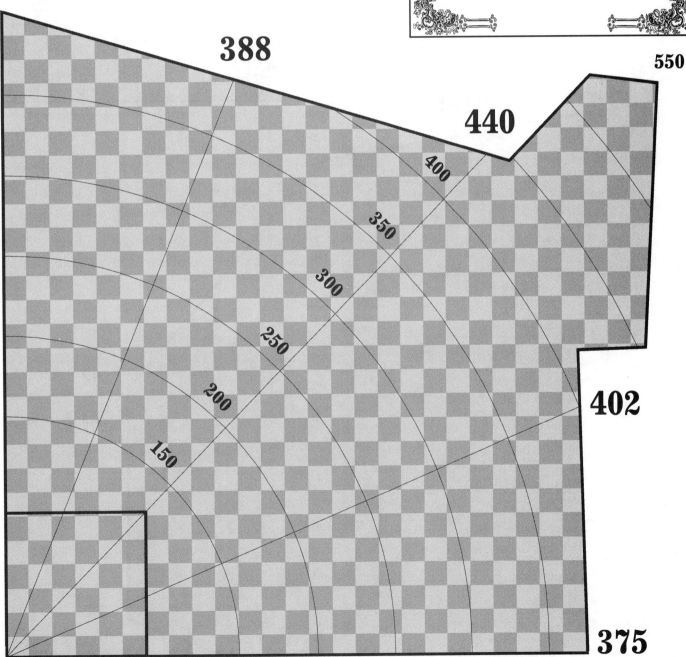

402

388

550

440

400

350

300

250

200

150

402

375

Braves Field Park Factors		
Year	R	HR
1931	97	67
1932	81	61
1933	86	99

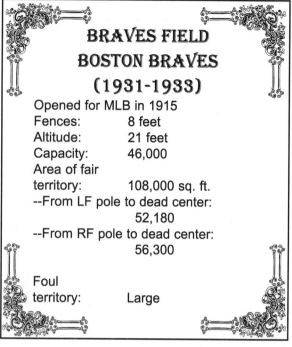

BRAVES FIELD
BOSTON BRAVES
(1931-1933)

Opened for MLB in 1915
Fences: 8 feet
Altitude: 21 feet
Capacity: 46,000
Area of fair
territory: 108,000 sq. ft.
--From LF pole to dead center:
                 52,180
--From RF pole to dead center:
                 56,300

Foul
territory: Large

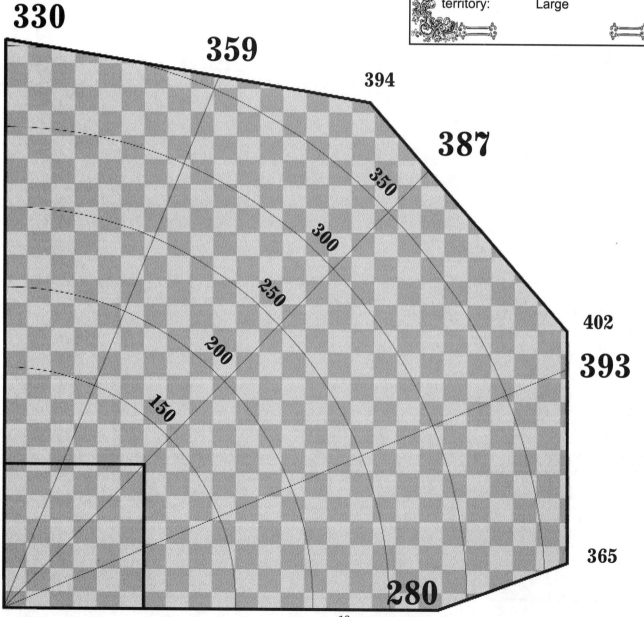

Braves Field Park Factors		
Year	R	HR
1949	89	60
1950	72	60
1951	96	74
1952	89	75

BRAVES FIELD
BOSTON BRAVES
(1949-1952)

Opened for MLB in 1915

Fences:	LF to R-C: 20 feet
	R-C to RF: 10 feet
Altitude:	21 feet
Capacity:	37,106
Area of fair territory:	103,000 sq. ft.
Foul territory:	Large

337 **365**

390

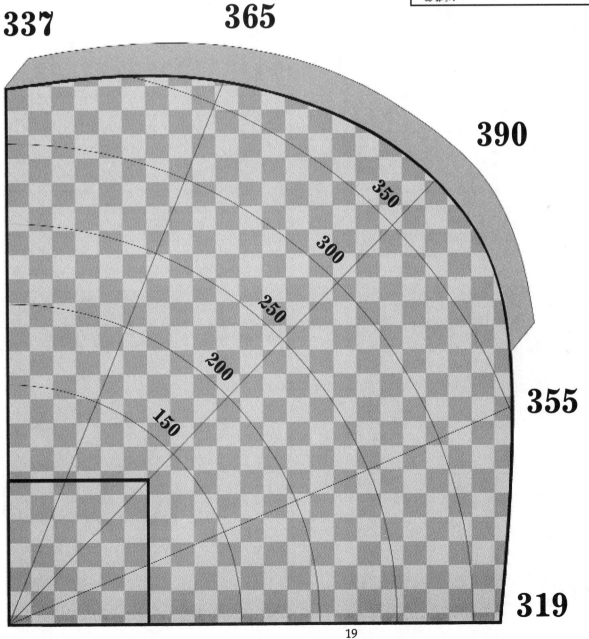

350

300

250

200

150

355

319

SOUTH END GROUNDS
HOME OF THE BOSTON BEANEATERS

The first South End Grounds looked more like a jail than a place of recreation. The baseball grounds were enclosed by a splintering wooden fence topped with hundreds of yards of spun barbed wire. In 1888, the park's concentration camp appearance was replaced with the facade of a theater. The park was given a semicircular double-decked grandstand reminiscent of Shakespeare's triple-decked Globe Theater. The park had several skyscraping spires, which helped the wandering fans find the park from a distance.

On May 15, 1894, the wooden palace burned to the ground, along with 170 buildings in Boston's South End. Because the park was underinsured, the owners rebuilt only as much as they could afford to. A single-deck grandstand replaced the double-decked beauty. The capacity of the park was slashed significantly.

The third version of the South End Grounds was a hitters' haven compared to its contemporary parks. The short distances down the lines rewarded sluggers with a good touch. Batters were twice as likely to hit homers in South End Grounds than in other parks of its time. The vast alleys rewarded hitters who could run. Runs piled up in a hurry. Right field rose slightly away from the the infield, tormenting right fielders and aiding offenses. The center fielders' defensive burden was greater than normal because the outfield mainly was one large center field.

A.G. Spalding

The double-decked South End Grounds was an attraction all its own, unlike the home team, which finished 30.5 games back in 1886. However, before the 1887 season, team officials acquired versatile Mike "King" Kelly from the Chicago Cubs. Worried about Kelly's hard-drinking, hard-living style, A.G. Spalding and Cap Anson sold Kelly to Boston for $10,000. Kelly's impact was felt immediately, as the lowly Beaneaters came within a game of the pennant in 1889. However, the untamable Kelly bolted the next season to join the Players League. Kelly returned to Boston for the 1891 season, but his better days were behind him; he faded from baseball by 1893. It was another great player who put Boston over the top: Hugh Duffy.

Cap Anson

In 1894, Duffy sizzled in the new South End Grounds, winning the Triple Crown with 18 homers, 145 runs batted in and an all-time high .440 batting average. Boston scored 1,220 runs that season, a record that still stands, and slammed 103 homers -- the last team with more than 100 homers until 1920. With Duffy, Boston won pennants in 1892, 1893, 1897 and 1898. For the last two pennants, Duffy was joined by Billy Hamilton and Jimmy Collins. Boston did not win another pennant until 1914, their last year at South End Grounds, and by then they were known as the Boston Braves.

King Kelly, Boston, 1887-89, 1891, 1892

Hugh Duffy

South End Grounds
Park Factors

Year	R	HR
1895	103	392
1896	117	197
1897	109	163
1898	104	272
1899	107	334
1900	148	326
1901	117	144

SOUTH END GROUNDS III
BOSTON BEANEATERS
(1895-1901)

Opened for MLB in 1894

Fences:	6 feet, except in RF: 20 feet
Altitude:	21 feet
Capacity:	5,800
Area of fair territory:	129,000 sq. ft.
Foul territory:	Large

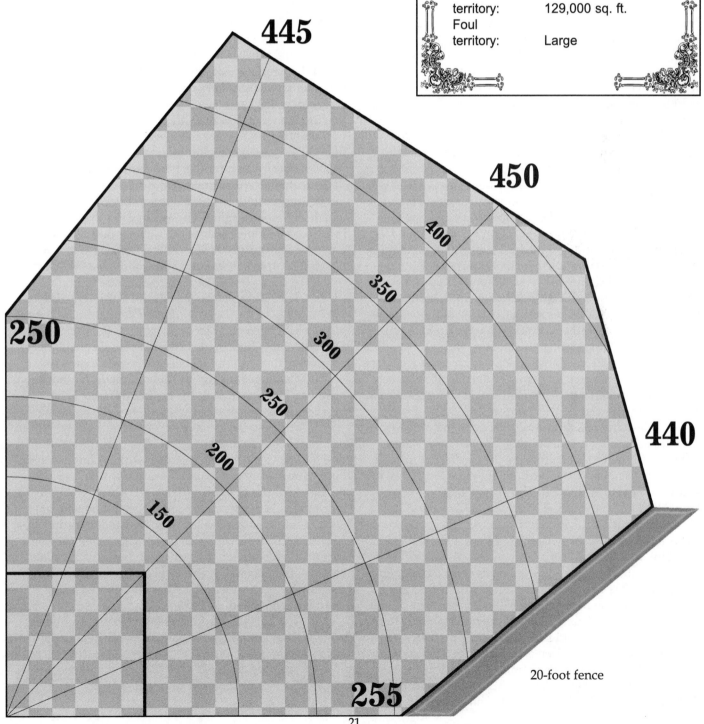

445

450

400

350

250

300

250

200

440

150

20-foot fence

255

ORIOLE PARK AT CAMDEN YARDS
HOME OF THE BALTIMORE ORIOLES

Oriole Park at Camden Yards marked the return of the classic ballpark design. The cookie-cutter stadiums of the '60s were the result of local governments playing major roles in ballpark construction. The local governments wanted to maximize their dollars, so they built multi-purpose stadiums, which could be used for both baseball and football. For a long time, ballparks have been shared by football and baseball teams, and football often had gotten the short end of the stick. The most obvious problem was the infield dirt. Capacity was a problem because football teams host nine to 12 games (including exhibitions) each season while baseball provides 81 or more games. In Chicago's Wrigley Field there was no room for the end zones, so the teams had to extend the field by covering the dugout steps with plywood. The corner of the end zone felt like a boxing ring. As professional football became more powerful, the league demanded more of its stadiums. The politicians aimed to please NFL owners as well as the baseball owners.

The first multi-purpose cookie-cutter stadium was RFK Stadium in Washington. It was hailed as a work of genius. The stands could be reshaped to accommodate either football or baseball. RFK Stadium was quickly followed by the Astrodome, Atlanta-Fulton County Stadium, Busch Stadium, Oakland-Alameda County Coliseum, Cinergy Field and Three Rivers Stadium. Except for Busch Stadium in St. Louis, little effort was spent to beautify the facade of the cookie-cutter stadiums. Most of them are like chickens without feathers. When you walk up to them, you see the walking ramps, something which was kept out of view in the classical parks. Their outside beauty was the equivalent of a concrete highway bridge. Football games demanded greater capacity, so the cookie-cutter stadiums became large bowls.

Kauffman Stadium was the beginning of the antithesis. Kauffman was built for baseball only. Kansas City still wanted to accommodate the Chiefs, but instead of making a cookie-cutter stadium, they constructed two stadiums next to each other. The second step on the path was Pilot Field (now called North AmeriCare Park) in downtown Buffalo, a city which was trying to build a downtown identity. New Comiskey Park, like Pilot Field, was built in the middle of a large metropolis instead of a removed suburb. These three ballfields were on the right path, but it was Oriole Park at Camden Yards that really brought all the elements together.

Camden Yards is not only downtown, but it recreates the facade of the old parks, enclosing the stairways with beautiful wrought iron and brick. The field was built asymmetrically, a key element missing from Royals Stadium, Pilot Field and New Comiskey Park. The city of Baltimore is clearly visible from the stands. In New Comiskey, the view of the surrounding ghetto is blocked by huge advertising panels. New Comiskey was received with great cheers at first, but after Camden Yards, it has fallen from grace. Camden Yards is the measuring stick against which all new parks are being judged.

Prevailing winds blow toward right field, helping lefthanded pull hitters and making this park a prolific home run stadium. The straight outfield walls play tricks on outfielders. Unlike rounded walls, where balls normally bounce back to the outfielders, balls at Camden Yards rebound toward center field.

Orel Hershiser once said in an interview with ESPN that straight walls are less forgiving to pitchers. For example, if the right field fence were rounded, there would be a belly between the 373 mark and the 318 mark, making the fence farther away from home plate than it is now. In other words, the actual size of right field is smaller than the dimensions would indicate.

First opened for the 1992 campaign, Camden Yards features natural grass and is easily accessible by public transportation. The Baltimore & Ohio Warehouse, which sits behind right field, was built in 1898 and closed in 1974. The Orioles restored it to enhance the park's ambiance; now, three of the eight floors house offices for the Orioles' front office staff. The warehouse runs parallel to the right field wall, about 60 feet behind it.

Babe Ruth's father ran Ruth's Cafe from 1906 to 1912 in the area that is now right-center field. The Babe himself was born two blocks away from the park. Coincidentally, Ruth signed his first professional baseball contract with the minor league Baltimore Orioles.

Camden Yards is not without modern innovations, however. The upper deck sits farther from the action because it was constructed without view-blocking supports. The upper decks have also been pushed upward in order to accommodate skyboxes. Camden Yards was designed to capitalize on nostalgia without forgetting the bottom line. Most of the park's seats surround the infield because fans prefer to sit closer to the action. (Fans are more likely to pay more for a seat "behind home plate," even if it is 100 rows behind home, than a first-row outfield seat.) The marketing tactic of maximizing the number of infield seats has left the park with few outfield seats. In contrast, the majority of the seats in Tiger Stadium are in the outfield -- a feature which has contributed to the demise of Tiger Stadium.

The fans have applauded Camden Yards' design, though. The park led the America League in attendance in 1995, '96 and '97.

From the left field pole to dead center, the AFT is 54,050. From dead center to the right field pole, the AFT is 52,570.

Park Factors

Year	Avg	R	H	2B	3B	HR	L-Avg	R-Avg	L-HR	R-HR
1992	95	98	95	85	103	113	94	95	151	99
1993	104	111	106	99	84	116	110	101	83	134
1994	103	113	102	86	68	121	106	100	146	110
1995	103	103	102	104	53	118	108	98	109	126
1996	96	89	94	82	93	97	95	97	97	96
1997	98	99	96	76	39	121	97	98	110	132

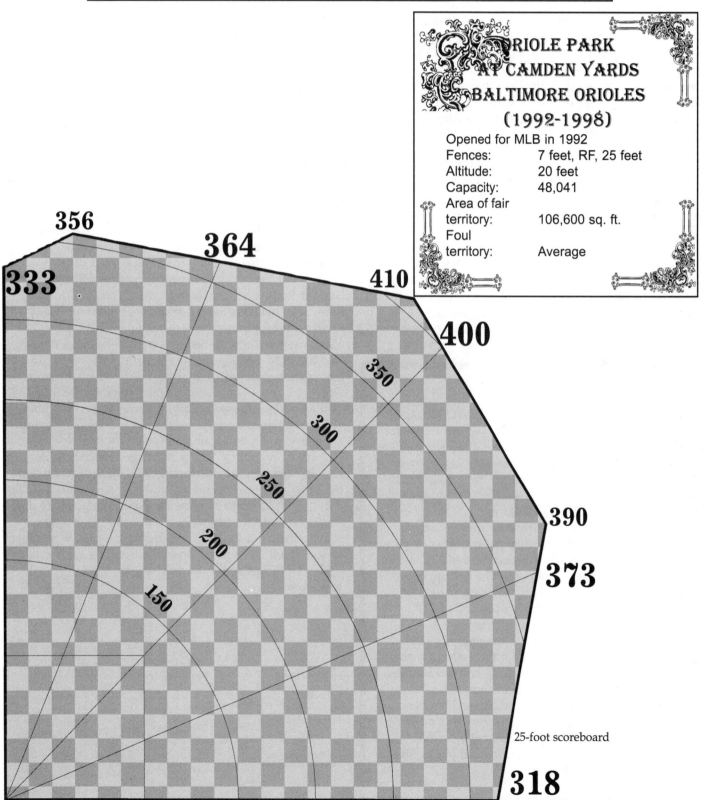

ORIOLE PARK
AT CAMDEN YARDS
BALTIMORE ORIOLES
(1992-1998)

Opened for MLB in 1992
Fences: 7 feet, RF, 25 feet
Altitude: 20 feet
Capacity: 48,041
Area of fair
territory: 106,600 sq. ft.
Foul
territory: Average

356
364
333
410
400
350
300
250
390
200
373
150
25-foot scoreboard
318

Memorial Stadium opened for baseball in 1954 when the St. Louis Browns left St. Louis to become the Baltimore Orioles. The stadium's reconstruction wasn't finished when the first game was played. The outfield lights had not been installed. Memorial Stadium was originally built for football in 1922. Basically, it began as a bowl before a baseball field was hammered into it. The result was short distances down the lines, but deep alleys as the outfield fences dropped back toward center field. This made the short distances down the lines deceiving because most of the outfield was very deep. Also, a hard-hit ball down the line would hit the curving wall and bounce toward center field. This allowed outfielders to bunch up toward center field and pinch off the gaps. With a deep outfield and large foul territory, Memorial Stadium was one of the American League's best pitchers' parks of its era.

The foul territory, following the shape of the bowl, increased as one moved from home plate toward first or third base. The seats between home plate and those bases were quite far away from the field. Normally, these are some of the best seats in a baseball stadium, but they weren't as good here. The bowl shape and the distance between the fans and the action revealed Memorial Stadium for what it really was: a football stadium at heart.

Despite the shortcomings of the stadium, it made

Boog Powell, Rats in the Tarp & Memorial Stadium

"There were rats in the tarp," Powell said. "When the fans started coming in and spilling popcorn, the rats would come out. But you know what? When it rained and they rolled out the tarp, there'd never be any rats in it."

Elrod Hendricks: "They were in the drain. That's why there were so many stray cats out in the bullpen."

--From *Ballpark: Camden Yards and the Building of the American Dream*, by Peter Richmond

it possible for Baltimore to once again be a major league city. In 1903 the first Baltimore Orioles moved to New York, eventually becoming the Yankees.

For the next half-century, the city of Baltimore lived with the stigma of being a minor league city. They knew they deserved better, and most importantly, they knew they could draw better than other cities could. Bill Veeck owned the St. Louis Browns, and he had a theory that he could make more money with promotions and a losing team than with a winning team and no promotions. One of his famed promotions was batting the 3-foot-7 Eddie Gaedel. However, Veeck's theory wasn't working as well as he hoped because his team was constantly being compared to the St. Louis Cardinals. After considering the attendance numbers, American League officials agreed that St. Louis could not support two ballclubs. They knew the Browns might become profitable in Baltimore, but they didn't want Veeck to increase his power. In fact, they didn't want him in the league at all. In April of 1953, Veeck sold Sportsman's Park to the Cardinals, and in September, he sold the Browns. As soon as the franchise had been sold, AL officials approved its move to Baltimore.

Earl Weaver

From 1968 until 1982, Earl Weaver managed the Baltimore Orioles to glory. He later came back for a couple more seasons, but retired for good after suffering his first losing record as a manager in 1986. Up until that season, he had managed the Orioles for 16 seasons, and they all were winning campaigns, an absolutely remarkable feat. Weaver made use of every player on his rosters, and when he added them all up, his teams were greater than the sum of their parts. Take 1981 as an example. His team scored 429 runs in that strike-shortened season. The Orioles' opponents scored 437. You'd figure they were a game or two under .500. Instead the team won 59 and lost 46. Despite Memorial Stadium hurting offensive production, Weaver believed in making outs only at home plate, meaning waiting for three-run homers and no liberties on the basepaths. It worked for him. You decide whether he was lucky or whether his handling of pitchers was the real reason he was successful. (He let pitchers call their own game.) When you decide whether to imitate him or not, keep in mind, Weaver was a genius and one of the best managers of all time.

Memorial Stadium Park Factors		
Year	R	HR
1962	87	74
1963	84	83
1964	108	97
1965	97	125
1966	100	101
1967	88	87
1968	102	93
1969	102	84

MEMORIAL STADIUM
BALTIMORE ORIOLES
(1963-1969)

Opened for MLB in 1954

Fences:	LF to L-C: 14 feet
	L-C to R-C: 6 feet
	R-C to RF: 14 feet
Altitude:	20 feet
Capacity:	60,000
Area of fair territory:	109,000 sq. ft.
Foul territory:	Average

370

309

410

350

300

250

200

150

370

309

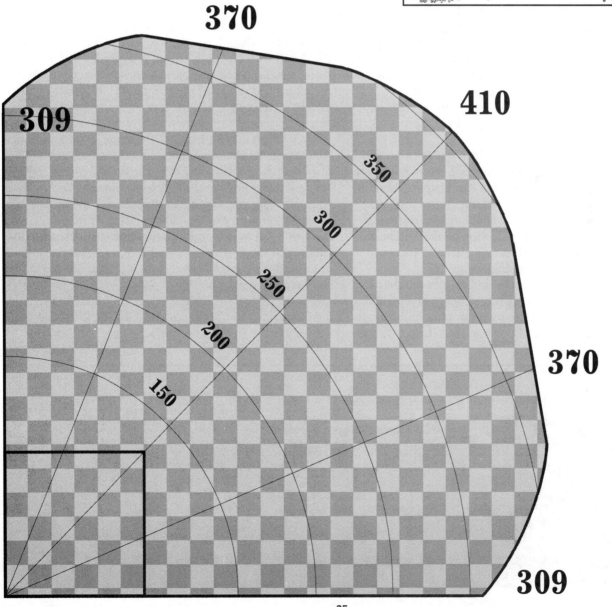

TERRAPIN PARK
HOME OF THE
FEDERAL LEAGUE BALTIMORE TERRAPINS
NEGRO AMERICAN LEAGUE BALTIMORE ELITE GIANTS
INTERNATIONAL LEAGUE BALTIMORE ORIOLES

In 1914, the Federal League shook up baseball by establishing a third major league to rival the National and American leagues. The league began when a group of wealthy businesspeople established the Federal League as a minor league in 1913. In 1914 they made their move, offering major-league money to several star players. Eighty-one big leaguers were enticed to join the new circuit by both higher salaries and the absence of the reserve clause in Federal League contracts. (Players hated the reserve clause because it prevented them from being free agents and getting fair-market salaries.)

The Federal League's life span was a short two years, but it left its mark on baseball. The Federal League renovated old ballparks and constructed new ones such as Wrigley Field in Chicago and Terrapin Park in Baltimore. The Federal League consisted of eight franchises: Baltimore, Brooklyn, Buffalo, Chicago, Kansas City, Pittsburgh, St. Louis, Indianapolis (1914 only) and Newark (1915 only).

The 1914 Terrapins marked the return of MLB to Baltimore. The last year of the National League Baltimore Orioles was 1899. In 1901, the American League placed a new Orioles team in Baltimore, but it left after the 1902 season to become the New York Highlanders (the same team that would be later known as the Yankees). The 1914 Terrapins won 84 games and lost 70. The 1915 team did an about-face, winning 47 games and losing 107.

The National and American Leagues fought back by increasing the salaries of their loyal star players, and blacklisting any players who would jump to the Federal League. The Feds retaliated by taking the NL and AL to court. The judge who presided over the case was Kenesaw Mountain Landis, who would later become baseball's first Commissioner. Landis sat on the case and encouraged the parties to settle out of court.

The case was settled on the following terms: (1) the AL St. Louis Browns franchise was awarded to a Federal League owner; (2) the Chicago Cubs were sold to another Fed owner; and (3) the Federal League's players were sold off to AL and NL franchises.

The owners of the Baltimore Terrapins refused to go along with the deal. They went back to court and pursued their case all the way to the U.S. Supreme Court, where it was dismissed. Justice Oliver Wendell Holmes ruled that the Terrapins had no remedy under Federal Anti-Trust laws because baseball was primarily a sport, not a business, and did not constitute "interstate commerce" in the sense that the law's framers had contemplated.

On the Terrapins' first Opening Day, they drew 30,000 fans, while the minor league Baltimore Orioles saw their attendance drop to 1,500. The arrival of the Terrapins brought hard times to the Orioles. While the Terrapins were drawing crowds in excess of 20,000, the Orioles were struggling with crowds of 200 or less. Unfortunately for the Orioles, the first year of Babe Ruth's pro career coincided with the first year of the FL. The O's had no choice but to sell their most prized commodity to the Boston Red Sox for a fraction of his future value. In 1915, the Orioles moved to Richmond, Virginia, but after the FL collapsed, the Orioles moved back to Baltimore. The Orioles were not only lucky to have the Terrapins go, but they also

Continued on Page 28

The 1921 Baltimore Orioles. Courtesy of the Library of Congress

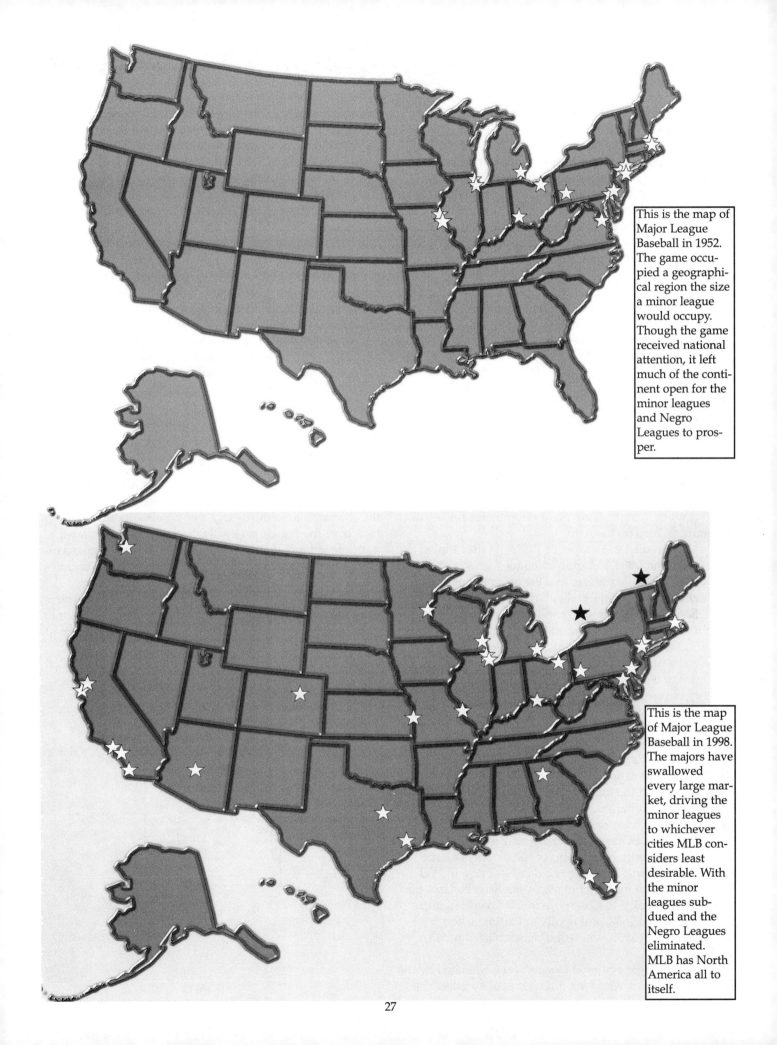

This is the map of Major League Baseball in 1952. The game occupied a geographical region the size a minor league would occupy. Though the game received national attention, it left much of the continent open for the minor leagues and Negro Leagues to prosper.

This is the map of Major League Baseball in 1998. The majors have swallowed every large market, driving the minor leagues to whichever cities MLB considers least desirable. With the minor leagues subdued and the Negro Leagues eliminated. MLB has North America all to itself.

inherited Terrapin Park, a major league venue few minor league teams could afford.

The Baltimore Orioles were led by their owner, Jack Dunn, a former major league ballplayer who now made his living as a one-man front office. Dunn had a tremendous eye for baseball talent. His teams won seven consecutive pennants from 1919 to 1925. Dunn made the rounds through the Baltimore area schools fishing for talent. In one of those schools, Dunn discovered Babe Ruth. Dunn assumed legal guardianship of the youth until the Babe was 21 years old.

Dunn discovered and developed another huge star who would partly make up for the loss of Ruth: Lefty Grove. When Grove pitched, the Orioles could beat any major league team. In 1925, Dunn finally sold Lefty for $100,600 (or about $920,000 in 1997 dollars) to the tightfisted Connie Mack. This is a far cry from what Dunn had been forced to sell Ruth for in 1914: $25,000. Dunn also threw in Ernie Shore to make the deal with Boston. Shore went 19-8 for Boston in 1915 with a 1.64 ERA.

By looking at the impact ex-Orioles had at the major league level, it is obvious that many were ready to play in the majors well before Dunn sold them. These players were desperate to gain major league recognition, but Dunn managed to keep them satisfied in the minors by paying them high wages and arranging for first-class accommodations on the road.

Dunn died in October of 1928, and the Orioles never were the same. The club owed its success to Dunn's eye for talent and to the fact that the International League was not required to subject its players to the major league draft. Major league teams were allowed to draft players from minor league teams for an insignificant fee of $1,000. This draft kept the minor leagues weak, and helped perpetuate the major league's monopoly of baseball. Many minor leagues assented to the draft in exchange for the security of being affiliated with the majors; however, Dunn's team proved that minor league teams were capable of surviving, enduring and thriving on their own if they were led by strong, competent business people.

In 1931, a new National Agreement restored the draft to the International League. Major league teams again plundered the minor league's talent, and few minor league teams ever approached the independence and success the Orioles once enjoyed.

After the Orioles' decline, a new team came to town: the Baltimore Elite Giants of the Negro National League. The Giants first originated in Nashville in 1921. Always in search for better markets, the team began a pilgrimage that took it to Columbus in 1935, Washington, D.C. in 1936 and 1937, and finally to Baltimore and Terrapin Park in 1938, where the Giants played for 13 years.

The Negro National League was dominated by the Homestead Grays, who won nine consecutive titles. The Giants were able to claim the 1939 championship, though, by defeating the Grays in a four-team postseason tournament. Among the Giants' biggest stars were Roy Campanella (1937-1942), Biz Mackey (1938-39) and Henry Kimbro (1938-40, 1942-51).

The Negro National League folded in 1948 and the Giants joined the Negro American League for the 1949 and 1950 seasons. In 1951, with the Negro Leagues in shambles, the Giants returned to Nashville for one final season. Then the team folded.

The period after World War II was devastating to every league except for the majors. Like a global extinction, minor leagues, Negro Leagues and women's leagues folded at an alarming rate. By 1954, the Negro Leagues had ceased to exist. The All-American Girls' Professional Baseball League folded after the 1954 season. Minor league attendance crashed from 42 million in 1939 to less than 10 million in 1963. The number of minor leagues shrunk from 59 to 21.

Television and major league franchise relocation were the major causes of the collapse. In the 1950s, the St. Louis Browns moved to Baltimore and became the latest incarnation of the Orioles; the Braves left Boston for Milwaukee; the Philadelphia A's left for Kansas City; the Giants left for San Francisco; and the Dodgers moved to the country's then-third-largest city. Subsequent expansion took over the remaining available markets. The number of minor leagues had been reduced to 18 by 1973. The majors had extended their monopoly across the midwest to the west coast, at the minors' expense.

However, the minor leagues are currently rising from the ashes. A ballpark construction boom -- which has gone largely unnoticed -- is a clear sign that a second golden age is coming. There are many reasons for the rebirth of the minors: an improving economy, a nostalgic atmosphere, and more accessible and affordable ballparks.

Terrapin Park Federal League Park Factors		
Year	R	HR
1914	98	146
1915	128	298

TERRAPIN PARK
BALTIMORE TERRAPINS
(Federal League)
BALTIMORE ELITE GIANTS
(Negro American League)
(1914-1943)

Opened for MLB in 1944
Fences:	LF to R-C: 12 feet
	R-C: 25 feet
	R-C to RF: 8 to 4 feet
Altitude:	20 feet
Capacity:	16,000
Area of fair territory:	106,000 sq. ft.
Foul territory:	Large

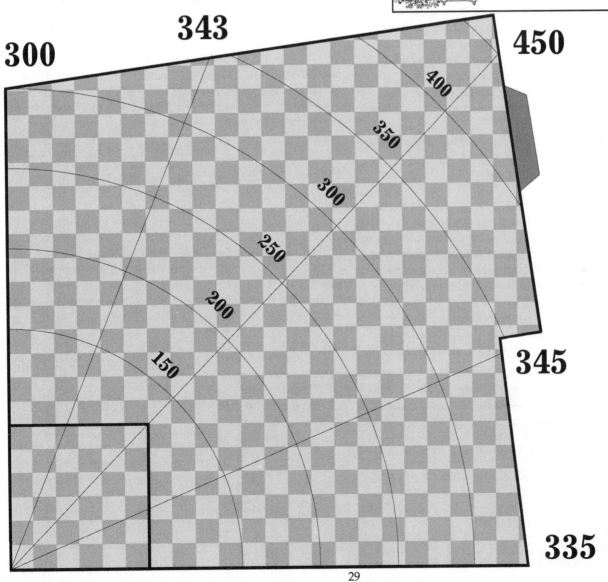

NEW FENWAY PARK
HOME OF THE BOSTON RED SOX

By Mat Olkin

Although it's nothing close to the home run haven it used to be, Fenway Park is still one of the best hitters' parks in the major leagues. The reasons for this are obvious: the foul territory is very small, especially near the foul poles, where it is virtually non-existent; the 17-foot high center field wall provides a good hitting background; and most importantly, all of the action unfolds in the shadow of every hitter's best friend, the "Green Monster."

The Monster, which was likely designed by a hitter but named by a pitcher, is one of the most recognizable features of any ballpark on earth. The 37-foot-high edifice can convert a rather ordinary flyball into a two-base hit or even a home run. By the same token, it can return a hard-hit drive to the left fielder so quickly that a slow or uninspired baserunner can be left with only a single and an expletive. For over 50 years, the left field line was listed at 315 feet, a more-than-generous estimate that was politely regarded as a charming little myth. In 1995, the Red Sox -- without an explanation, or even an announcement -- changed the official measurement to "310," which is seen as a compromise between the original figure and the actual distance.

It's often been assumed that the Wall benefits only righthanded hitters, but that's not necessarily the case. Righthanded hitters seem to gain more in the home run department, but certain types of lefthanded hitters can use the Wall quite effectively to boost their batting average. Among righthanded hitters, the ones who benefit the most are pull hitters who loft the ball, like Joe Carter and Mark McGwire. A hitter with quick wrists like John Valentin or the young Jody Reed can do quite well by sending balls down the left field line. The lefthanded hitters who've gained the most have been the ones who've learned to hit the ball to left field consistently. Fred Lynn was able to do that, and Wade Boggs made himself a Hall-of-Famer by learning to pull in his hands and send liners into left field.

Photo by Mat Olkin

Among the current Red Sox, Troy O'Leary and Reggie Jefferson have become the most proficient at feeding the Monster.

The Wall was constructed in 1933 as part of a massive overhaul of Fenway undertaken by new owner Tom Yawkey. Three years later, a 23-foot-high screen was installed atop the wall. A ladder -- which is in play -- runs to the top of the Wall in left field. At the end of batting practice, a member of the grounds crew climbs the ladder and retrieves baseballs from the net, strolling precariously atop the Monster, high above the field.

An often-overlooked aspect of the Wall is the conflicting set of defensive demands it places on the left fielder. On one hand, it can be tremendously forgiving to a player with little foot speed or poor defensive instincts (Mike Greenwell was saddled with both deficiencies; although he survived for a decade in Fenway's outfield, it was said that National League clubs categorically refused to consider trading for him, apparently convinced that he couldn't cover the turf fields of the Senior Circuit). But on the other hand, the Wall requires a Boston left fielder to learn to play its tricky rebounds. As a rule, the ball caroms away from the left field line, but judging the ball's intended point of return can require some complex calculations. The instant the ball is hit, the left fielder must judge the strength of the drive, as well as how far up the wall the ball is likely to hit. If he is able to do that consistently, he'll be in position to quickly field and return the ball to the infield as often as possible. An adept fielder can throw out overaggressive baserunners and turn many

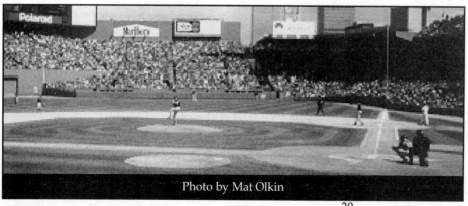
Photo by Mat Olkin

doubles into singles over the course of a season. Carl Yastrzemski was the master at this. Jim Rice became surprisingly proficient at fielding the Monster and played it as well as anyone.

One of the features that used to make the park such a favorite of longball hitters was the summer breeze that blew out from behind the grandstands and into the outfield. The winds were especially prevalent in June, July

Photo by Mat Olkin

and August. In 1982 and 1983, private suites were constructed on the grandstand roof along the left and right field lines, largely cutting off the wind. Since that time, Fenway has a distinctly average home run park. More recently, some Red Sox hitters have blamed the death of the winds on the construction of the "600 Club," a new seating section that was added in 1989. The 600 Club sits directly behind home plate, and its addition necessitated the construction of a new, higher press box. Upon closer scrutiny, it's clear that the new construction did not significantly alter the characteristics of the park. (What's more, the 600 Club theory's biggest adherents tended to be the players who sought to defend their own declining power numbers during the late 1980s.) The park can still be a surprisingly unfriendly place to hit in April and May, when a chill breeze often blows in from the northeast.

An often-overlooked aspect of the park is its enormous right field area, which is one of the biggest in the

majors. The right field line is deceptively short at 302 feet; it immediately drops back to over 380 feet, and the narrow slice of shallow fair territory near the foul pole hardly provides a good target for a lefthanded pull hitter (Ted Williams was one of the few who was able to target it with any success). Fenway may be the one park in the majors where the right fielder's defensive responsibilities eclipse those of the center fielder. The right fielder has more territory to cover, and a strong throwing arm is a necessity. The deepest park of the park lies in right-center field and is known as the "triangle." This is where the 17-foot center field fence meets the bullpen fence, forming a nearly-90-degree angle with its farthest point 420 feet from home plate. A drive that reaches either wall of the triangle on the fly is apt to take several unpredictable caroms before being retrieved, and it's not surprising that most Fenway triples are hit to this part of the park.

The high center field fence provides another advantage to the hitter, forming a good "hitter's eye" for Fenway batsmen. Most pitchers' release points allow the hitter to view a pitch against the wall's solid green background, rather than the sea of multicolored bleacher shirts above the wall. It has been said that a lefthanded pitcher with an overhand motion can reach "over the top" of the wall and into the sea of shirts to camouflage his pitches during the daytime, but it's never been proven that lefthanders enjoy any real advantage there during the day.

It's also been said that lefthanded pitchers can't win in Fenway, but this is another overstatement that isn't supported by history. Most of the Red Sox' pennant-winning clubs have had quality southpaws (Mel Parnell, Bill Lee and Bruce Hurst come to mind), and it's generally true that any pitcher can survive there if he keeps the ball on the ground and isn't afraid to pitch inside.

Fenway has a history of memorable moments as

Photo by Mat Olkin

31

Fenway fits in one quirky Boston city block.
Satellite Photo by SOVINFORMSPUTNIK & Aerial Images, Inc.

A Tale of Two Fenways

Fenway Park is really two ballparks fitted into one. The AFT to the right of center field is one of the largest in the majors. The AFT from the LF pole to dead CF: 44,410 square feet. The AFT from the RF pole to dead CF: 54,120 square feet. Now, the two area numbers above include the infield, but since all infields have the same area, let's eliminate the infield and compare the LF and RF outfields by comparing the areas beyond 300 feet away from home. Then, RF is 207 percent larger than LF.

voluminous as any current park's. One of the most unforgettable spectacles of the last 30 years was the sight of Boston's Carlton Fisk furiously waving his game-winning home run fair-fair-FAIR!!! in the sixth game of the 1975 World Series.

Earlier in the same contest, Dwight Evans' over-the-shoulder catch in the deepest part of right field resulted in a double play and probably saved a home run; any Boston fan over the age of 30 can still replay the magical stretch-twist-and-throw in his or her mind. On a more painful note, Bucky Dent's windblown popup in the 1978 playoff game has come to represent the ill fortune that inevitably strikes the Sox whenever they venture too close to the promised land. For pure entertainment value, Jose Canseco's only career mound appearance in 1993 was a once-in-a-lifetime event. The most recent addition to the highlight film may be Jay Buhner's home run-saving catch in right field, where he caught the ball in midair while diving into the bullpen, only to pop back up over the fence with the ball held triumphantly aloft.

MO

Within Fenway Park is a luxurious section called the 600 Club. The Red Sox want a new ballpark with more luxury suites. These are the rules of the 600 Club:

"NOTE: The 600 Club has an established dress code that is enforced and applicable in all areas of the club, including dining and lounge areas. Jeans of any kind, sweatpants, T-shirts, tank tops, shorts and sneakers are not permitted. "
--From the Boston Red Sox' official Web site.

What can be more anti-baseball than those rules? Yet, in order to create more luxury suites, the Red Sox will tear down Fenway Park. The team's choices are:

One of the best ballparks of all-time
or
**"Theatre-style seats,
Fine dining before the games,
Private entrance to Fenway Park,
Exclusive amenities"**

It seems to me that the Red Sox are in the wrong business. Perhaps they should open a chain of restaurants instead. They are going to tear down a park loved by the masses, so people seeking exclusivity can wine and dine a safe distance away from the masses? And taxpayers are going to shell out millions for the benefit of such few people?

OP

Park Factors										
Year	Avg	R	H	2B	3B	HR	L-Avg	R-Avg	L-HR	R-HR
1992	110	112	113	126	94	89	109	111	80	94
1993	110	120	114	141	103	77	116	106	74	81
1994	106	107	110	104	95	101	106	109	132	83
1995	107	101	108	127	106	78	103	110	59	94
1996	108	113	111	127	115	116	110	107	114	117
1997	100	96	101	118	100	85	107	95	97	77

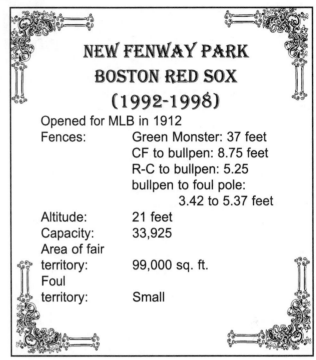

NEW FENWAY PARK
BOSTON RED SOX
(1992-1998)

Opened for MLB in 1912

Fences:	Green Monster: 37 feet
	CF to bullpen: 8.75 feet
	R-C to bullpen: 5.25
	bullpen to foul pole:
	3.42 to 5.37 feet
Altitude:	21 feet
Capacity:	33,925
Area of fair territory:	99,000 sq. ft.
Foul territory:	Small

The Green Monster: 37-Foot Fence

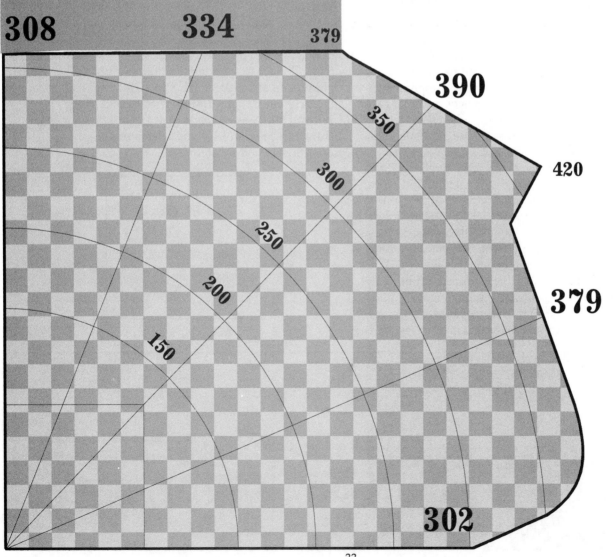

OLD FENWAY PARK
HOME OF THE BOSTON RED SOX

Old Fenway Park didn't look at all like today's Fenway. There was no Green Monster. The two Fenways share the same plot of land and the same name, but the old and new Fenways must be considered different parks. Old Fenway was quirky, too, with a 324-foot left field line and a mammoth 500-foot center field.

The first game at old Fennie was held on April 20, 1912. The formal ceremonies for opening day weren't held until the next month. Former Boston mayor and U.S. Congressman John Francis "Honey Fitz" Kennedy, the grandfather of President John F. Kennedy, threw out the first pitch at Boston's new jewel. Five months later, the second game of the 1912 World Series was played at Fenway Park. The game was called with the score 6-6 after the bottom of the 11th inning because of darkness. Two Giants had been caught stealing on the top of the 11th and the team failed to score. McGraw's Giants won Game Seven easily 11-4. Of course, the series was not over. Because of the tie, there was a Game Eight.

The final game was epic. A beaten man came out the winner. A hero failed because of a teammate. And a man went down in history not for the 2,100 putouts he made in his career, but for muffing a ball that was easier to catch than to drop. The Giants scored first, bringing one run home in the third inning. The Giants nursed that run until the bottom of the seventh inning, when Boston tied the score. Smokey Joe Wood had lost close games in both of his World Series starts despite posting a 34-5 record during the regular season, but he came in to relieve, holding the Giants scoreless in the top of the eighth and ninth. Christy Mathewson, now a weathered veteran, was pitching a complete game when he saw the Giants score a run for him on the top of the 10th. Wood looked poised to lose his third game of the series, but in the bottom of the 10th, baseball magic again acted in its mysterious way. Fred Snodgrass, the Giants center fielder, dropped a routine flyball. Snodgrass almost redeemed himself by making an incredible catch on a sinking line drive, but Mathewson was now laboring. He walked the next batter and up came

Tris Speaker. A miscommunication between Giants first baseman Fred Merkle and catcher Chief Meyers gave Speaker another chance after his foul pop dropped untouched. Spoke responded by driving in the tying run. Mathewson walked the next batter intentionally, but Larry Gardner came through with a flyout to right field to bring home the winning run. The game was over. Mathewson had lost his second game of the series despite a a 1.26 ERA. In the following years, Snodgrass established himself as one of the best fielders in the league, but it was too late to change his eventual epitaph.

The Boston fans went crazy. Fenway, they said, was their good-luck charm. The team proceeded to win three more World Series, thanks in part to the pitching of a young lefty named Babe Ruth. The 1918 championship was the last the Red Sox enjoyed to this day. The team was mismanaged and fell into financial difficulties. Owner Harry Frazee tried to get back into the black by selling Ruth to the New York Yankees. Fenway was left to rot, but it didn't. Instead it caught fire. The park was rebuilt for the 1934 season and in 1936, the Green Monster was erected in left field. Before the fire, Fenway was a pitchers' park and an awful place to for a longball hitter. The old Fens' outfield was a hard place to play, too. Left field had no warning track, but rather a 10-foot rise, named Duffy's Cliff for Duffy Lewis' mastery of it. Duffy's Cliff was leveled in 1934 and later buried under the Green Monster.

Old Fenway Park Park Factors		
Year	R	HR
1921	95	37
1922	93	36
1923	107	45
1924	106	52
1925	95	56

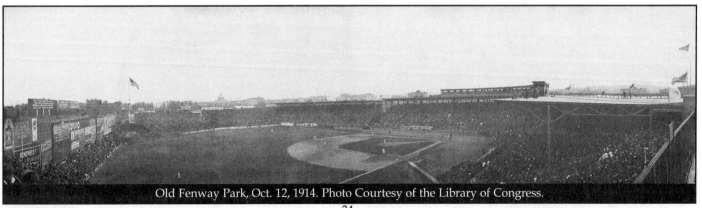

Old Fenway Park, Oct. 12, 1914. Photo Courtesy of the Library of Congress.

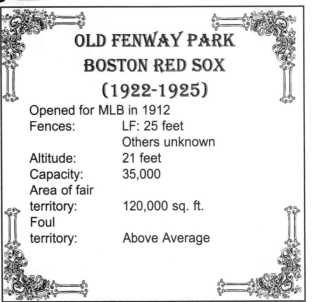

OLD FENWAY PARK
BOSTON RED SOX
(1922-1925)

Opened for MLB in 1912
Fences: LF: 25 feet
                Others unknown
Altitude: 21 feet
Capacity: 35,000
Area of fair
territory: 120,000 sq. ft.
Foul
territory: Above Average

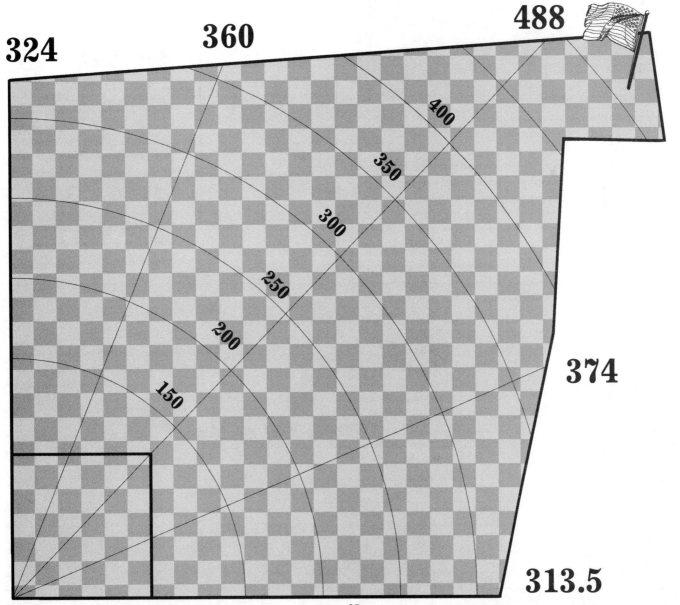

324   360   488

400

350

300

250

200

150

374

313.5

HUNTINGTON AVENUE GROUNDS
HOME OF THE BOSTON RED SOX

The Huntington Avenue Grounds were hastily built to house the Red Sox of the outlaw American League. The site chosen was a former circus lot, so sandy and salty that grass would not grow in the areas around home plate, the foul lines and deep center field. The park was huge, with tall wooden fences to keep people from watching the games for free. The wooden fences were riddled with holes as poor fans would rather see the action 400 feet away than not at all. The knotholes in the wood provided a better view than expected because the field sunk toward home plate.

of-nine series. Boston hit 16 triples to Pittsburgh's nine. The crowds at Huntington Avenue Grounds overflowed onto the field, as was the custom in those days. By allowing the fans on the field, Huntington Avenue Grounds increased its capacity from 11,500 to 18,801 in Game Three.

Huntington Avenue Grounds in 1903.
Courtesy of the Library of Congress

Huntington Avenue Grounds was the site of the first World Series between the American and National Leagues after the two leagues agreed to work together instead of escalating player prices by raiding each other's rosters. In 1903, many considered the upstart league weaker than the NL, but the Boston Pilgrims (soon to be known as Red Sox) showed the mighty Pittsburgh Pirates that the AL could play baseball with the best of them. Cy Young and Bill Dinneen combined to win five games in the best-

Huntington Avenue Grounds Park Factors

Year	R	HR
1901	84	109
1902	96	104
1903	120	196
1904	105	151
1905	102	195
1906	106	182
1907	102	133

Cy Young warming up. Notice the poor condition of the grass, a far cry from today's ballparks. Photo courtesy of the Library of Congress.

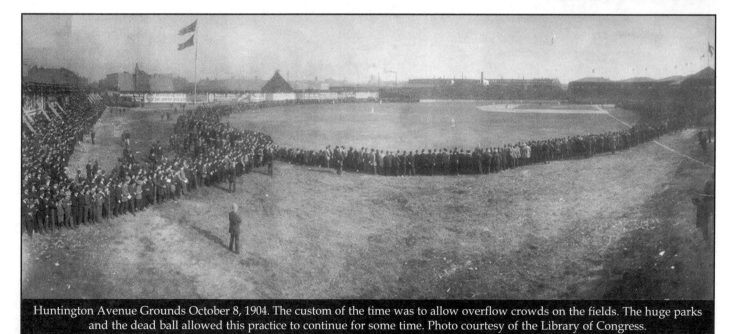

Huntington Avenue Grounds October 8, 1904. The custom of the time was to allow overflow crowds on the fields. The huge parks and the dead ball allowed this practice to continue for some time. Photo courtesy of the Library of Congress.

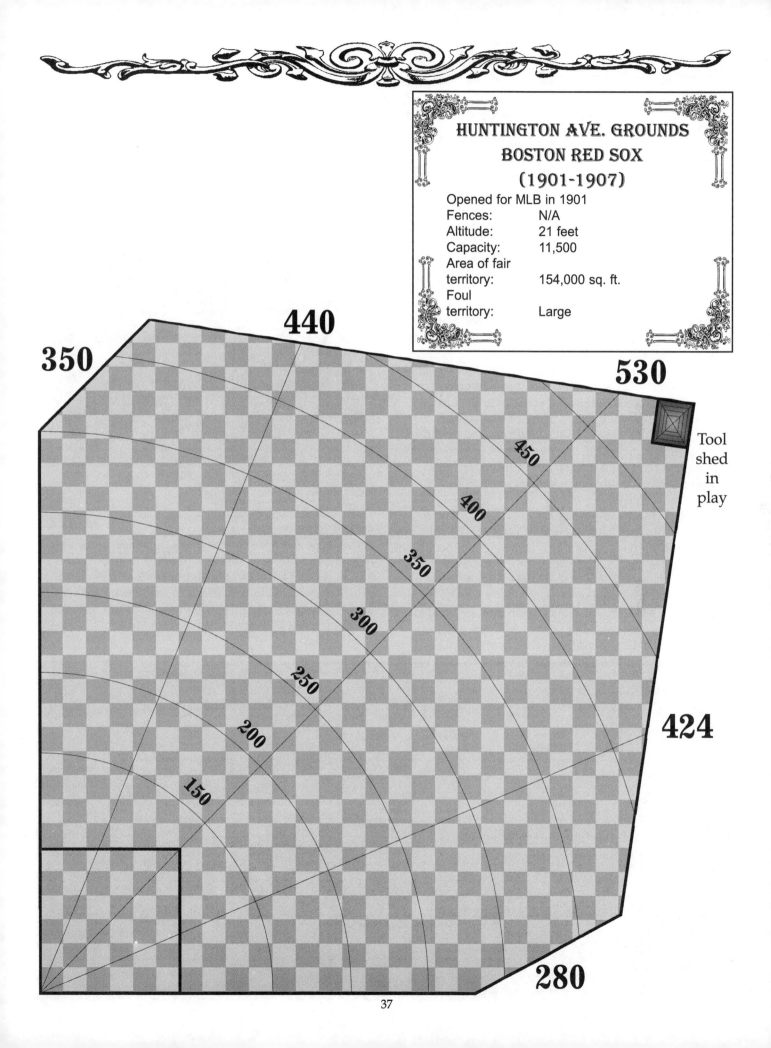

HUNTINGTON AVE. GROUNDS
BOSTON RED SOX
(1901-1907)

Opened for MLB in 1901
Fences: N/A
Altitude: 21 feet
Capacity: 11,500
Area of fair
territory: 154,000 sq. ft.
Foul
territory: Large

440

350

530

450

400

350

300

250

200

150

Tool
shed
in
play

424

280

WRIGLEY FIELD
HOME OF THE CHICAGO CUBS

Wrigley Field is the perfect ballpark. It is one of the few places in Chicago where people can enjoy the blue sky, the cotton clouds and the colors of the sunset. Normally, Chicago's North Side residents have no reason to look up (and I don't mean the standings here). Multi-story buildings act like horse blinders, channeling people's vision toward the car in front of them. The buildings block the sky, replacing the sun with brick. Even at night, there's no reason to look up at the sky. There are no stars. The Chicago night sky is an inhospitable place that glows angrily orange from the refracted light of street lamps. It's as if the city resides inside a jack-o-lantern.

However, in Wrigley Field the urbanites can get back in touch with nature. The sun is soaked up by tanning skin. The green of the field pours over the fans, cleansing them of their daily visions of rust-stained cement and broken glass. The ivy, first planted by Bill Veeck in 1937, waves lazily in the breeze. The park's spa atmosphere can be glimpsed by the hundreds of thousands of commuters that pass by Wrigley in noisy gray trains.

Few parks tempt people like Wrigley. Many ballparks are completely surrounded by cement. The concrete facades don't entice fans as much as the sight of people sitting in the bleachers having fun. From outside Wrigley Field, you can see people in the stands, and this lures more fans than any advertisement can.

Wrigley Field and its neighborhood are bonded together like a tree that absorbs the metal fence against which it leans. Home runs that sail out of Wrigley have

landed in people's bedrooms, breaking windows as high up as the third floor. The roof tops of the neighboring buildings often are packed with hundreds of fans; from inside the park, it can be difficult to tell where Wrigley Field ends and the neighborhood begins. In fact, the area in Chicago near Wrigley Field is referred to as Wrigleyville.

Photo by Oscar Palacios

For decades batters have complained about the late afternoon shadows in Wrigley Field. Typically, home plate would be deep in darkness, yet the pitchers mound may be under blindingly brilliant light. This effect makes it very difficult to pick up a 90+ MPH delivery of a closer late in the game. The late afternoon shadows became more distracting, ironically, after the lights were installed for the 1988 season. The shadows of the light posts reach the pitcher's mound earlier, meaning batters must battle the dreaded shadows half an inning earlier than before the lights were installed.

The "wells" in the outfield add extra excitement to deep fly balls. One or two feet to the left or to the right can be the difference between a long out or a short home run. As the wells turn inward toward the  infield, the stands run closer to home plate than the foul poles. While tracking a fly, many outfielders stand against the wells ready to drift either way. It can be hard to tell whether the ball is going to go out until the outfielder takes one final step and either catches the ball or looks up at a souvenir.

The wells are not the only quirks to Wrigley's outfield walls. Behind the soft-looking vines stands a solid brick wall. Outfielders must have strong fundamentals to play the wall properly; many have pulled up short in fear or hit the bricks at an unsafe speed. The wall is at its most intimidating in the first month of the season, when the vines have yet to regenerate leaves from their winter hibernation. After the leaves have grown back, balls hit into the ivy are sometimes lost and declared ground-rule doubles.

The wall is topped with a basket that extends five feet into the playing field, making the top of the wall closer to the plate than the markers indicate. The basket was installed to prevent fans from falling onto the field. The colorful "Bleacher Bums" used to try to tightrope the top of the wall-- an amazing feat considering their alcohol consumption.

But it isn't only the neighborhood that makes Wrigley Field great. Every seat is both close to the action and within range of foul balls. For kids, a great seat is one where you can catch a souvenir. There are far too many seats in the majors that cannot be reached by baseballs. Then again, like many great marketing tools, foul balls can also backfire. Even fans waiting to buy food below the stands have to watch out for foul balls. There also have been quite a few broken fingers in the stands. You have to be awake in Wrigley.

Wrigley Field is the only remaining Federal League ballpark. Originally called Weeghman Park, the field was built in 1914. The Chicago Whales called the park home for two seasons until the collapse of the Federal League. The park was bankrolled by Charles Weeghman, who hired architect Zachary Taylor Davis to design it. Davis also designed Comiskey Park. Wrigley Field was the first major league park on the north side of the city, which was the underdeveloped part of town at the time and much less popular than the South Side. After the Federal

League folded, Weeghman was allowed to buy the Cubs, and he moved the team to his park. In 1918, Weeghman lost much of his fortune in the sugar futures business. He was forced to sell his interests in the Cubs to William Wrigley Jr., the heir to the Wrigley chewing gum empire.

The park has endured many changes. Originally, center field was 440 feet deep, but the park began to change as the need for increased capacity grew. In 1926, the park was renamed Wrigley Field. The single-decked grandstand was replaced by a double-decker for the 1927 season, and the original bleachers were removed at that point. New temporary bleachers were installed outside the park on Waveland and Sheffield avenues for the 1929, 1932 and 1935 seasons.

In 1937, Bill Veeck added the distinct Wrigley Field features of the scoreboard, the ivy, and the bleachers. The outfield dimensions have not changed since the 1938 season. All these changes increased the capacity from 14,000 in 1914 to over 38,000 in 1938.

Though Wrigley Field remained the only major league park without lights until 1988, Phil Wrigley had the lights inside the the park back in 1941. Wrigley ultimately donated them to the World War II effort instead.

One morning in July of 1997, closer Mark Wohlers and his Atlanta Braves were in Wrigley Field for a doubleheader. Wohlers wanted to play catch and started yelling for a partner. Finally, pitching coach Leo Mazzone came over and played catch with the 6-foot-4 giant.

"Leo, look how beautiful this park is," Wohlers said as if he were looking at a natural wonder like the Grand Canyon or the Carlsbad Caverns. Despite being a seven-year veteran, Wohlers was talking like a rookie, beyond himself.

"Leo, look how beautiful this place is. God, can you imagine playing here all year?" Then Wohlers imagined playing in Wrigley all year. His grin went away, but it came back and he added, "The wind is blowing in."

Wind is not the only element that plays a significant role at Wrigley. The sun makes its right field one of the toughest to play in the majors. Because the games are mostly played in the afternoon, the sun makes it harsh for outfielders. The Wrigley grandstand is fairly low and does a poor job blocking the sun. To make matters worse, pitchers warm up in foul territory, and the bullpen mounds extend about five feet into fair territory. As outfielders range towards the foul lines, they have to deal with these mounds down the left- and right-field lines.

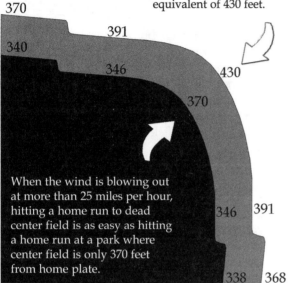

370

391

340

When the wind is blowing in at more than 25 miles per hour, the distance from home plate to center field becomes the equivalent of 430 feet.

346

430

370

When the wind is blowing out at more than 25 miles per hour, hitting a home run to dead center field is as easy as hitting a home run at a park where center field is only 370 feet from home plate.

346   391

338   368

The winds in Wrigley Field have a tremendous effect on the baseball played there. With a stiff wind blowing in, the park acts as if it were one of the largest in the majors. A wind blowing in at an average of 25 miles per hour or more can make the park play as if it were 430 feet to center field. While a constant 25-MPH wind may sound like an anomaly, it's not uncommon in Chicago. Conversely, a stiff wind blowing out makes the park an easy place to homer. Balls that normally would be 350-foot outs to the power alleys can become wind-blown homers. On days he was scheduled to pitch, Cy Young Award-winner Mike Scott refused to watch batting practice if the wind was blowing out -- he found it too demoralizing. When the wind blows, even the flyballs that remain in the park are no picnic to field, as the wind can play tricks with them.

As part of a tradition, visiting teams' veterans convince the club's rookies to spray-paint a certain part of this anatomically correct horse. If the horse is painted, the veterans say, the team will have a good season, and the rookies will have long careers. However, the veterans usually alert the police in advance, and the joke is to have the rookies "booked." The General Philip Sheridan statue is a few blocks from Wrigley Field at the Belmont exit of Lake Shore Drive.

Sheridan was a successful Civil War general as well as a notorious Indian hater. He helped popularize the idea that killing buffaloes was the most effective way to eradicate the Indians.

Photo by Oscar Palacios.

A packed Wrigley Field July 27, 1929. Source Library of Congress. Photo by Kaufmann & Fabry Co.

Most ballparks have thousands of parking spots, creating a buffer between the stadium and the surrounding neighborhood. Not Wrigley Field. With people sitting on the roofs of the neighboring buildings to watch ballgames, sometimes it is difficult to say where the neighborhood ends and Wrigley Field begins. Wrigley's neighborhood is called Wrigleyville.

Unless you know a secret parking spot, take the Elevated train to Wrigley. It is a quarter of a block east of the ballpark. The stands are fully visible to commuters on the train, tempting the commuters to go to the park.

Photo by Satellite Photo by SOVIN-FORMSPUTNIK & Aerial Images, Inc. Taken in 1989.

More Wrigley Field photos. Right, the infield without shadows. Left, the quirky Wrigley outfield, and the legendary center field scoreboard.
Photos by Oscar Palacios.

Old Wrigley
Park Factors

Year	R	HR
1928	82	64
1929	96	115
1930	113	127
1931	89	82
1932	105	88
1933	89	134
1934	89	111
1935	92	92
1936	105	96
1937	105	101

Park Factors

Year	Avg	R	H	2B	3B	HR	L-Avg	R-Avg	L-HR	R-HR
1992	98	101	100	98	158	102	101	95	82	121
1993	102	106	102	109	124	116	106	99	83	162
1994	94	84	94	80	73	97	103	89	144	79
1995	103	102	102	100	83	109	104	103	99	115
1996	99	104	101	96	102	108	102	98	82	124
1997	103	114	105	78	79	148	106	101	101	176

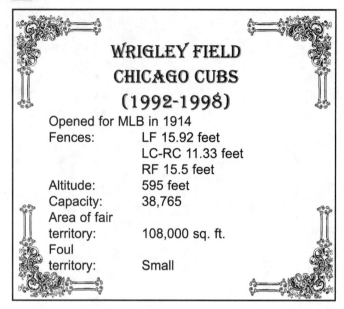

WRIGLEY FIELD
CHICAGO CUBS
(1992-1998)

Opened for MLB in 1914

Fences:	LF 15.92 feet
	LC-RC 11.33 feet
	RF 15.5 feet
Altitude:	595 feet
Capacity:	38,765
Area of fair territory:	108,000 sq. ft.
Foul territory:	Small

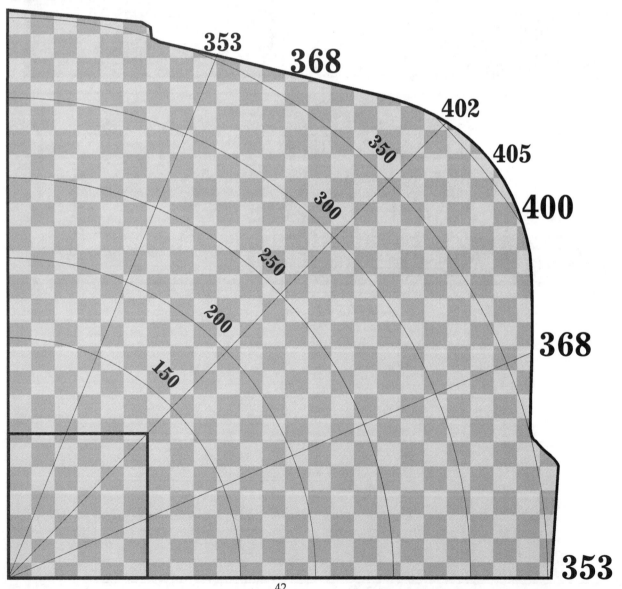

355

353

368

402

350

405

300

400

250

200

368

150

353

OLD WRIGLEY FIELD
CHICAGO CUBS
(1928-1937)

Opened for MLB in 1914
Fences: LF 8 feet
                  CF 3.5 feet
                  RF 7.5 feet
Altitude: 595 feet
Capacity: 40,000
Area of fair
territory: 113,000 sq. ft.
Foul
territory: Small

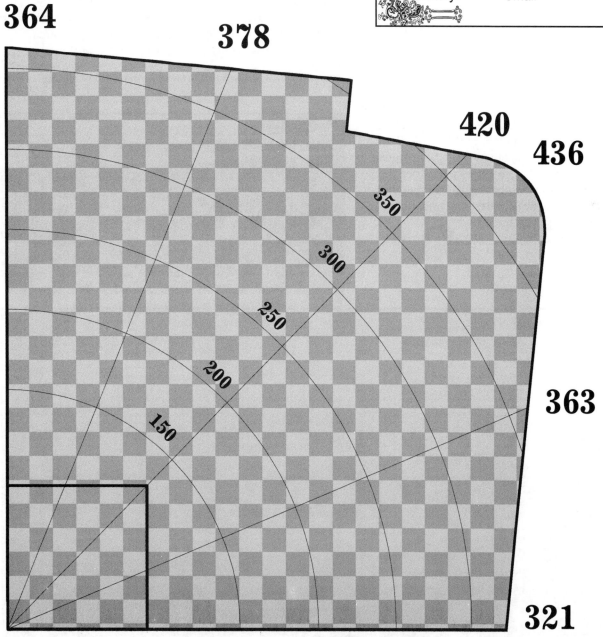

364 378 420 436 350 300 250 200 150 363 321

WEST SIDE GROUNDS
HOME OF THE CHICAGO CUBS

The West Side Grounds was a huge park and a good fit for its team and time. The outfield was so spacious that the grass in deep center was hardly ever cut and stood waist high. The Chicago Cubs mastered the art of scoring by scratching and clawing for one run at a time. They moved their baserunners a base at a time via the hit-and-run, the bunt and the stolen base. Most importantly, they made sure they made productive outs, advancing baserunners even when they failed to hit safely. On top of playing smart offensive baseball, their infield defense was sharp, featuring Joe Tinker at short, Johnny Evers at second and Frank Chance at first base.

Chance became the Cubs manager in 1905 and took his team to the World Series the following year with a 116-36 record. Unfortunately for the Cubbies, the "Hitless Wonders" Chicago White Sox (who hit .230 as a team in 1906 to earn the nickname) won the series in six games. The Cubs returned to the World Series in 1907 and destroyed the Detroit Tigers by winning four, tying one game and losing none. Orval Overall and Mordecai "Three Finger" Brown helped hold the Tigers to six runs in those five games. In 1908, the Cubs made it to the World Series for the third straight year and again mastered the Tigers. Tinker hit the first homer in World Series play since 1903. Tiger catcher Boss Schmidt was not only 1-for-14 at the plate, but also let the Cubs steal 15 bases against him. In 1909, the Cubs won 104 games, but failed to make the World Series. The Cubs' glory years had ended.

When baseball was young, baseball teams used to go by several names. Many names were given to the teams by reporters and fans. Teams just went by the name of their cities, and people could call them whatever they wanted. Official team names were a later invention. Here are the teams used for the Chicago National League Baseball Club before becoming widely known as the Cubs:

White Stockings (1876-1894), Colts (1887-1906), Ex-Colts (1898), Black Stockings (1888-1889), Rainmakers (1898), Orphans (1898), Cowboys (1899), Rough Riders (1899-1900), Remnants (1901-1902), Recruits (1902), Panamas (1903), Zephyrs (1905), Nationals (1905-1907), Spuds (1906), Trojans (1913) and Cubs (1902-present).

West Side Grounds, Aug. 30, 1908. Photo by Geo. R. Lawrence Co. Courtesy of the Library of Congress.

West Side Grounds, Giants vs. Cubs, Aug. 30, 1908. Photo by Geo. R. Lawrence Co. Courtesy of the Library of Congress.

WEST SIDE GROUNDS
CHICAGO CUBS
(1894-1915)

Opened for MLB in 1893
Fences: Unknown
Altitude: 595 feet
Capacity: 16,000
Area of fair
territory: 149,000 sq. ft.
Foul
territory: Huge

West Side Grounds Park Factors		
Year	R	HR
1894	121	58
1895	101	128
1896	118	113
1897	97	84
1898	101	46
1899	90	115
1900	80	40
1901	105	56
1902	85	44
1903	84	57
1904	96	74

West Side Grounds Park Factors		
Year	R	HR
1905	102	80
1906	103	67
1907	108	45
1908	106	160
1909	89	45
1910	93	108
1911	91	90
1912	108	111
1913	94	135
1914	95	117
1915	107	140

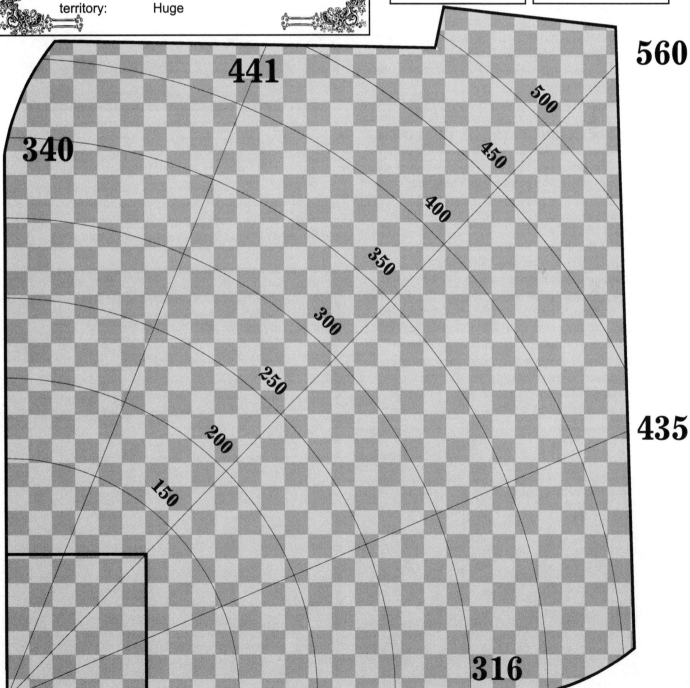

NEW COMISKEY PARK
HOME OF THE CHICAGO WHITE SOX

Just like in the old Comiskey Park, hitters have a hard time in this stadium, although changes were made to make the new Comiskey more hitter friendly. Unlike old Comiskey, the new park has a hitting background, towering walls block the wind (in the old park, winds used to swirl over the left field roof, killing long drives hit down that line), and a realigned diamond so that the wind that does get through helps drives toward right field while hardly affecting flyballs to left. In the new alignment, a player running home from third is running west, instead of south like in several old parks. The traditional design was adopted so hitters would not have the sun in their eyes while at the plate. New Comiskey's towering outer walls block out the sun.

The new stands are light blue and give outfielders a hard time seeing flyballs as they leave the infield. Many flyballs never rise above the stands. Spectators in the worst seats always look down, even at towering pop-ups.

New Comiskey has an infield as true as any other in the majors, resulting in fewer errors. The dimensions in the outfield are generous to pitchers. The outfield territory is above average in size. Overall, New Comiskey is a pitchers' park.

The fact that New Comiskey could have been styled like Oriole Park at Camden Yards eats at Chicagoans. New Comiskey is symmetrical. The exterior is fitting for Los Angeles or Las Vegas, but not the iron and brick look of the South Side of Chicago. The fans in the upper deck are far removed from the action and 60 feet higher than the upper deck at old Comiskey. It is very difficult to catch a foul ball because of the distance of the seats from the field. Generally, criticism of New Comiskey's is justified. However, the White Sox gave the fans what they thought they wanted: unobstructed seats,

skyboxes, great food, cleanliness, and a site in the same neighborhood as the old park. The last point is irrelevant, however, since traffic rarely filters through the surrounding streets. A buffer of parking lots keeps the fans' money in Comiskey. They even have cops guiding traffic from a highway ramp into the parking lots. Going to New Comiskey is like going to a movie theater. You see the show, spend your money in the building and go home.

The columnless design of New Comiskey resulted in no seats with obstructed view, but also in a very steep and distant upperdeck. Photo by Oscar Palacios.

Today, New Comiskey is viewed as a joke in Chicago. The fans complain that they are too far away from the action. They complain the field is symmetrical. They complained that the stadium is not Camden Yards.

However, those were not most people's first impressions. This is what people said about Old Comiskey and New Comiskey as the rookie stadium made its debut:

"This is the best baseball can offer," Commissioner Fay Vincent said.

"Why is that stupid thing [Old Comiskey] still there?" Ozzie Guillen asked. *"This place, you want to come here early."*

"The new park seemed to retain the intimacy of the old one," wrote Chicago Tribune reporter Ed Sherman.

"[Fans] couldn't see how (in the old park), after it rained, you'd be in water up to your ankles walking just from our dugout to our bullpen," White Sox reliever Bobby Thigpen.

"Memories aren't in the ballpark. Memories are between your ears," White Sox catcher Carlton Fisk added. *"After going to that ballpark all these years, this feels like I've been in a time capsule. It's like riding on a horse to riding on the Challenger."*

Maybe that wasn't a bad analogy by Fisk because just like the Challenger had a few successful runs, New Comiskey had a few hurrahs. Now they are both known as disasters.

New Comiskey is a lesson that when you build a ballpark, don't cater to the players. Just because they play in ballparks doesn't mean they know what a good ballpark is.

Sources: Chicago Tribune, Thursday, April 18, 1991, edition and Friday, April 19, 1991 edition.

New Comiskey Park Factors

Year	Avg	R	H	2B	3B	HR	L-Avg	R-Avg	L-HR	R-HR
1992	95	89	93	77	79	99	97	94	117	90
1993	101	98	100	85	96	115	99	104	111	116
1994	98	90	96	97	78	92	87	108	74	106
1995	98	93	93	92	195	76	95	100	58	89
1996	95	83	92	75	76	85	92	98	73	94
1997	96	91	94	106	163	81	96	96	59	99

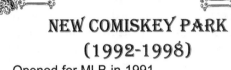

NEW COMISKEY PARK
(1992-1998)

Opened for MLB in 1991

Fences:	8 feet
Altitude:	595 feet
Capacity:	44,321
Area of fair territory:	110,000 sq. ft.
Foul territory:	Average

347   **375**

400

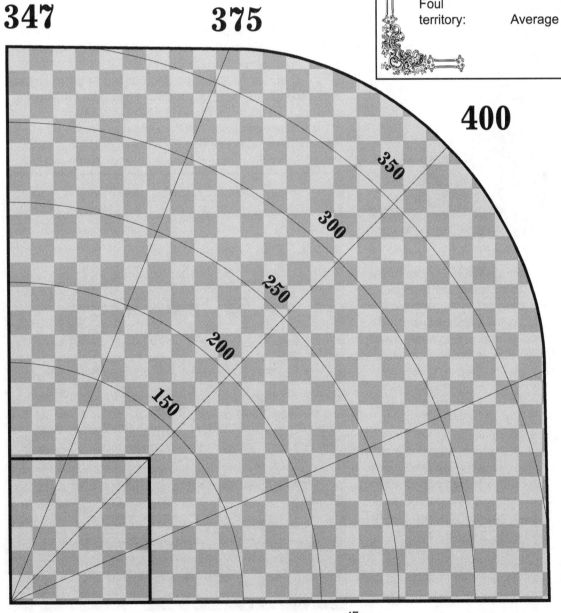

350

300

250

200

150

375

347

OLD COMISKEY PARK
HOME OF THE CHICAGO WHITE SOX

Charles Comiskey wanted a ballpark where home runs would not come cheap, and he built one. White Sox pitcher "Big Ed" Walsh helped with the design, making it a pitchers' haven. What made Old Comiskey the prototypical pitchers' park were the outfield dimensions. The fences were far enough to steal homers away from batters, but close enough to stop balls from rolling too deep, turning would-be triples into long doubles. In addition, the grass was generally kept long, slowing down rollers headed toward the outfield.

The "Old Roman," Charles Comiskey.

A pitcher's strategy can change dramatically in a park like Old Comiskey. The diminished home run threat allows pitchers to attack the strike zone rather than pick at the corners. The higher percentage of strikes reduces the number of at-bats going to full counts, and, consequently reduces the number of pitches per out. Also, more strikes result in fewer walks and, therefore, fewer baserunners. Fewer baserunners, in turn, allow pitchers to pitch out of the stretch less often. Not only does the stretch delivery rob pitchers of three to five miles an hour from their fastball, but it also hurts their stamina. Pitchers still have to get batters out, but letting a hurler pitch in a park like Old Comiskey was like letting a major league batter hit with an aluminum bat. Pitchers got away with more mistakes at Comiskey Park than they did at the average park of its era.

My last game at Old Comiskey was in July of 1990, a couple of months before the park was torn down. I was sitting in the lower deck of the left field bleachers, below a colony of pigeons. I spent the whole game looking up, waiting for the birds to get me. Fortunately it was poster day, so at least I was able to cover myself. I was sitting next to a post that was flaking paint. It felt more like I

was sitting under a rusting bridge than in a park. The White Sox had a no-hitter thrown against them that afternoon, yet they won the game 4-0. The pigeons kept me preoccupied, so I can't tell you much about the game.

Sitting in the outfield, it was evident something had to be done because the park's deterioration was overpowering. The facade of the park was not much to look at either: flaking white paint on old bricks. At one point, Charles Comiskey wanted the park to look like a Roman temple with elaborate columns and engravings. However, he decided to save money and left the park unfinished. The exterior bricks were added later, and Bill Veeck painted them white when he took over the team.

For years, White Sox officials threatened to leave the park. The team had its eyes on suburban Addison, Milwaukee and St. Petersburg, Florida. The White Sox even played 20 games as the home team in Milwaukee's County Stadium in 1968 and 1969. (Milwaukee was without a major league team at that point.)

Like an execution carried out late to avoid controversy, the Illinois General Assembly passed a bill at midnight of June 30, 1988, funding a new stadium.

The demolition of Old Comiskey erased the diamond where the White Sox played two of their three World Series, including their last championship in 1917.

This is the site of Old Comiskey Park as seen from New Comiskey Park. Old Comiskey is now a parking lot serving as a buffer between the New Comiskey and its neighborhood. The politicians voted to build New Comiskey Park to keep the White Sox in town, so the surrounding neighborhood would reap the financial benefits a major league team brings to a city. However, New Comiskey might as well be in the suburbs. The parking lots to the north, west and south, and the highway to the east, prevent New Comiskey from having much financial impact on its neighborhood. The buffering of Comiskey Park was created so people would spend concession and parking money in Comiskey instead of elsewhere. Despite the new stadium, the White Sox remained in an economically depressed area. Neither the neighborhood, the team, Old Comiskey or the taxpayers benefitted from the new stadium's construction. The only people who benefitted were the politicians and the contractors.

The park also took it with many memories of the golden era of the Negro Leagues. Chicago held the first Negro League All-Star Game in 1933. All but one of the games were played annually at Comiskey until 1950.

Many suggest the drawing ability of the Negro League All-Star Game was an important factor in integration. The attendance of the game grew to over 50,000 fans. The All-Star Game was the peak of the Negro League season, greater than the Negro League World Series. Alex Radcliffe and Buck Leonard played in the most All-Star Games, 11 each. Leonard also led the games in homers and RBI with three and 11, respectively. Josh Gibson flashed a .483 batting average. Mule Suttles slugged .882.

The demolition of Comiskey also erased the playing field of the infamous 1919 World Series. Eight players were barred for life in 1920 for throwing the Series the year before.

In 1910, White Sox cather Billy Sullivan travelled to Ireland and brought back grass for the new park. A green brick was placed on top of the sod on St. Patrick's Day, and the brick became the park's cornerstone.

When the Allyn family owned the team, they carpeted the infield with Astroturf as a cost-cutting measure. The turf remained in place from 1969 until 1976, when Bill Veeck regained ownership of the team and replaced the Astroturf with natural grass.

The first official night game in Comiskey was held on August 14, 1939. Johnny Rigney hurled a three-hitter and beat the St. Louis Browns by a score of 5-2 before a crowd of 30,000. The first attempt at night baseball in Comiskey was held as early as August 27, 1910, by George F. Cahill. The exhibition game was called a success, but plans for night baseball were dropped at that point. Thus Cincinnati became the first major league team with lights in 1935.

However, Comiskey Park was first when it came to electric scoreboards. A center field scoreboard was

installed in 1951. In 1960, Bill Veeck converted it into his "Exploding Scoreboard." He stuffed it with fireworks and adorned with it lighted pinwheels. Not satisfied, Veeck turned it into a true monster when he gave the scoreboard the sounds of crashes, shrieks, locomotives, sirens and live battles. This concert of sounds and fireworks went into action whenever a Sox player homered. The scoreboard was a big hit with the fans and a great annoyance to the opposition.

One of the original pinwheels from Old Comiskey now lights up after Cub homers on top of a private rooftop across the street from Wrigley Field.

Old Comiskey visible through light clouds. Photo courtesy of SOVINFORMSPUTNIK & Aerial Images, Inc. Taken in 1989.

The area surrounding Comiskey Park changed dramatically after the park was built in 1910. Between 1935 and 1970, more than five million African-Americans migrated from the South to the North. Black migrants overwhelmed the available housing in the South Side of Chicago. The landlords saw the demand for their apartments remain great even when they didn't take care of them. They also divided normal apartments into one-room studios. The neighborhoods became poorer and denser. The black middle class was pushed from its neighborhoods by the poorer migrants. In the 1930s and 1940s, the South Side was the capital of black America. It was home to the brightest black sports star, Joe Louis, the only black Congressman, William Dawson, and the best black newspaper, the Chicago Defender. The African-American population in Chicago swelled from 278,000 in the 1930s to 813,000 in 1950. The migration rate peaked at 2,200 black people moving to Chicago a week. The ballpark's neighborhood turned from an integrated middle class mix, to a segregated, poor black community.

The coup de grâce happened in 1962, when Mayor Richard Daley, the father of the current Chicago mayor, built 28 identical, 16-story buildings called the Robert Taylor Homes. The housing project was designed to house African-Americans and not let them spread to the rest of the city. To make sure of this, Daley built the Dan Ryan Expressway to the west of the projects, so the tenants could not cross over easily. To the east, the lake provided a natural border. The projects housed 40,000 people. On the other side of highway was Comiskey Park. Because of the neighborhood changes, the White Sox began having attendance problems. The people closest to the park were poor and chose not to attend ball games. Those who attended had long distances to travel.

Before the Chicago White Sox played in Old Comiskey Park, they played in South Side Park from April of 1901 to June of 1910. Its capacity was about 15,000, but on sellout dates, fans were allowed to watch from the playing field, as was the custom back then. After the White Sox left, the ballpark was used by several Negro League teams.

Photos courtesy of the Library of Congress. Top: South Side Park, Aug. 14, 1904. Photo by Geo. R. Lawrence Co. Middle: South Side Park, Oct. 9, 1909. Bottom: South Side Park, Oct. 14, 1906.

Old Comiskey Park Factors

Year	R	HR
1986	101	76
1987	118	81
1988	96	78
1989	87	66
1990	103	82

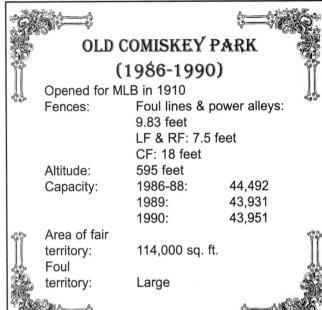

OLD COMISKEY PARK
(1986-1990)

Opened for MLB in 1910

Fences:	Foul lines & power alleys: 9.83 feet
	LF & RF: 7.5 feet
	CF: 18 feet
Altitude:	595 feet
Capacity:	1986-88: 44,492
	1989: 43,931
	1990: 43,951
Area of fair territory:	114,000 sq. ft.
Foul territory:	Large

347 **372** **382** **417**

409

350

300

415

250

382

372

200

150

347

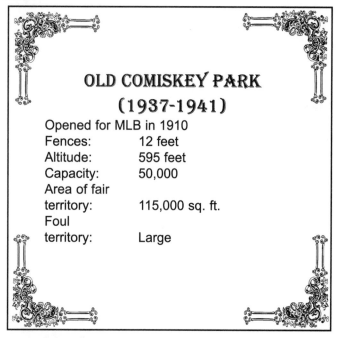

Old Comiskey Park Factors

Year	R	HR
1937	102	125
1938	94	67
1939	110	120
1940	105	122
1941	83	72

OLD COMISKEY PARK
(1937-1941)

Opened for MLB in 1910

Fences:	12 feet
Altitude:	595 feet
Capacity:	50,000
Area of fair territory:	115,000 sq. ft.
Foul territory:	Large

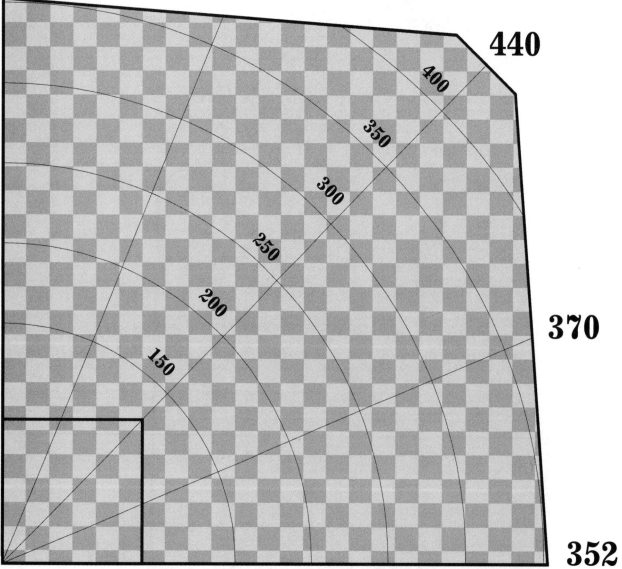

352

370

440

400

350

300

250

200

150

370

352

PARK FACTORS

Throughout this book, you have seen the term "park factor." If you are new to the study of baseball statistics, this term may be foreign to you. Don't worry, we're not going to take points away from you or ridicule you because you don't know park factors. Instead, we'll explain what they mean.

Park factors tell you whether a park favors a certain statistic. For example, in 1997, all National League batters hit 118 homer runs in 5,071 at-bats at Atlanta's Turner Field, a frequency of .0233 home runs per at-bat (we excluded all interleague games when calculating the factors). In Braves' road games, the frequency was .0277 home runs per at-bat. This means it was harder to homer at Turner Field than it was in the other National League ballparks, on average, in 1997.

If you divide .0233 by .0277, you get 0.84. This number is multiplied by 100 to make it more recognizable: 84. What does a park factor of 84 mean? It means that it was 16 percent tougher for players to hit a home run at Turner Field in 1997 than it was in other National League parks.

A park factor of 100 indicates neutrality. The higher the park factor is over 100, the more favorable the park is for that statistic. The lower the factor is under 100, the less favorable the park is for that statistic.

The following are the park factors for New Comiskey Park in 1992:

R	95
H	89
2B	93
3B	77
HR	79
L-Avg	99
R-Avg	97
L-HR	94
R-HR	117

The run factor (R) of 95, which tells us that it was five percent harder to score runs in New Comiskey Park in 1992 than it was in the other American League parks. It was 11 percent harder to get a hit, seven percent harder to get a double, 23 percent harder to get a triple and 21 percent harder to homer. "L-Avg" means batting average by lefthanded batters. We present some lefty-righty breakdowns for modern parks because asymmetric ballparks have different effects on righthanded or lefthanded hitters. For modern parks, we have the data to create separate park factors for lefties and righties.

A L-HR factor of 94 means that lefthanded hitters had a harder time homering in New Comiskey in 1992 than in the other AL stadiums. A R-HR factor of 117 means righthanded hitters had an easier time homering at New Comiskey in 1992 than they did at the other AL parks.

Now, you shouldn't just look at one year to determine if a park helps or hurts a certain statistic. Using several seasons' worth of data allows anomalies to even out. Sometimes park factors change from year to year not due to normal variations, but rather to changes in the other ballparks. Imagine that you have a league with nine ballparks identical to Dodger Stadium. Because all the ballparks are the same, then all the factors would bunch around 100 (statistical variations would give you a few over 100 and a few under). Well, if you add Coors Field to this happy league of Dodger Stadiums, the park factors will change for all nine parks, even though their dimensions did not change.

But now that we've added Coors Field to this league, the average for league average has moved. If the pre-Coors HR factor for a given park was 100, the post-Coors HR factor may drop to, say, 95. The Coors HR factor would be 145, so the league-average HR factor would remain 100, as it necessarily must.

On the other hand, if we had a league with nine Coors and only one Dodger Stadium, the HR factor for the Coors Stadiums may be only 105 (while the HR factor for Dodger Stadium may be 55). If you looked at one of the Coors and saw that its HR factor was 105, you might dismiss it as only a slightly above-average home-run park.

So we have to be careful when looking at park factors, especially when looking at historical park factors. Remember that a HR factor of 200 in 1890 may not mean the same thing as a HR factor of 200 in 1990. The HR factor of 200 in 1890 was when the park was compared to other 1890 parks. There is no absolute park factor.

That's why analyzing the dimensions, shapes, AFTs (areas of fair territories) and altitudes of ballparks helps. The park factor is just a tool to help you understand a park. It works best when used in combination with other tools, rather than all by itself.

We have broken down the park factors year-by-year so you can better analyze them. Other publications have park factors spanning 50 or more years. That makes their park factors useless, because in 50 years, a park's dimensions may change drastically (just look at Braves Field). By listing the park factors annually, you can begin to understand why they are the way they are, and why they have changed: "Oh, yeah -- in 1935 they reduced the distance down the line by 30 feet, so the home run factor increased."

Here's one more note on the historical parks. As you have noticed, we have fewer park factors for the historical parks. That is simply because we have less data on them to analyze. We imagine that someday, we may be able to calculate the L-HR factor for the Polo Grounds. Who knows; the data could be out there somewhere. We simply haven't had the time to peek under enough rocks. Also, the historical park factors were not determined on an at-bat basis (as the modern park factors are). They were determined by games played, which is less precise.

I hope you're now an expert on park factors. They add a lot of value to this book, in my humble opinion.

As most have noticed, we are in the middle of a prolific home run era. The most popular explanation for this phenomenon is that expansion has diluted pitching, and that the present major league talent is weak. I'd like to argue that this is not the case.

It can be difficult to argue against the popular belief. Has expansion diluted talent so that homers come more easily? To test this theory, we would have to come up with a method for rating the strength of leagues across different eras. Was the National League in 1997 weaker or stronger than the National League in 1964? Many people have tried to answer this question by comparing batting averages, runs per game, home runs per game, etc. The problem with this approach is that it's difficult to say whether an increase in runs per game would be due to the pitching getting weaker, or the offensive talent getting deeper. Others have argued that they can calculate the strength of the leagues by comparing the errors per game. This theory is a good one because fewer errors per game would mean that the defensive talent in a league had improved. Unfortunately, there are other factors, apart from talent, that can affect the number of errors per game: better equipment and better fields, for example.

However, I have an idea about how to measure the strengths of a league: examining pitchers' batting averages.

Imagine that you're an Average Joe, walking by your neighborhood park, and a group of weekend warriors are having a pick-up baseball game. They are one person short, so they yell at you and ask you to join the game. Well, the talent level of this neighborhood game is not very good, so your batting average could be around .200 if you played enough games with these people.

Now imagine you're in the stands watching a minor league game. You make a great catch, and a la Bill Veeck, they give you a contract based on your spectacular catch. Well, the talent level in this minor league is much higher than in your neighborhood, so your batting average could be around .100 if you played enough in this minor league.

Now imagine that for whatever reason, despite your sorry batting average, you bring people to the stands and they call you to the Show. Now you're in for it. The talent level in the majors is unbelievable, and you manage to hit only .030.

If you buy my premise, you accept that an Average Joe's batting average would keep getting lower as the Average Joe moves up the talent ladder of leagues. If we were only lucky enough to have Average Joes coming up to the plate year after year, then we could measure the strengths of the leagues through the ages. Luckily for us, we do have Average Joes: pitchers.

Normally, pitchers don't get brought up to the majors because of their hitting abilities. Steve Stone was never in danger of getting demoted because of he went 0-for-34 in 1971 with the San Francisco Giants. Neither his .147 on-base percentage nor his .110 slugging percentage threatened his career. Pitchers are our "control group" when studying the strength of the leagues.

The following numbers are the pitchers' batting averages and the (real) hitters' batting averages for both leagues, and the difference between them. The difference is important because if they used a rabbit ball, both pitchers' averages and hitters' averages would increase. A livelier ball could make pitchers appear to be better hitters when in fact, compared to professional hitters, they may be getting worse. Now, talking about rabbit and livelier balls may give you the idea that I love conspiracy theories, but in fact, the official baseball rules do allow for variations in the size and weight of the ball (they even allow variation on the seams and construction material). The rules say that a baseball shall weigh between five and 5.25 ounces. The rules then allow for a five percent variation from year to year. Five percent means a 315-foot long out could become a 331-foot homer. The rules also say that the ball should measure between nine and 9.25 inches in circumference. This also creates for interesting variations. All this means is that if the owners thought that better pitching would be good for the game, they could do more than simply increase the height of the mound, as they did in 1969. The same would be true if they thought more offense would be better for the game.

Anyway, here are the numbers:

	Pitchers			Non-Pitchers			Diff
Year	H	AB	AVG	H	AB	AVG	
1903	1402	7495	.187	18375	67947	.270	.083
1904	1625	8819	.184	18738	73669	.254	.070
1905	1421	8213	.173	18850	73523	.256	.083
1906	1404	7970	.176	18340	72099	.254	.078
1907	1321	7732	.171	18376	72573	.253	.082
1908	1314	7739	.170	17965	72916	.246	.077
1909	1249	7685	.163	18397	72857	.253	.090
1910	1400	7717	.181	18923	73743	.257	.075
1911	1488	7851	.190	20401	74315	.275	.085
1912	1432	7496	.191	20572	74426	.276	.085
1913	1298	7371	.176	19710	73789	.267	.091
1914	1927	11138	.173	29194	111397	.262	.089
1915	1880	10736	.175	28537	110822	.258	.082
1916	1191	7178	.166	19057	74610	.255	.089
1917	1279	7342	.174	19072	74589	.256	.081
1918	1167	6297	.185	15700	60287	.260	.075
1919	1248	6666	.187	18188	67369	.270	.083
1920	1538	7603	.202	21523	75960	.283	.081
1921	1617	7631	.212	22889	76797	.298	.086
1922	1616	7886	.205	22720	76549	.297	.092
1923	1727	8183	.211	22286	76519	.291	.080
1924	1668	7821	.213	22401	76315	.294	.080
1925	1577	7654	.206	23233	77422	.300	.094
1926	1537	7613	.202	21784	75642	.288	.086
1927	1521	7494	.203	22247	76426	.291	.088

	Pitchers			Non-Pitchers			Diff
Year	H	AB	AVG	H	AB	AVG	
1928	1437	7394	.194	22126	76550	.289	.095
1929	1507	7580	.199	22966	77141	.298	.099
1930	1663	7688	.216	23748	78359	.303	.087
1931	1459	7634	.191	22388	78446	.285	.094
1932	1442	7590	.190	22508	79134	.284	.094
1933	1412	7573	.186	21418	77192	.277	.091
1934	1493	7825	.191	22364	77721	.288	.097
1935	1471	7525	.195	22590	78839	.287	.091
1936	1511	7728	.196	23352	79911	.292	.097
1937	1451	7592	.191	22318	78371	.285	.094
1938	1357	7350	.185	21936	77662	.282	.098
1939	1384	7296	.190	21987	77584	.283	.094
1940	1310	7255	.181	21692	78747	.275	.095
1941	1249	7243	.172	21282	78612	.271	.098
1942	1178	7070	.167	19998	76661	.261	.094
1943	1269	7136	.178	20198	77565	.260	.083
1944	1314	7311	.180	20993	78354	.268	.088
1945	1314	7206	.182	20663	77243	.268	.085
1946	1201	6941	.173	20354	77392	.263	.090
1947	1259	7106	.177	20744	77330	.268	.091
1948	1266	7009	.181	20836	76930	.271	.090
1949	1219	6952	.175	20860	77065	.271	.095
1950	1269	7135	.178	21248	77508	.274	.096
1951	1307	6974	.187	20808	77813	.267	.080
1952	1136	7056	.161	20071	76842	.261	.100
1953	1198	6816	.176	21218	77998	.272	.096
1954	1126	6912	.163	20774	76993	.270	.107
1955	1153	6631	.174	20453	76936	.266	.092
1956	1111	6485	.171	20534	77317	.266	.094
1957	1041	6544	.159	20810	78293	.266	.107
1958	1054	6414	.164	20562	77404	.266	.101
1959	1000	6481	.154	20635	77809	.265	.111
1960	973	6288	.155	20461	77726	.263	.109
1961	1183	7415	.160	23883	89617	.267	.107
1962	1248	8338	.150	27273	102350	.266	.117
1963	1153	8170	.141	25890	101644	.255	.114
1964	1138	8218	.138	26531	102246	.259	.121
1965	1065	8012	.133	25887	101727	.254	.122
1966	1203	8095	.149	26004	101372	.257	.108
1967	1096	7977	.137	25366	101225	.251	.113
1968	1062	8022	.132	24646	100590	.245	.113
1969	1347	9663	.139	31234	121624	.257	.117
1970	1414	9693	.146	32141	122447	.262	.117
1971	1430	9615	.149	31117	120929	.257	.109
1972	1350	9230	.146	29084	115598	.252	.105
1973	714	4767	.150	33296	127596	.261	.111
1974	778	4712	.165	33191	127544	.260	.095
1975	697	4656	.150	33166	126817	.262	.112
1976	672	4495	.149	32926	127030	.259	.110
1977	716	4506	.159	37321	139468	.268	.109
1978	672	4528	.148	35836	137039	.262	.113
1979	683	4537	.151	37228	138255	.269	.119
1980	691	4439	.156	37453	139721	.268	.112
1981	419	2797	.150	23738	91670	.259	.109
1982	674	4470	.151	36977	139679	.265	.114
1983	653	4458	.146	36790	139080	.265	.118
1984	654	4438	.147	36727	139391	.263	.116
1985	596	4273	.139	36182	138802	.261	.121
1986	597	4338	.138	36283	138768	.261	.124
1987	595	4296	.139	37300	139799	.267	.128

	Pitchers			Non-Pitchers			Diff
Year	H	AB	AVG	H	AB	AVG	
1988	570	4281	.133	35674	138287	.258	.125
1989	592	4259	.139	35701	138562	.258	.119
1990	572	4131	.138	36245	138637	.261	.123
1991	555	4007	.139	36003	138960	.259	.121
1992	567	4110	.138	35977	138785	.259	.121
1993	722	4768	.151	40366	150227	.269	.117
1994	522	3384	.154	29221	106882	.273	.119
1995	616	4147	.149	36359	134424	.270	.122
1996	693	4691	.148	41627	152110	.274	.126
1997	650	4697	.138	40821	150741	.271	.133

As you can see, the difference between pitchers' batting averages and hitters' batting averages were never greater than in 1997 (.133). This is a solid indication that baseball in 1997 was considerably stronger than in 1958 (.101).

After adding two new expansion teams in 1998, you would expect the talent level to be somewhat weaker. In fact, it did become weaker, as this theory predicted it would. With the 1998 season almost over, the differential is coming in at .125--making the league weaker than in 1998, but not significantly weaker.

By adding two teams in 1998, we increased the number of teams from 28 to 30--an increase of seven percent. You would expect the talent level to go down about 7 percent, plus or minus some variation. Well, the difference between .133 and .125 is 6.4 percent.

There is more evidence to support this theory. In 1943, when World War II had thinned talent not just in the majors, but also in the minors, where the potential major-league replacements lay, the differential between pitchers' batting averages and hitters' batting averages was .083, the lowest differential since 1924.

It wasn't until the effect of integration was felt in the '50s that the differential passed the .100 mark. The Latin American invasion added more talent to the majors, increasing the differential to .117 in 1962. Starting in 1952, when integration truly began to take effect, the differential grew 17 percent over the next 10 years. The black population made up 9.9 percent of the population in 1950 and 10.5 percent in 1960, so allowing this segment of the population to play should have resulted in an increase of talent of about ten percent. The influx of Latino talent only boosted the talent level in the league even more.

Let's go back to the home-run increase we're currently experiencing. Expansion has somewhat diluted the pitching talent in 1998, but it seems to have dropped only to '96 levels. It looks like other factors may have more to do with the home run explosion: smaller strike zones (no longer shoulders to knees, but waist to knees), stronger athletes, and, most importantly, smaller ballparks.

Pitching is as strong these days as ever. Medical advances have also added to the talent pool (Roger Clemens underwent shoulder surgery in 1985). One mustn't overlook the presence of Latino and black talent. This is the golden age of baseball.

1943: WWII dilutes the talent--PD reaches a 19-year low.
1966: the full effect of African-American and Latino integration is felt.
1971-76: the closing of the Cuban talent pipeline is felt.
1997-98: Asian and Cuban pitchers offset expansion's stress on pitching (Livan Hernandez, Orlando Hernandez, Rolando Arrojo, Hideki Irabu, Shigetoshi Hasegawa have 67 career wins and 53 career losses combined at the time of this writing).

CINERGY FIELD/RIVERFRONT STADIUM
HOME OF THE CINCINNATI REDS

The naming of ballparks became complicated after the 1950s. Teams began to leave cities, so naming ballparks after teams became risky. When city, county and state governments began building stadiums, the governments gave them safer names, such as County Stadium, Three Rivers Stadium or Riverfront Stadium. Fans complained that the names were too hard to remember and lacked baseball flavor. The fans said they missed the days when ballparks were named after powerful people such as Wrigley, Crosley or Griffith.

What baseball fans hate the most, however, is change. Once again, parks are being named after powerful people and companies, yet fans still complain. They may have a point, though. Can you tell which home teams play with these parks? Turner Field, 3Com Park, Pro Player Stadium, Qualcomm Stadium, Edison International Field, Bank One Ballpark, and Cinergy Field. If you got all of them right, you deserve a major league contract.

Well, I'll give you the answer for one right away. Cincinnati's Riverfront Stadium is now called Cinergy Field. The name may shock a few fans, but in some ways it is a return to the old days.

There is a legacy about governments building stadiums that cannot be changed as easily as a name. Cinergy Field is one of the so-called "cookie-cutter" stadiums. It was built by the city of Cincinnati. On behalf of taxpayers, the city tried to build a park that could earn as much revenue as possible; therefore, the city looked for an additional source of revenue other than the Reds, and it found one: the National Football League. With the promise of an expansion NFL team, the city went ahead and built the multi-purpose stadium.

The generation of cookie-cutter stadiums originated with RFK Stadium in Washington. The park had retractable seats that allowed a swift conversion from a baseball field to a football field and vice versa. The next evolutionary step was the Astrodome, with its luxury suites (skyboxes) and Astroturf. In the next generation of parks, the result was Riverfront/Cinergy, Three Rivers, Veterans Stadium, Busch Stadium and Atlanta-Fulton County Stadium. Cinergy Field added a few things to the evolution of these parks. It was the first to use synthetic turf all over the infield, leaving only small dirt patches around the bases.

The synthetic turf can make Cinergy Field a horrible place to play or watch summer baseball. On July 26, 1997, Atlanta Brave shortstop Jeff Blauser discovered his cleats had melted after the field temperature reached 120 degrees. The next day, the temperature rose even higher in the afternoon sun. The mercury reached 152 degrees on the field -- the equivalent of trying to play baseball while sitting in your car on a 100+ degree day, with the air conditioner off, the windows rolled up and the sun incinerating your dashboard. Imagine trying to pitch when your brain is being boiled. That's what Greg Maddux had to do on July 27, 1997. He said he felt mentally burned, physically burned, mush-brained. Over a hundred fans had to receive treatment for heat exposure.

Unlike other "cookie-cutter" stadiums, which are surrounded by seas of parking spaces, Cinergy's parking lots are underground, below the field. Cinergy Field satellite photo courtesy of the United States Goelogical Survey.

Park Factors

Year	Avg	R	H	2B	3B	HR	L-Avg	R-Avg	L-HR	R-HR
1992	97	103	95	103	82	139	105	91	109	159
1993	99	98	96	100	59	106	98	99	158	91
1994	95	98	94	109	86	98	94	95	77	112
1995	100	95	98	107	90	87	104	99	119	73
1996	98	100	96	109	117	98	102	96	109	91
1997	102	106	101	115	112	108	106	98	137	94

CINERGY FIELD
CINCINNATI REDS
(1992-1998)

Artificial turf
Opened for MLB in 1970

Fences:	8 feet
Altitude:	550 feet
Capacity:	52,952 (baseball)
Area of fair territory:	112,000 sq. ft.
Foul territory:	Small

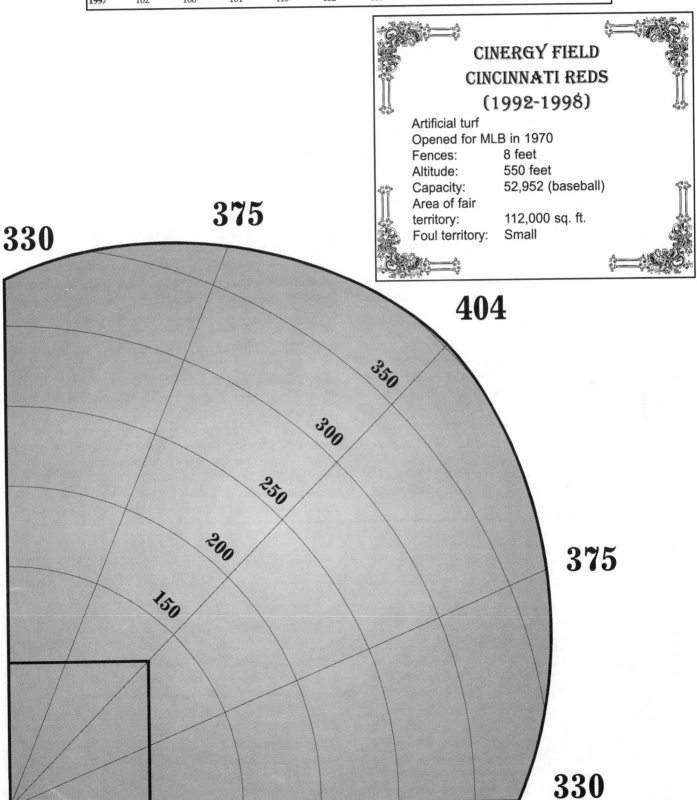

CROSLEY FIELD
HOME OF THE CINCINNATI REDS

In 1912, the Cincinnati Reds moved from Palace of the Fans to Redland Field. In 1934, the park was renamed Crosley Field in honor of the Reds' owner, Powel Crosley. Originally, Redland Field was different from what it later became. The park was symmetrical, measuring 360 feet down the lines and 420 to straightaway center. Following the 1926 season, home plate was moved out 20 feet and the playing field was rotated slightly, in order to increase capacity.

In 1935, Crosley became the first park in the majors to host a night game. President Franklin Delano Roosevelt flipped a special switch in the White House that turned on the lights. Night games were astronomically successful, and most major league teams ultimately were forced to follow suit, despite many owners' dislike of night baseball.

The park's dimensions changed again for the 1938 season when home plate was moved another 20 feet towards center, resulting in the following dimensions: 328 to the left field foul pole, 387 to center field, and 366 to the right field pole. Even so, the fences remained too deep to reach with regularity, and Crosley remained a pitchers' park.

For 1953 through 1957, Crosley was a hitters' park, as home plate was again moved toward center field. An inner fence in right field cut the distance to the right field pole from 366 feet to 342, and center field became much shallower. Crosley became an easy place to score runs and to hit homers, yielding about 10 percent more runs and homers than average. Even more runs would have been scored if the size of the foul territory behind home not been allowed to grow to to 78 feet (about 18 feet longer than average). The inner fence in right field was removed after the '57 season.

The Reds transplanted Crosley's home plate to Riverfront Stadium (now Cinergy Field) when they left their old park in 1970. Crosley was used as a car junkyard for two years before being torn down. Many parts of the old park were auctioned off. Larry Luebbers, from Union, Kentucky, bought several pieces of the stadium. On his ranch, he began to reconstruct the old park. His version of it included 400 seats, the 60-foot flagpole, the scoreboard, the ticket office and some of the original walls. He also recreated the 40-foot incline that gave outfielders so much trouble as they backpedaled uphill towards the wall. Originally, Crosley's incline existed only in left field. In 1936, it was extended from foul pole to foul pole. Due to the incline, Crosley was exempted from having a warning track.

All seemed perfect with Luebbers' private Crosley, but like many mothers who have thrown out invaluable baseball cards, Luebbers' mother sold the land and old Crosley was thrown out as garbage. By some sort of divine intervention, a man named Mark Rohr discovered a few of Luebbers' pieces in a faraway dump site. Rohr roamed to the ends of the Earth to recover the rest of the missing pieces. Some seats were discovered -- still in use -- in a softball complex. Others were found in a skating rink. In the end, he received help from the Reds, and through his efforts, Crosley rose again in 1988, 16 years after being torn down. The revived park is now in Blue Ash, Ohio, about a half hour from downtown Cincinnati.

Businesses in the area of Cincy where Crosley once stood proudly display authentic red seats on their lawns. The terrace that went up to meet the walls is still visible, half-covered by pavement. Don't believe it? Take a drive around York, Findlay and Dalton streets. You'll see old Crosley.

Palace of the Fans was Cincinnati's home from 1902 to 1911. Photograph taken April 14, 1905. Courtesy of the Library of Congress.

Crosley Field
Park Factors

Year	R	HR
1953	102	116
1954	112	170
1955	113	130
1956	117	128
1957	118	149

CROSLEY FIELD
CINCINNATI REDS
(1953-1957)

Opened for MLB in 1912

Fences:	LF: 18 feet
	Scoreboard in L-C: 37 feet
	L-C to R-C: 18 feet
	RF: 10 feet
Altitude:	550 feet
Capacity:	20,000
Area of fair territory:	104,000 sq. ft.
Foul territory:	Average

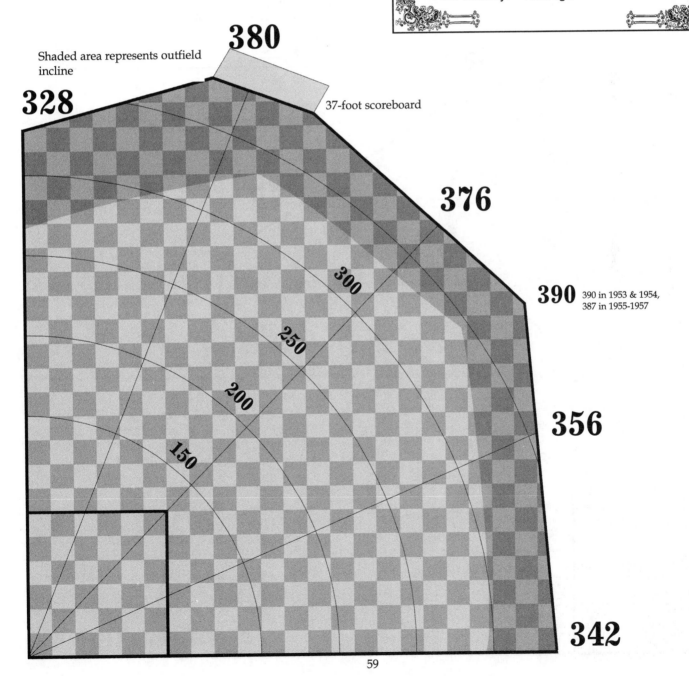

Shaded area represents outfield incline

328

380

37-foot scoreboard

376

390 — 390 in 1953 & 1954, 387 in 1955-1957

356

342

300

250

200

150

CROSLEY FIELD
CINCINNATI REDS
(1938-1941)

Opened for MLB in 1912

Fences:	LF: 18 feet
	Scoreboard in L-C: 30 feet
	L-C to R-C: 18 feet
	RF: 7.5 feet
Altitude:	550 feet
Capacity:	20,000
Area of fair territory:	108,000 sq. ft.
Foul territory:	Small

380

328

387

399

350

300

250

200

150

364

366

Redland Field
Park Factors

Year	R	HR
1912	81	22
1913	109	73
1914	113	25
1915	106	44
1916	99	41
1917	90	39
1918	97	58
1919	103	56
1920	76	16

REDLAND FIELD
CINCINNATI REDS
(1912-1920)

Opened for MLB in 1912	
Fences:	Unknown
Altitude:	550 feet
Capacity:	25,000
Area of fair territory:	118,000 sq. ft.
Foul territory:	Average

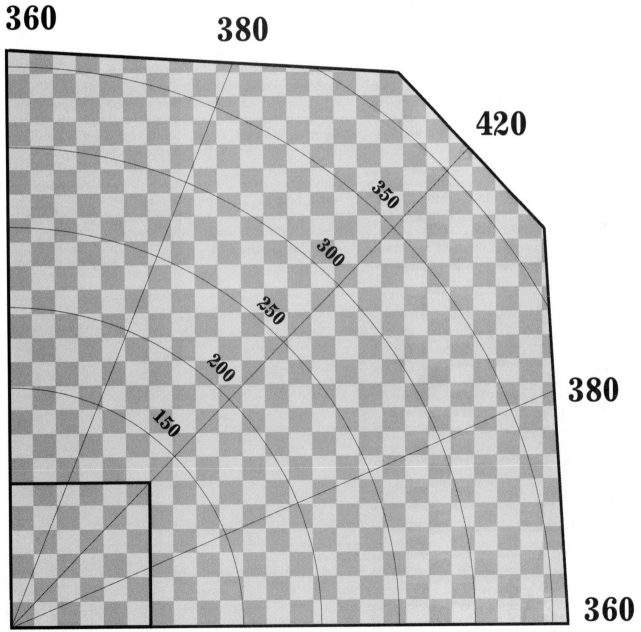

JACOBS FIELD
HOME OF THE CLEVELAND INDIANS

A very confused child once asked me, "How can the Detroit Lions call themselves the *Detroit* Lions if they play in Pontiac? And how can the Giants call themselves the *New York* Giants if they play in the Meadowlands?" I had no answer. Some city's names are just part of team's nicknames... not unlike a "Hawaiian" souvenir made in a third-world country.

"Cleveland," however, is not a just a name next to "Indians." Jacobs Field is a jewel in the heart of downtown Cleveland. It is the shining symbol of a city that has reinvented itself. The Indians are now winners and play in a city that again knows how to win. From Jacobs Field, Cleveland looks beautiful. It has made the locals realize, "Wow, forget the jokes, Cleveland is a big-time city." Although the park was built only a few years ago, it fits so perfectly in its location that it now is difficult to imagine Cleveland without it. The strong identification of the team with the city changed Cleveland from a medium-sized baseball market into a big-time baseball town, and other baseball owners noticed. Fans who would not dare go to Cleveland Stadium now follow the team to Detroit, Chicago, and even Milwaukee to watch their dear Indians, because all the home games are sold out.

There are people who still criticize baseball in Cleveland, perhaps out of habit. Some announcers complain that it's too cold in the late spring or early fall. But are Clevelanders really afraid of the cold? Pampered sportscasters are not qualified to judge. Go to the stands and ask the fans. They'll tell you it's *Cleveland*, for crying out loud. As long as there isn't a foot of lake effect snow, let's play ball!

It's true that curveball pitchers may have a hard time getting a feel for their pitch when it's cold. They like moisture on their hands to grip the seams, and they like the cowhide to give in slightly. In the cold, pitchers' hands dry out instead of sweat, and pitchers are forced to go to great lengths to keep their hands warm. Plus, the ball's cover hardens. The worst thing for a curveball pitcher is to stay out in the cold longer than necessary. If an inning drags out longer, even if it is by bloop singles, curveball pitchers make themselves more susceptible to walking people or giving up clean hits because the longer they stay out in the cold, the more they risk losing the feeling for the curve .

Batters are less intellectual when it comes to cold weather. All they want is to keep from having balls busted on their fists. Hitting a ball in cold weather with a wooden bat is like taking a full uppercut at an oak tree.

However, it isn't always cold in Cleveland. Runs pile up in the summertime at the Jake. Despite the straight, asymmetrical walls and the funny bounces they produce, the lack of foul territory keeps the number of triples around the average. And forget about the constant homer highlights seen on ESPN -- Jacobs Field is a *below*-average home run park. The park really is a doubles park. In some years, it may produce up to 20 percent more doubles than the average American League park.

Jacobs Field is part of the Gateway Sports and Entertainment Complex, which includes Jacobs Field and the NBA Gund Arena, home of the Cleveland Cavaliers. Although the complex provides the grand-scale architectural beauty that Cleveland had lacked for years, Jacobs Field is not without its critics. It was given "the mother-of-all" private-sector tax-free incentives to operate in downtown Cleveland. Many Cleveland taxpayers do not approve of their tax dollars being spent to subside Major League Baseball and the NBA. Doomsayers predict that the property tax revenue the city could have collected from the site will be sorely missed, and that the missing revenue will result in the eventual underfinancing of Cleveland's public schools.

Park Factors										
Year	Avg	R	H	2B	3B	HR	L-Avg	R-Avg	L-HR	R-HR
1994	101	108	105	121	80	118	99	103	121	118
1995	96	87	95	94	107	88	100	92	91	86
1996	99	105	101	121	102	84	99	103	78	89
1997	99	97	97	98	72	85	103	97	97	75

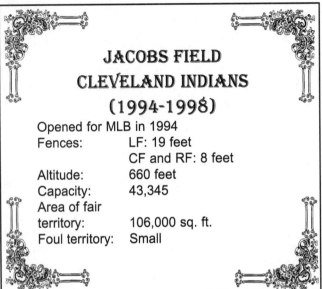

JACOBS FIELD
CLEVELAND INDIANS
(1994-1998)

Opened for MLB in 1994
Fences:	LF: 19 feet
	CF and RF: 8 feet
Altitude:	660 feet
Capacity:	43,345
Area of fair territory:	106,000 sq. ft.
Foul territory:	Small

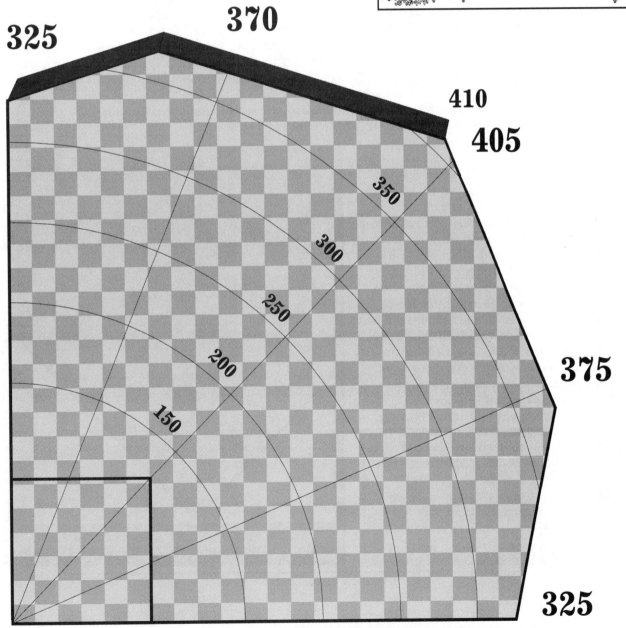

325

370

410

405

350

300

250

200

150

375

325

CLEVELAND STADIUM
HOME OF THE CLEVELAND INDIANS

Bob DiBiasio, the Indians' vice-president, said the club chose to increase the size of Cleveland Stadium for 1991 because they were out-homered 2-to-1 at home the previous year. The Indians expected to feature speed in 1991, so they increased left field from 377 to 390, left-center from 387 to 400, center from 400 to 415, right-center from 395 to 400 and right field from 385 to 390.

Then the Indians went out and acquired Glenallen Hill and Reggie Jefferson--both power hitters--to complement a young Albert Belle. In 1990 the team finished with a 77-85 record. In 1991, they ended up at 57-105. The '91 Indians hit 22 homers at home and 57 on the road. Although they expected to have a running team in 1991, Cleveland had only two players with more than eight stolen bases. The '91 team was a power team, and management hurt its own chances by making Cleveland Stadium an impossible home run park. Unfortunately, it is illegal to change a park's dimension in the middle of the season, so the Indians had to wait until 1992 to change the park back to favor power hitters. The 1992 Indians slammed 62 home runs at Cleveland Stadium, 40 more than the previous season. They also won 19 more games. The moral of story is: either build the right team for your park, or build the right park for your team.

The new dimensions used in Cleveland Stadium in 1992 and 1993 resulted in a friendlier park for lefthanded home run hitters. The dimensions to left field were slightly larger, making the park an average place to homer for righthanded pull hitters. The new dimensions made doubles and triples rarer than normal, making the park an average place to score, despite the abundance of homers.

The 1992 and 1993 seasons were the last two for the park, which first opened its gates in 1932. Between 1932 and 1946, the Indians played at both League Park and Cleveland Stadium. Team officials would schedule games with potentially high attendance at Cleveland Stadium because it could accommodate about 53,000 more people than League Park. Owner Bill Veeck decided to use Cleveland Stadium on a full-time basis beginning in 1947.

Because of its large capacity, Cleveland Stadium hosted the All-Star Game four times; only New York and Chicago have hosted more games than Cleveland. Though the game was hyped by a *Chicago Tribune* writer, the game's origin was a charity game between the American League All-Stars and the Indians in 1911. The purpose of the game was to raise money for the widow of Indians' pitcher Addie Joss, who died of tubercular meningitis prior to the season. The first official All-Star Game was held in Chicago in 1933.

Cleveland Stadium was abandoned by two major professional teams in the 1990s. The Indians moved out in favor of Jacobs Field, and the Cleveland Browns moved to Baltimore.

In their new park, the Indians in effect became a large-market team, drawing big crowds on a daily basis. It had been difficult to attract fans to the "Mistake by the Lake," as Cleveland Stadium was nicknamed. In Jacbos Field the autumn nights don't seem as cold. Depression-era Cleveland Stadium reminded the city of the image it wanted to erase. Jacobs Field represents everything about Cleveland that the city wants to show the rest of the world.

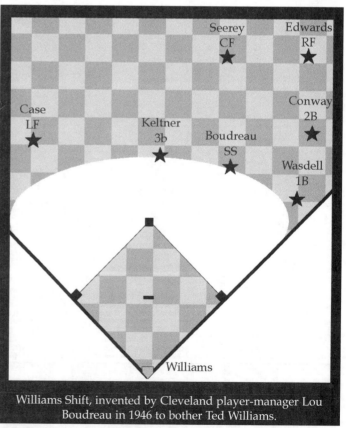

Williams Shift, invented by Cleveland player-manager Lou Boudreau in 1946 to bother Ted Williams.

Hank Aaron said that part of the reason why the NL went 28-5-1 against the AL after the 1950 season was because the AL was slow in integrating. In 1959 the NL had eight black players in the All-Star Game while the AL had only one, and that angered black players. He said the black NL players wanted to show the AL, so they played harder and won.

Park Factors

Year	Avg	R	H	2B	3B	HR	L-Avg	R-Avg	L-HR	R-HR
1992	108	116	111	111	93	116	104	111	113	119
1993	94	85	89	98	77	93	94	93	105	87

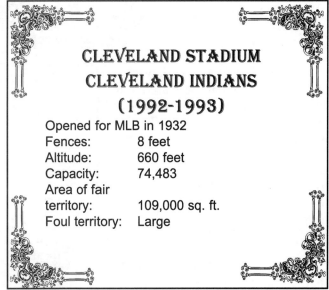

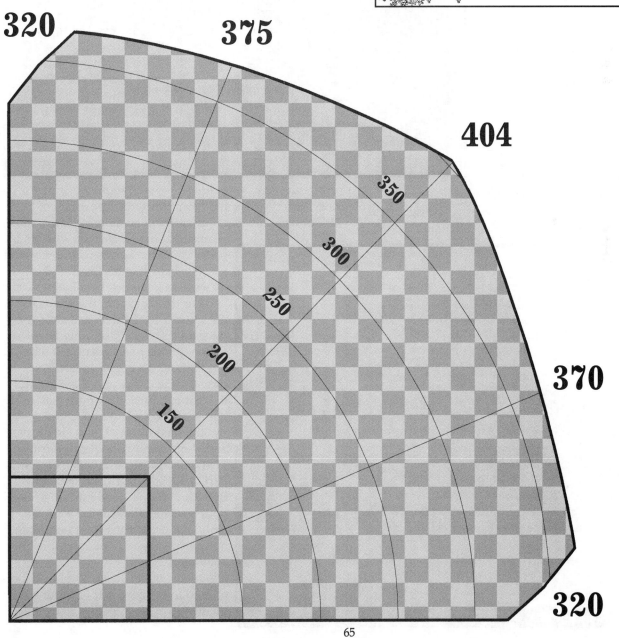

320 375

404

370

350 300 250 200 150

320

LEAGUE PARK
HOME OF THE CLEVELAND INDIANS

The first League Park was built in 1891. The park was used from 1901 to 1909 by the Cleveland Indians of the new American League. The field was ragged. The ballpark was an unattractive wooden hull. Like many other AL teams, Cleveland was using its ballpark temporarily. When the Indians felt stable, they built a new ballpark, also called League Park. The new League Park opened its doors in 1910.

The new ballpark had an odd shape, almost as if right field was missing. The irregular shape was the result of the owners of a saloon and two homes refusing to sell their properties. Therefore, the park never reached the dimensions first envisioned.

From 1910 to 1919, the park had a gargantuan left field, measuring 505 feet to deepest left-center field. In 1920, new seats were added in left field, reducing the distances. Also in 1920, a 45-foot barrier was installed in right field to prevent balls from leaving the park too easily. The right field wall became a fan favorite because balls that hit the wall's

League Park, courtesy of the Library of Congress.

protruding steel supports rebounded unpredictably. A 25-foot chicken-wire screen comprised the upper half of the 45-foot wall, causing outfielders even more problems. Steel beams held up the chicken wire, and balls hitting the beams would rebound sharply. Balls that hit the wire, however, were liable to drop straight down.

For the most part, the winds blew out toward left field. Fortunately for pitchers, left field was rather deep. Even with the wind gusting, it was difficult to hit a homer to left. The spacious left field area and the high wall in right cut down the number of homers for both lefthanded and righthanded hitters. Many long drives ended up as only doubles and triples. This didn't necessarily make League Park a pitchers' park, though. Lazy flyballs to right turned into singles or doubles when they hit the wall. Although home runs were rarer than normal at League Park, runs still abounded.

Many great Cleveland players performed in League Park. Cy Young won the first game ever played at the origi-

League Park, courtesy of the Library of Congress.

66

nal League Park for Cleveland. Tris Speaker led the Indians to a World Championship as a player-manager in 1920. In the same World Series, Indians' second baseman Bill Wambsganss started an unassisted triple play. Napoleon Lajoie played 12-plus dominant seasons for the Indians, who for a time were called the Naps in his honor. Bob Feller struck out 17 batters in one game in 1936. Babe Ruth hit his 500th homer down the right field line in 1929. The Washington Senators stole eight bases in the first inning in 1915.

A precursor to the modern All-Star Game was played on July 11, 1911. In that contest, a team of American League "All-Stars" played the Naps, raising a sum equivalent to $165,000 in 1996 dollars for Addie Joss's widow and nine-year-old son. Joss had been a standout Indians pitcher, but succumbed to tubercular meningitis only two days after his 31st birthday. The All-Star Game as we know it came into being in 1933.

Between 1932 and 1946, the Indians played their day games at League Park and their night games at Municipal Stadium. Because of Municipal's large capacity, important weekday games were also played there. The Indians moved permanently to Municipal Stadium in 1948.

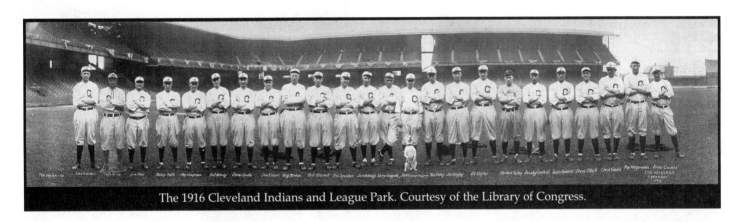

The 1916 Cleveland Indians and League Park. Courtesy of the Library of Congress.

This photo is of an amateur game at Brookside Stadium in Cleveland between the Cleveland White Autos and Omaha, Nebraska on October 10, 1915. The attendance was reported between 85,000 and 115,000. The huge crowd is a reminder that Major League Baseball's supremacy was less secure in its infancy than it is today. Photo courtesy of the Library of Congress.

League Park Park Factors		
Year	R	HR
1910	105	47
1911	104	119
1912	102	63
1913	113	59
1914	108	50
1915	109	71
1916	100	68
1917	127	76
1918	120	43
1919	112	60

League Park Park Factors		
Year	R	HR
1921	95	42
1922	109	52
1923	104	64
1924	95	61
1925	117	85
1926	93	60
1927	94	49
1928	116	41
1929	99	69

LEAGUE PARK
CLEVELAND INDIANS
(1921-1929)

Opened for MLB in 1910
Fences: LF: 5 feet
                   L-C: 10 feet
                   CF-RF: 45 feet
Altitude: 660 feet
Capacity: 21,414
Area of fair
territory: 103,000 sq. ft.
Foul territory: Average

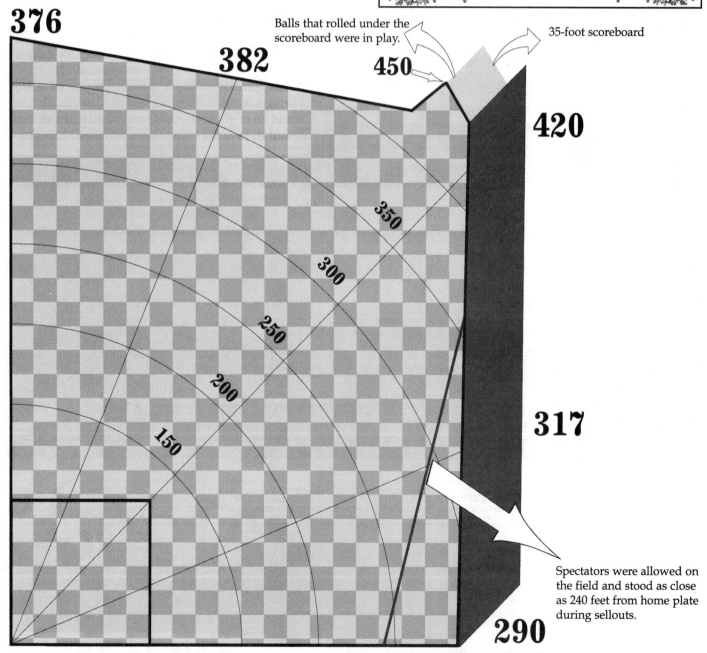

376

382

450

Balls that rolled under the scoreboard were in play.

35-foot scoreboard

420

350

300

250

200

150

317

Spectators were allowed on the field and stood as close as 240 feet from home plate during sellouts.

290

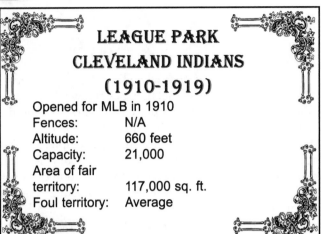

LEAGUE PARK
CLEVELAND INDIANS
(1910-1919)

Opened for MLB in 1910
Fences: N/A
Altitude: 660 feet
Capacity: 21,000
Area of fair
territory: 117,000 sq. ft.
Foul territory: Average

385 **428** **505**

420

350

300

250

200

150

317

290

COORS FIELD
HOME OF THE COLORADO ROCKIES

It's safe to say that when the founding fathers of baseball invented the game, they never envisioned that the game would be played in a place like Denver, Colorado. Denver's altitude distorts the game of baseball in ways that could not have been foreseen. For example, a 400-foot homer at sea level would sail 430 feet at Coors Field. But there are other, more subtle ways the elevation can hurt pitchers. For example, curveballs break about 25 percent less in the thin air.

Robert K. Adair wrote in his book *The Physics of Baseball* that in Coors Field, balls travel into the outfield much more quickly, leaving outfielders less time to react. As a result, an outfielder's range may be reduced by as much as eight feet. The same is true to a lesser extent for infielders; their range may reduced by six to 12 inches. They say (all too often) that baseball is a game of inches, and there's no better illustration than this. The effects could be the difference between an out or a double down the line.

Compared to today's parks, Coors Field is large, yet it remains a home run haven. In fact, the long measurements have resulted in more triples and doubles being hit at this park than at any other in the majors. In addition, Coors has a hard infield. Balls skip through the infield as if they were hit in an empty parking lot. Even pitchers who successfully keep the ball on the ground may find themselves singled to death.

Coors Field puts unique demands on managers, who must be patient and leave their starting pitcher in the game, even when they seem to be getting hit hard. Going to the bullpen too early can be dangerous, since it's all too easy to empty out an entire bullpen in nine innings. As the home team, the Rockies often are forced to carry an extra pitcher at the expense of a bench player.

Coors has another terrifying effect. More hits and runs means pitchers have to throw more pitches in order to work a given number of innings. More pitches means the staff will have more wear and tear, and more injuries. Even bad pitchers have value here because they allow managers to save their better pitchers in blowouts.

The park factors below show that triples occur far more frequently in Coors Field than in the rest of the National League parks. It should be obvious why this happens. There are three characteristics that make a park a triples haven: 1) the right field corner is far from home plate; 2) substantial foul territory exists down the right field line; and 3) the outfield walls are quirky.

Coors qualifies on all three counts. It's 350 feet down the right field line; this gives runners about two extra seconds to reach third base on balls hit to the wall, compared to a park with a 325-foot right field fence.

The large foul territory down the right field line helps as well. In parks where there is little foul territory, a ball hit down the line will often rebound toward the right fielder. In Coors, there is substantial foul territory between the foul line and the wall, and a ball hit down the right field line may travel all the way into the corner before the fielder can retrieve it. By the time the fielder chases it down, he's wasted a few seconds while moving farther away from third base.

Finally, the shape of Coors' walls is conducive to three base hits. Its straight walls create awkward bounces, sending caroms off at an angle rather than directly back to the fielder. Outfielders in Coors have a dilemma when tracking a line drive heading toward the right field corner, where two sections of the fence come together at an angle, about 10 feet from the foul pole. If the ball hits the fence to the left of the angle, it will bounce back toward the infield, but a line drive that hits the section of the wall between the angle and the foul pole will ricochet towards center field, parallel to the outfield wall. Many outfielders have run all-out toward the right field corner only to have the ball bounce back past them with impossible speed.

Coors Field Fun Fact
by John Sasman

Games when the losing team scored 10 or more runs between 1995 and August 29, 1998:

	Number	Total Games	Rate
In Coors	17	301	once every 17.7 games
Other NL parks	18	4122	once every 229.0 games

Park Factors

Year	Avg	R	H	2B	3B	HR	L-Avg	R-Avg	L-HR	R-HR
1995	126	164	135	123	275	189	119	130	144	215
1996	132	172	146	130	136	166	122	137	156	169
1997	118	133	126	116	113	119	117	119	94	140

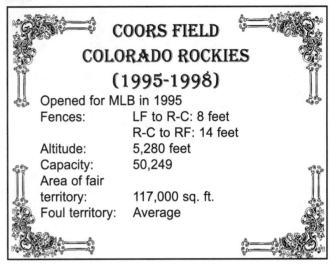

Opened for MLB in 1995
Fences: LF to R-C: 8 feet
                  R-C to RF: 14 feet

Altitude: 5,280 feet
Capacity: 50,249
Area of fair
territory: 117,000 sq. ft.
Foul territory: Average

347
390
415
350
300
250
200
150
375
350

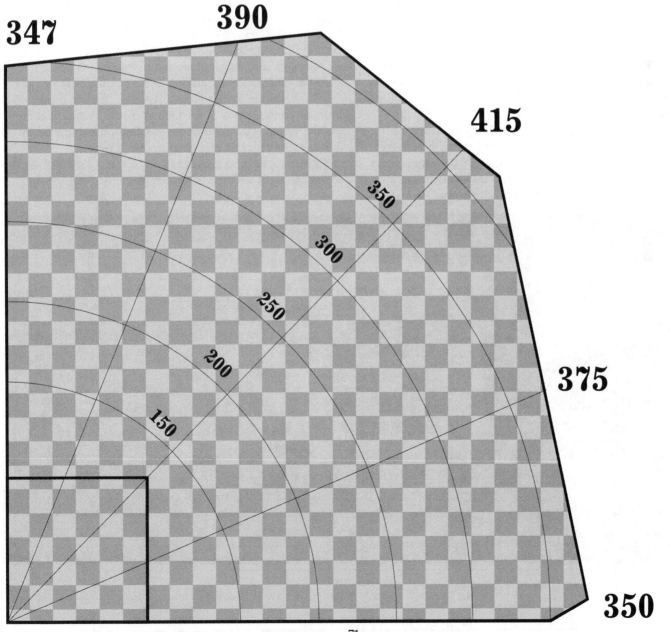

MILE HIGH STADIUM
HOME OF THE COLORADO ROCKIES

Although it hosted major league baseball for only two seasons, Mile High Stadium and baseball go way back. Even before it was the home of the NFL Denver Broncos, Mile High was the home of the Triple-A Denver Bears. Originally built in 1947, the stadium was first known as Bears Stadium. Capacity was increased a few more times until it more or less arrived at its current form in 1968, when it was rededicated and renamed Mile High Stadium.

The Colorado Rockies played for two years at Mile High while their new home, Coors Field was being built. Game after game, the Rockies put football-sized crowds in the stands. In 1994, they drew a record 4.49 million fans. On Opening Day of their maiden season, the Rockies drew 80,227 people. While playing at Mile High, the Rockies drew better than 70,000 people on 21 occasions. In the 135 dates played at Mile High, the average attendance per game was 57,051. Though support for the Rockies remains astronomically high, all these records appear safe for now since Coors Field seats only 50,249, about 25,000 less than Mile High.

Colorado's staggering attendance figures sent every marketing department in Major League Baseball scrambling, but people who were affected the most were pitchers. Due to the altitude, the ball travels extremely well in Denver. This factor alone produces more home runs and more hits because the faster the ball travels, the less likely it is to be caught anywhere on the field. The dimensions of Mile High Stadium were generous, turning some potential homers into triples. Right field was enormous -- 370 down the line and quickly falling back to 400 feet in the power alley. The result was that triples were three times more abundant at Mile High than at the average National League park. Many homers still were hit at Mile High, but the effect was not outrageous (it was only about 15 percent better than the average park). Over the same two-year period, a comparable number of homers were hit at Riverfront Stadium (now Cinergy Field).

What drove the pitchers crazy were singles and triples. In 1993 and '94, there were 304 homers hit at Mile High by the home and visiting teams. In the same period, there were 150 triples hit. In the Rockies' road games, there were 264 homers and only 47 triples. The additional number of triples and singles resulted in more runs being scored at this park than anywhere else in the majors.

After the Rockies left Mile High, the stadium returned to the hands of the Denver Broncos and was the stage of the magical 1997 Broncos Championship season. The Broncos are now campaigning for a new stadium, however, since Mile High has no luxury boxes. It's future is uncertain.

Mile High Stadium, as seen by a Soviet spy satellite. The left-field seats have been pushed outward to convert Mile High into a baseball facility. The seats are retracted to convert the field for the Denver Broncos.
Satellite photo by SOVINFORMSPUTNIK & Aerial Images, Inc.

					Park Factors					
Year	Avg	R	H	2B	3B	HR	L-Avg	R-Avg	L-HR	R-HR
1993	118	152	123	112	291	127	112	121	87	146
1994	114	132	118	105	348	98	102	122	69	112

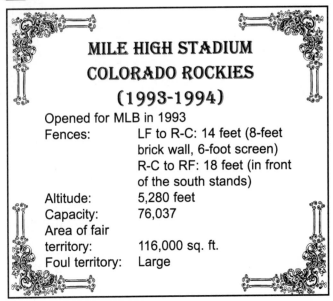

333   **366**

423

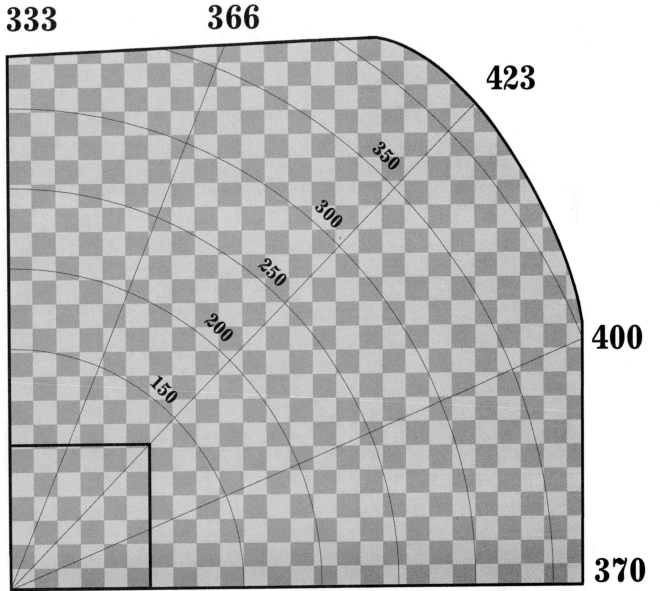

400

370

TIGER STADIUM
HOME OF THE DETROIT TIGERS

I have met many people who say they are from Detroit, but as we go deeper into our conversation, it turns out they really live in Mt. Clemens, Farmington Hills, Sterling Heights, Dearborn, Southfield or some other Detroit suburb. It seems like no one lives *in* Detroit anymore, although a million people still do.

Detroit lost 14.6 percent of its population in the 1980s, and has lost 32 percent of its population since 1970. It bothers people in Detroit that their city has not adjusted to the post-industrialist world. It eats at them that their city is considered an "urban basket-case." And it pains them to see the buildings from Detroit's golden era crumbling. Decay is omnipresent.

Those that remain in the city have searched for a magic bullet, and Cleveland's plan gave them an idea: revitalize downtown with a new stadium. The last serious talks on a new park were held in the mid-1980s, when Detroit had little concrete proof (e.g., Cleveland) of what a new ballpark could do for a downtown area. It's a good thing the city did not choose to build then, for Detroit would have ended up with a stadium like New Comiskey Park or Skydome.

Recently, though, Detroit voters passed a referendum approving the construction of a new sports complex for the Tigers and NFL Lions. This new complex is supposed to be Detroit's magic bullet. It is hoped that the two adjacent stadiums will bring money back into the heart of Detroit. The project is expected to cost $505 million.

The thinking is that if that much money is spent in Detroit, more will follow, from others. Confidence in Detroit will soar, they say, and the city will be reborn. On clear nights people will gaze toward the city and see two shining new gems downtown. Detroiters will be proud to live here. Politicians will be re-elected. People will move back into the city, showering it with tax revenue.

Can a new sports complex revitalize a city that has been burning, in one way or another, since the 1967 riots? Perhaps the expectations are too high here; if so, the sports complex may be set up to be a disastrous failure. On the other hand, $505 million can buy more than a couple of air fresheners.

The attitude in Detroit is that if the new complex can revitalize downtown, then Tiger Stadium should be plowed under. After all, the city has enough old buildings. There is more than baseball at stake here, they say; last year, Detroit gave out 86 permits for new housing constructions, and 8,432 for housing demolitions. But orthodox baseball fans are appalled at the idea of sacrificing Tiger Stadium.

Tiger Stadium will be mourned, no doubt. But if Detroit is finally revitalized after several other failed attempts, it will be a testimony to the power of sports. Then again, Detroit may not be revived; either way, Tiger Stadium will be gone.

Good luck, Detroit. You're about to make a sacrifice of mythical proportions. Tiger Stadium is a jewel in the firmament of ballparks. May Al Kaline, Hank Greenberg, Heinie Manush, Mickey Cochrane, George Kell, Sam Crawford, Charlie Gehringer, Ty Cobb, Harry Heilmann, Hughie Jennings and Hal Newhouser forgive you.

Satellite photo by SOVINFORMSPUTNIK & Aerial Images, Inc.

Park Factors

Year	Avg	R	H	2B	3B	HR	L-Avg	R-Avg	L-HR	R-HR
1992	100	101	101	102	84	118	103	98	141	109
1993	97	99	95	88	89	125	99	95	128	124
1994	101	102	101	88	135	107	95	106	108	106
1995	99	109	97	90	120	131	94	103	148	121
1996	96	97	95	94	70	108	95	96	106	110
1997	94	101	92	87	113	118	97	91	129	110

TIGER STADIUM
DETROIT TIGERS
(1992-1998)

Opened for MLB in 1912
Fences:	6.5 feet, except CF: 5.5
Altitude:	585 feet
Capacity:	46,945
Area of fair territory:	113,000 sq. ft.
Foul territory:	Small

The dark line inside the right field line represents where the second deck of seats overhangs the first deck. The second deck is 10 feet closer to home plate than the first deck. Meaning a towering fly ball may only need to travel 315 feet down the right field line to be a home run, while a grounder may roll 325 feet down the same right field line.

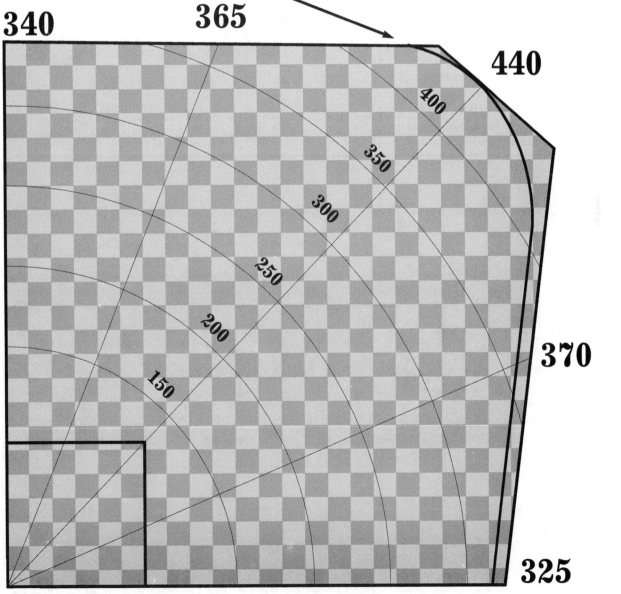

340   365   440   400   350   300   250   200   150   370   325

Navin Field, named after team co-owner Frank Navin, was built on the same site where Bennett Park stood between 1896 and 1911. In 1938, the park was renamed for its new owner, Walter Briggs. The park was rechristened (again) as Tiger Stadium in 1961.

When Navin Field was built on the site where Bennett park had stood, the infield was turned 80 degrees. Before the switch, lefthanded and righthanded hitters had to bat while facing into the afternoon sun. A double-decked grandstand replaced Bennett's simple grandstand. The homes beyond left field and the industrial buildings beyond right field were purchased by the team, and the ballpark was expanded to cover the entire city block for the first time. For the 1938 season, Navin Field was rebuilt again; the makeover was so complete that the newer Navin can be considered a whole new stadium. Cherry Street was pushed away from the park to increase the size of the stadium's city block.

The popularity of Ty Cobb and the influx of workers at Ford Motors were the reasons that capacity had to be increased. Bennett proved too small, and shortly thereafter, Navin proved too small, also. When Navin was replaced by the modern Tiger Stadium, the team used up all of the available land. The modern overhang in right field, which hangs 10 feet into the playing field, was an attempt to increase capacity without cutting into the playing field. The overhang results in more homers for lefties.

While managing the Tigers, Cobb used to install temporary bleachers in the right field wall indentation. Any fly balls landing in this bleacher area were ruled doubles, and Cobb used the bleachers as part of his defensive strategy--a practice that is now illegal. Cobb's Lake was an area near home plate soaked with water to deaden Cobb's bunts.

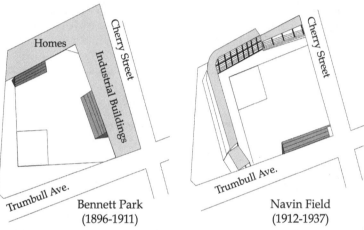

Bennett Park (1896-1911)

Navin Field (1912-1937)

Before Navin Field, the Tigers played at Bennett Stadium. The two photographs show that the Tigers needed a bigger park. If you look on the right of the bottom photo, you'll see that park officials hung sheets so people couldn't see the game from outside the stadium. Nonetheless, fans still managed a peek by climbing the power poles. Photos courtesy of the Library of Congress.

Navin Field
Park Factors

Year	R	HR
1927	122	107
1928	102	97
1929	100	97

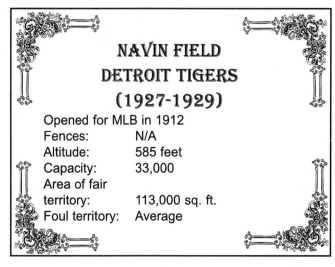

NAVIN FIELD
DETROIT TIGERS
(1927-1929)

Opened for MLB in 1912	
Fences:	N/A
Altitude:	585 feet
Capacity:	33,000
Area of fair territory:	113,000 sq. ft.
Foul territory:	Average

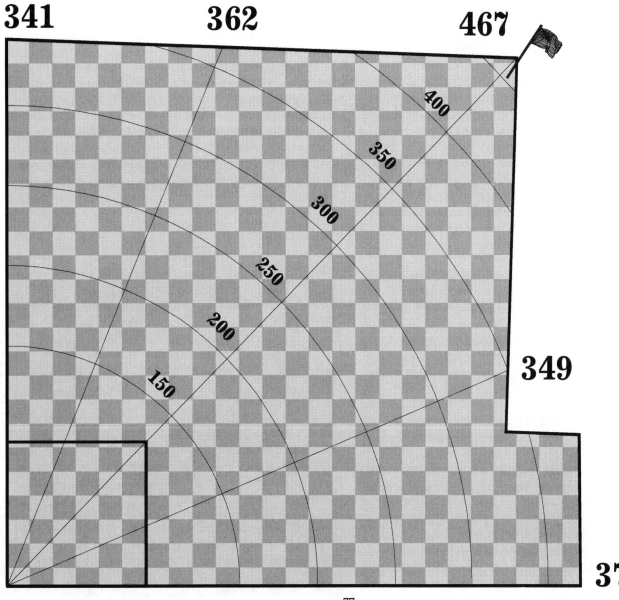

341   362   467

400
350
300
250
200
150

349

371

PRO PLAYER STADIUM
HOME OF THE FLORIDA MARLINS

I've flown to Miami dozens of times. Flying over the city, I wonder what in the world I'm doing living in a cold-weather city like Chicago. Southern Florida has gorgeous beaches. Boats sail up and down the waters as far as your eyes can see. The beach houses give the appearance of a city in constant relaxation. Flying over Miami at night is a different experience, however. The landscape below looks confusing. Clusters of city lights are surrounded by areas of deep darkness, which I imagine to be either canals or warm, primeval swamps. Pro Player Stadium has a similar appearance at night. Flying over it, you see the darkness of the Snake Creek Canal and of the acres of parking lots that surround it. In the middle of the darkness, the park shines like a galaxy unto itself with its pedestrian tunnels coiling upward. Only the shining green grass reveals the grounds to be a place where people come to watch poetry performed by people.

From ground level, there's no doubting the Miami flavor in the stadium. There are over 1,000 palm trees. It is the only park in the majors that plays salsa and other Caribbean music between innings.

Pro Player Stadium was constructed for the Miami Dolphins for the 1987 season. The construction was privately funded, largely through the sale of 10-year leases of executives suites at $30,000 to $90,000 per year and club seats for $800 to $1,800 a year. On March 7, 1990, Wayne Huizenga bought 15 percent of the Dolphins and 50 percent of their stadium in order to bring an expansion baseball team to Miami. The National League granted him a franchise in July of 1991. In 1994, Huizenga bought the remaining 85 percent of the Dolphins and the other 50 percent of the stadium.

Huizenga began his business career in 1962 when he bought a one-truck waste collection route in Ft. Lauderdale. In 1971, Huizenga joined forces with a relative to buy Waste Management Inc. of Chicago. Huizenga's Midas touch continued as he purchased Blockbuster Video in 1987. In addition to owning the Dolphins and the Florida Marlins, the magnate also owns the NHL Florida Panthers.

Huizenga's fortune enabled the Marlins to become the fastest expansion team to win a World Series. Huizenga went on a shopping spree before the 1997 season that brought Alex Fernandez, Bobby Bonilla, Moises Alou, Dennis Cook, John Cangelosi and Jim Eisenreich to the Marlins. Like a teenager bragging to his friends about an expensive car, he joyously announced before the 1997 season that even if every game was a sellout, the team would lose $10 million for the year. His mood changed during the season because the fans did not flock to the stadium as he thought they would. The team also appeared to be in turmoil in the middle of the season when Gary Sheffield complained that management needed to go out and get more players. Manager Jim Leyland responded that they had gotten the players, and that the players who already were there needed to perform, hinting at Sheffield's season-long slump. Huizenga then shocked Florida fans by announcing he would sell the Marlins because the team was losing too much money. Huizenga made a similar announcement about his Florida Panthers, and the NHL team responded by reaching the finals. His threat to the Marlins worked, too.

The Miami fans finally became excited about the Marlins as the championship became a clear possibility; however, when the Marlins finally won it all, the fans froze. No one rushed onto the field. Admittedly, there were enough security guards on the field to repel an amphibious invasion. Nevertheless, they should have rushed the field and celebrated. Leyland looked silly running around the field with only a group of photographers chasing him like flies.

Right after the championship, Huizenga dismantled the team to cut payroll and make the team more attractive to prospective buyers. Had the team not been dismantled, it may have repeated as World Champions, if you put a lot of weight on pitching. In 1997, Kevin Brown, Al Leiter, Rick Helling, Tony Saunders, Dennis Cook and Robb Nen all thrived as ex-Marlins in 1998. Things might have been very different had they remained with Florida.

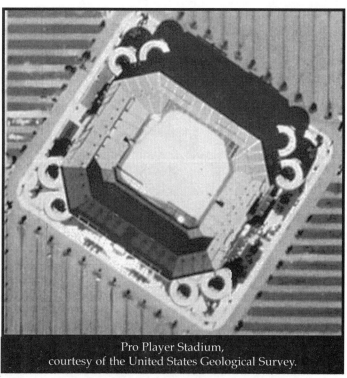

Pro Player Stadium,
courtesy of the United States Geological Survey.

78

Park Factors

Year	Avg	R	H	2B	3B	HR	L-Avg	R-Avg	L-HR	R-HR
1994	109	121	113	104	158	108	108	109	115	107
1995	102	95	103	86	149	83	100	103	70	89
1996	93	87	88	81	124	85	92	93	59	95
1997	96	92	93	88	105	91	97	96	87	93

PRO PLAYER STADIUM
FLORIDA MARLINS
(1994-1998)

Opened for MLB in 1993

Fences: 8 feet
L-C Scoreboard 33 feet

Altitude: 10 feet

Capacity: 47,662 (baseball)

Area of fair territory: 115,000 sq. ft.

Foul territory: Above Average

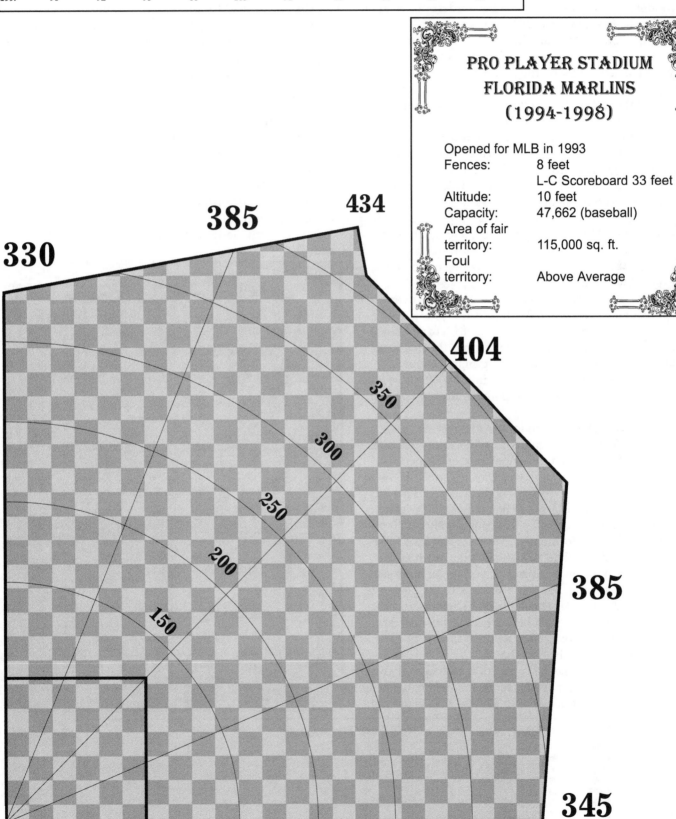

THE ASTRODOME
HOME OF THE HOUSTON ASTROS

Despite changes to the dimensions of the park, the Astrodome continues to be one of the hardest places to hit. Opposing batters complain that they have a hard time reading the spin on the ball when it leaves the pitcher's hand. The difficulties opposing offenses have adapting to the park may explain why the Astros have had only one losing season at home since 1976. Compared to the home records of the rest of the league, Houston should have had four losing seasons at home since 1976.

Batters tend to strike out more often at the Astrodome than in other parks. Having pitchers like Nolan Ryan, J.R. Richard and Mike Scott pitching for Houston helps, but all pitchers tend to strike out more people in Houston than at other parks.

In 1981, Houston pitchers held opponents to 3.01 runs per game. At home, they were even tougher--2.08 runs per game, breaking the record for fewest runs allowed per home game, previously owned by the 1906 Chicago White Sox.

Today's Astrodome is the smallest it has ever been. The power alleys measured 390 feet in 1977, but have been reduced to the current 375. In addition, the current fences stand 10 feet tall, compared to the original 16. Thanks to these changes, Jeff Bagwell and Craig Biggio should become Houston's franchise leaders in most offensive categories. It doesn't hurt that they're tremendously talented, either.

In the past, the Astrodome had concealed great offensive performances because it had handicapped hitters to a greater extent than it does now. One of the performances obscured by the park was Dickie Thon's 1983 season. An outstanding shortstop, Thon smacked 20 homers that year--16 on the road. Had Thon played in Wrigley Field or Fenway Park, he may had consistently hit 30-plus homers a season. Unfortunately, Thon was hit by a Mike Torrez pitch in April of 1984, virtually blinding him. He made an amazing comeback and played for 10 more seasons after the beaning, but was a shadow of the player he once was. With one eye, Thon still hit 15 homers and batted .271 in 1989. Along with J.R. Richard, whose career was cut short by a stroke, Thon will remain one of Houston's greatest might-have-beens.

When the Astrodome first opened, it had natural grass. The stadium had a clear ceiling so the sunlight could keep the grass healthy. But players complained they could not see because of the glare. Some players wore their batting helmets on the field for protection, and they were given orange sunglasses to fight the glare. Managers ordered outfielders to always back each other up, but the outfielders got too tired. The end to the glare came when the ceiling was painted. Unfortunately, the grass died, and Astroturf had to be invented. Astroturf makes this park an average doubles park because balls roll easily to the wall and sometimes take high bounces. Fewer errors than normal are made at the Astrodome.

Originally, the Houston National League team was called the Colt .45s, but they changed their name to the Astros when the Astrodome opened. The dome opened as a marvel of engineering, and compared to Houston's previous park, Colt Stadium, the Astrodome was the best stadium ever.

The Astrodome. Photos courtesy of the Houston Astros.

Park Factors										
Year	Avg	R	H	2B	3B	HR	L-Avg	R-Avg	L-HR	R-HR
1992	96	87	99	94	90	73	93	98	75	71
1993	96	93	94	99	103	89	90	102	67	110
1994	98	93	96	98	89	101	111	90	115	94
1995	90	77	87	90	78	66	91	89	40	82
1996	95	85	95	110	71	77	95	95	86	74
1997	94	88	92	100	186	79	95	94	77	79

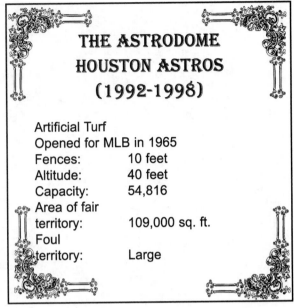

THE ASTRODOME
HOUSTON ASTROS
(1992-1998)

Artificial Turf
Opened for MLB in 1965
Fences: 10 feet
Altitude: 40 feet
Capacity: 54,816
Area of fair
territory: 109,000 sq. ft.
Foul
territory: Large

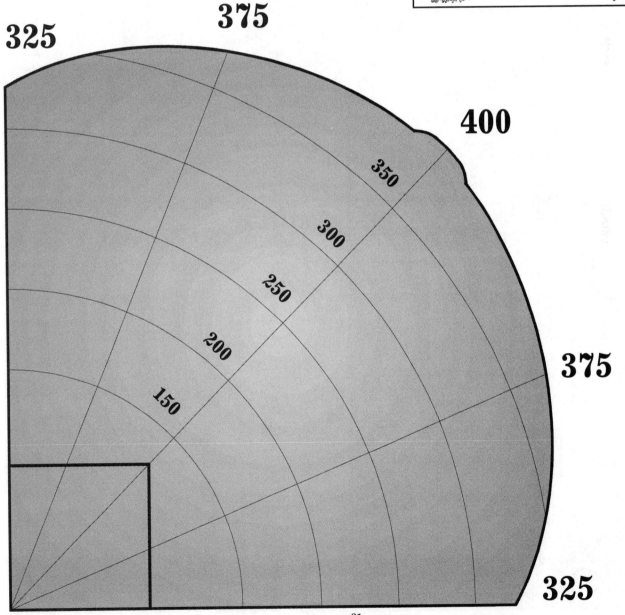

325 **375**

400

350

300

250

200

150

375

325

Like many ballparks built after 1960, the Astrodome is disconnected from its neighborhood because it is surrounded by thousands of parking spaces. Satellite photo courtesy of the United States Geological Survey.

Astrodome Park Factors		
Year	R	HR
1966	94	66
1967	91	42
1968	100	63

THE ASTRODOME
HOUSTON ASTROS
(1966-1968)

Artificial Turf
Opened for MLB in 1965

Fences:	16 feet
Altitude:	40 feet
Capacity:	1966-67: 46,000
	1968-74: 44,500
Area of fair territory:	116,000 sq. ft.
Foul territory:	Average

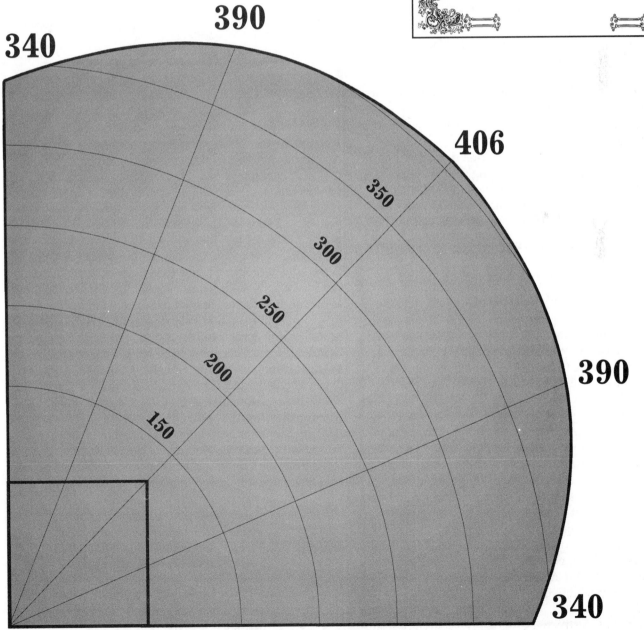

390

340

406

350

300

250

200

150

390

340

When Houston was awarded a major league franchise in 1960, officials planned for the Astrodome to be ready by Opening Day in 1962. When it became evident the construction of the park was behind schedule, team officials scrambled to build the team a temporary place to play. The result was nothing but an overembellished high school stadium: Colt Stadium. The park had an uncovered grandstand wrapped around the infield. Because of the heat and the sun, Houston was the first franchise allowed to play Sunday night games.

The lighting in Colt Stadium was poor, making it difficult for the hitters to see the ball. The park was huge, a breeze blew stubbornly toward home plate from right field, and the humidity made the balls heavy. These characteristics made the park nightmarish for hitters. Colt was not much friendlier to pitchers because the heat hurt their stamina. During a single doubleheader, 100 fans needed first aid due to the heat.

Equally troubling to fans were the mosquitoes. The grounds crew sprayed the field between innings with insecticide to keep the pests under control. Colt first baseman Rusty Staub joked that mosquito repellent was part of the team's equipment.

The Astrodome, the world's first domed stadium, finally opened in April of 1965, leaving Colt abandoned until 1970. Then it was bought and moved to Mexico.

If only other parks could have been as lucky as Colt. Imagine somewhere in the canyonlands of Utah or

Arizona a vast area where the historic ballparks would be relocated, stone by stone. There, against the golden sunsets, would stand Ebbets Field, Shibe Park, Old Comiskey Park, the Polo Grounds. Whoever ran the place would be preparing a spot for Tiger Stadium... I'd better stop before giving Las Vegas any ideas.

However, Colt Stadium was not moved to the desert. It was shipped to the twin cities of Torreon and Gomez Palacio, neither of which list the old Colt Stadium as one of their top tourists attractions.

Just in case Ross Perot is reading, the huge sucking sound in Houston is not because of NAFTA or because Colt Stadium has been imported back. The mosquitoes are salivating upon reviewing Houston's plans for a new stadium. The Ballpark at Union Station will have a retractable dome, but it will remain open as much as possible. It is scheduled to open in March of 2000. It will have natural grass. Bring your insect repellent.

Scouting Report on Mosquitoes

Mosquitoes can suck up to three times their weight in blood. (If only Milwaukee fans were as lucky when it came to beer!) The pests have sensors telling them when it's time to stop feasting, or else they would explode and die.

However, being a mosquito is harder than it seems. They run the risk of being squashed every time they step up for a drink. It's dangerous to poke a host for a drink, and this poking has to be repeated several times because blood vessels intersect with only five percent of people's skin. Once the critter has located an area rich in blood, it releases dilators and thinners to keep the liquid flowing.

Fortunately, only females suck blood, and they do it solely to obtain extra protein for egg production. Males, on the other hand, drink nectar from flowers their whole peaceful lives.

Colt Stadium Park Factors		
Year	R	HR
1962	87	64
1963	84	60
1964	91	72

Opened for MLB in 1962
Fences: LF & RF: 8 feet
                 CF: 30 feet
Altitude: 40 feet
Capacity: 32,601
Area of fair
territory: 124,000 sq. ft.
Foul
territory: Large

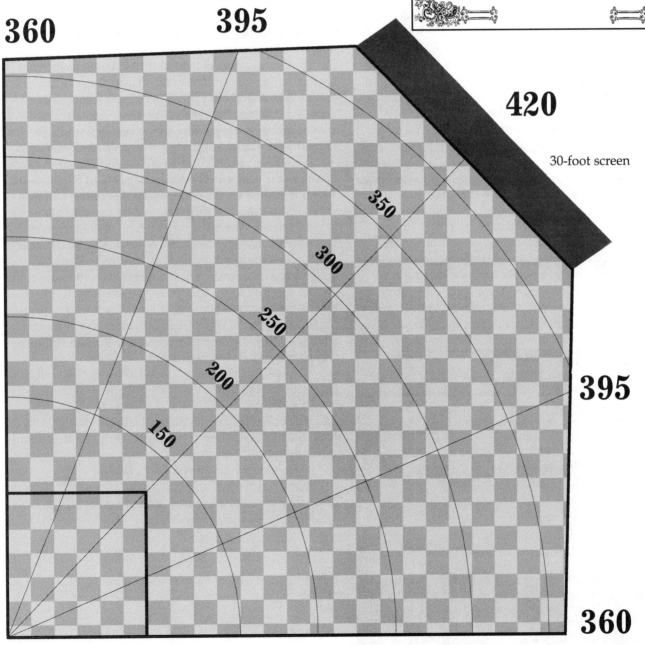

360   **395**

420

30-foot screen

350

300

250

200

150

395

360

Owen Bush Stadium was a spacious park, which rewarded teams that played solid fundamental baseball -- successful hit-and-runs, productive outs, bunting and heads-up baseball. Home runs were rare; therefore, offenses had to use more imaginative ways to score.

Though the park was simple, basically a square, the same cannot be said about its tenant. At first the Indianapolis Clowns were more like a traveling circus, emphasizing comedy acts as much as baseball. The economic times were hard and gimmicks proved successful in attracting crowds. The Clowns created "Shadow Ball," where they performed a believable game without a real baseball. They pitched, threw runners out, made diving catches, all before a crowd who could not believe there was no ball. The performing team began as the Miami Giants and evolved into the Ethiopian Clowns. When the Clowns moved to Indianapolis in 1939, they got serious and played solid baseball.

The 1947 Clowns included the great second baseman Newt Allen and the formidable third baseman Willie Wells. But the Clowns' golden era arrived at the same time integration crippled the Negro Leagues. By 1951 the Clowns were losing fans because small-town people did not have to wait for traveling teams to come through their town any more. Without the World War II gas restriction and with the modern highways, fans could now travel to major league cities. Television beamed baseball to any small town hidden within the tall grasses of the prairie.

In 1952, the Clowns signed Hank Aaron. The young man was a different player from the slugger who terrorized the majors until 1976. Aaron was a shortstop who hit cross-handed, meaning the righthanded batter placed his left hand higher up on the bat than his right hand. By the time Aaron joined the Clowns, owner Syd

Interest in Toni Stone grew in the 1980s. St. Paul, Minnesota, her home town, proclaimed March 6, 1990, "Toni Stone Day." The Great American Theater in St. Paul presented a play based on her life in 1997. The St. Paul City Council voted in December of 1996 to dedicate a ballpark to her.

Pollock was dealing with increasing economic difficulties. The team hardly ever played in Indianapolis anymore, barnstorming wherever possible to increase revenue. Pollock sold Aaron after he'd played one season with the team to the Boston Braves for $10,000.

It did not take Pollock long before finding another popular attraction. He signed a woman named Marcenia Lyle Alberga to play second base. Originally signed as a gimmick, she performed well, hitting .243 in 50 games in 1953. She played by the easier-to-market name Toni Stone.

Stone was not well received by the majority of the players. She was teased, thrown at and spiked. However, she endured, earning the praise of her Hall-of-Fame manager, Oscar Charleston.

Stone was traded to the Kansas City Monarchs the next season. The Monarchs were a solid baseball team and the move resulted in Stone playing in fewer games. She retired at the end of the 1954 season after two years of playing at the highest level of competition achieved by any woman in baseball before her.

The Clowns' Negro American League reorganized itself with 10 teams after 1947. By 1951 the league was down to six team. By 1953, the NAL was down to the Clowns, Monarchs, Birmingham Black Barons and Memphis Red Sox. Their level of play had also deteriorated significantly.

The Monarchs toured the nation for the last time in 1964. The Indianapolis Clowns managed to stay alive until the mid-1970s because of their comedy acts.

Bush Stadium served for many years as a minor league stadium. The Triple-A Indianapolis team has now left Bush Stadium for a downtown gem called Victory Field. This 1993 photo is courtesy of the United States Geological Survey.

**OWEN BUSH STADIUM
INDIANAPOLIS CLOWNS
(1944, 1946-1950)**

Opened in 1938
Fences: Unknown
Altitude: 710 feet
Capacity: 13,254
Area of fair
territory: 125,000 sq. ft.
Foul
territory: Large

350 **381** **500**

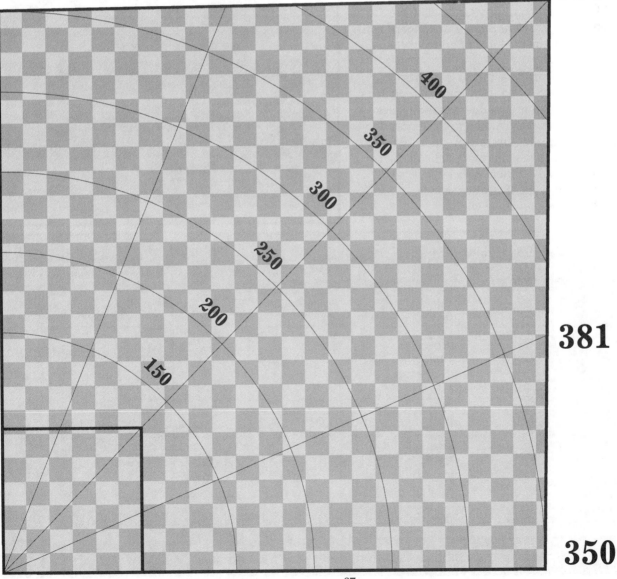

381

350

KAUFFMAN STADIUM
HOME OF THE KANSAS CITY ROYALS

Kauffman Stadium is a park in constant motion. Its 322-foot waterfall is far more attractive than advertising billboards. The park's full beauty blossomed when the artificial turf was replaced with natural grass in 1995. With the fading rug removed, Kauffman Stadium has deservedly taken its place as one of the most beautiful stadiums in the country.

Constructed in 1973, Royals Stadium, as it was first called, was built for baseball only. It was renamed Kauffman Stadium on July 2, 1993. Instead of making it a multi-purpose facility, a second stadium, Arrowhead Stadium, was built one block away. Both stadiums form the Truman Sports Complex. Despite the success of the complex, it was not copied until the 1990s. In 1991, New Comiskey Park became the first major league park since Kauffman to be built strictly for baseball. Camden Yards followed, adding another old twist to baseball parks: asymmetry. Like Kauffman, Camden Yards will have a football partner next door. The new Lions and Tigers' complex in Detroit will continue the trend of adjacent stadiums.

Kauffman Stadium photos courtesy of the Kansas City Royals.

The change from artificial turf to grass has changed baseball in this park. It is now more of a pitchers' park than ever. The number of hits, doubles and triples have been reduced significantly. Although the fences down the line and in the power alleys were brought in 10 feet in 1995, homering at the park remains more difficult than at a neutral park (about 15 percent more difficult). Lefthanded hitters enjoy a slight advantage in home runs because of the prevailing winds.

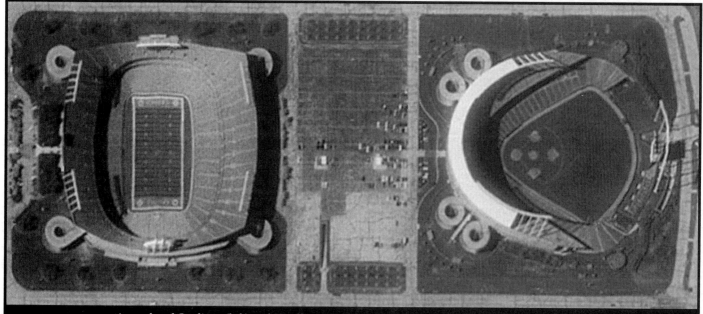

Arrowhead Stadium (left) and Kauffman Stadium (right) form the Truman Sports Complex. This photo is courtesy of the United States Geological Survey.

Park Factors										
Year	Avg	R	H	2B	3B	HR	L-Avg	R-Avg	L-HR	R-HR
1995	100	92	99	102	122	82	99	102	106	67
1996	97	95	98	97	167	88	98	97	77	96
1997	105	109	107	91	166	111	104	105	130	100

KAUFFMAN STADIUM
KANSAS CITY ROYALS
(1995-1998)

Opened in 1973
Fences: 8 feet
Altitude: 750 feet
Capacity: 40,625
Area of fair
territory: 110,000 sq. ft.
Foul
territory: Average

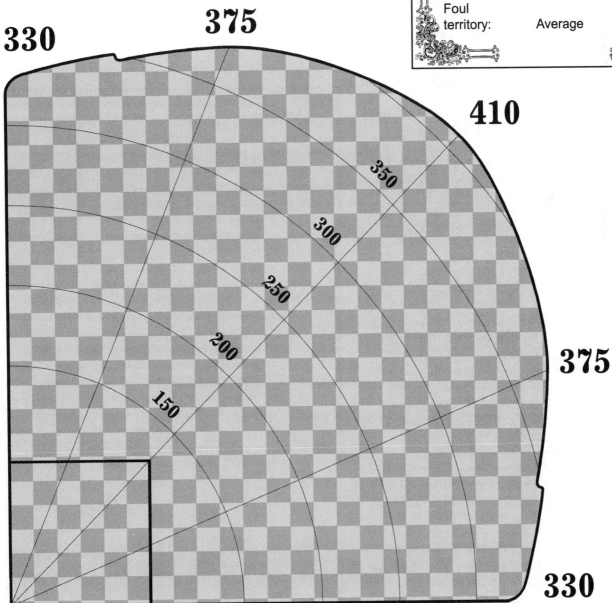

330
375
410
350
300
250
200
150
375
330

MUEHLEBACH FIELD
HOME OF THE KANSAS CITY MONARCHS

Muehlebach Field was built in 1923 by George Muehlebach, the owner of the Yankees' minor league team, the Kansas City Blues. Unlike many minor league owners who cut costs by giving new parks a small playing field, Muehlebach created a large ballfield, measuring 350 feet down the lines, 408 to left-center and 450 feet to center field. A pitchers' park, Muehlebach Field rewarded offenses with daring baserunners. Runs had to be manufactured base by base because home runs were rare.

Though built for the Blues, greatness played on the field when they were away. Muehlebach Field was the home of Kansas City's other team, the Kansas City Monarchs. The Negro League team was the brainchild of James Leslie Wilkinson, a white businessman and son of the president of the Algona Normal College. After an injury ended his playing days, Wilkinson organized the All Nations team, which toured the Midwest, barnstorming against semi-pro teams and professional black teams. As a result of the success and the contacts created by the All Nations club, Wilkinson created the Kansas City Monarchs in 1920.

The Monarchs took the Negro National League by storm, winning pennants in 1923, 1924, 1925 and 1929. Those pennants were won at a time when the black population in Kansas City was small -- only about 30,000. The crowds for Monarchs games averaged about 5,000 on Sundays, but only a few hundred on weekdays. Wilkinson created several promotions in order to pack the stands, such as admitting ladies and children free on certain days. The Monarchs were loved like alumni love their college. They even had a booster team to help increase attendance. The Booster Club organized the Opening Day Parade, a procession that rounded up people throughout town and ended at Muehlebach Field.

The Negro National League of the 1920s was like the National Association of Professional Base Ball Players of 1871-1875 (the precursor to the National League). The fans at Muehlebach Field were notorious for their rowdyism despite the large number of women on the stands. Unlike the 1870s, much of the rowdiness in Muehlebach Field was illegal because it was in the midst of Prohibition.

Black baseball was young in those days and susceptible to the smallest of economic environmental changes. Unfortunately, a cataclysm was ahead: the Great Depression. Wilkinson and the Monarchs battled the Great Depression by abandoning the Negro National League in 1931. By that time, the NNL was mortally wounded by the Depression and the death of its czar, Rube Foster, in 1930. The black population in Kansas City, like the rest of the country, was hit heavily by the Depression. The Monarchs could not stay in a city indefinitely because the dollars would run out. Instead, like a hunting and gathering band, Wilkinson led his group across the land in search for better prospects. As the number of contests played at Muehlebach Field declined, the Monarchs' affiliation to Kansas City became merely nominal.

In 1929, Wilkinson bought a portable light system. Although the lights were poor, they enabled the club to survive until the Depression ended. What followed those dark years was the golden age of the Negro Leagues. The Monarchs joined the Negro American League in 1936 and continued their dominance, winning pennants in 1937, 1939, 1940, 1941, 1942, and 1946. Kansas City had its team back, and greatness was again displayed on a daily basis at Muehlebach Field.

There have been plenty of colorful players in baseball, but few as colorful as Satchel Paige. Unfortunately, his adventures sometimes carried a price. Here's a short piece from the *Chicago Defender*, July 24, 1943:

(Unable to corral Satchel, circuit court workers had no choice but to hand him a divorce petition from his wife as he was getting off the mound on "Paige Day" in Chicago.)

Notice was served on the sensational baseball player by two deputies as he left the mound following participation in a doubleheader played in his honor before more than 22,000 howling fans.

In her bill of complaint, the wife accuses the fast ball pitcher of wedding a woman... during his diamond sojourn in Puerto Rico in 1940.

The wife states that Satchel has a $30,000 art collection [$278,797 in 1997 dollars] in a $25,000 [$232,331 in 1997] building in Kansas City, and that his annual income is in the neighborhood of $40,000 [$371,729].

She asks for $400 [$3,717] per month alimony and $500 [$4,647] lawyer's fee.

It is not known whether he paid.

Just for the record, Paige pitched five innings of no-hit ball in one of the games that day, earning a 1-0 victory over the New York Cubans.

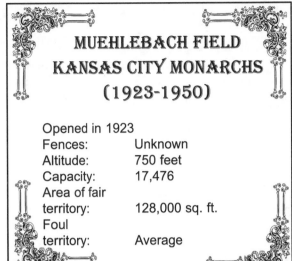

MUEHLEBACH FIELD
KANSAS CITY MONARCHS
(1923-1950)

Opened in 1923
Fences: Unknown
Altitude: 750 feet
Capacity: 17,476
Area of fair
territory: 128,000 sq. ft.
Foul
territory: Average

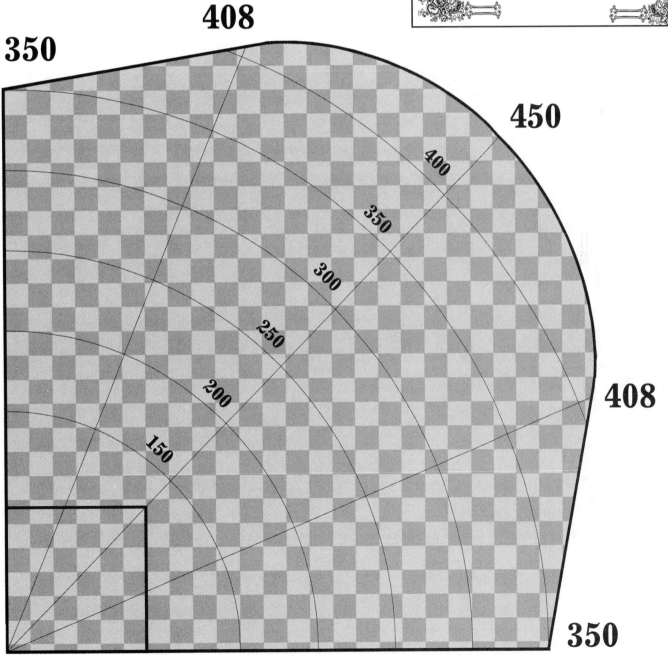

350 **408** **450**

400

350

300

250

200

150

408

350

DODGER STADIUM
HOME OF LOS ANGELES DODGERS

To Brooklynites, not only was the news of the Dodgers' move shocking, but the team's destination was simply incomprehensible. To them, there wasn't much of a difference in the team moving to Los Angeles or Tahiti. Los Angeles has palm trees--how foreign. West Coast people didn't get to the park by train. And they were digging out a new park from a mountain, like Mt. Rushmore, Crazy Horse or the Sphinx.

Between 1958 and 1961, the team played its home games in Los Angeles Coliseum while waiting for Dodger Stadium to be built. Walter O'Malley had a hard time acquiring Chavez Ravine. He eventually had to trade LA Wrigley Field to the City of Los Angeles for the land containing Chavez Ravine. Even after the deal had gone through, O'Malley had to survive a series of court challenges.

Nonetheless, the park opened in 1962 and become an instant success. The team found a home like no other. In 1978, Dodger Stadium became the first park to exceed three million in attendance. The crowds have kept on coming, eclipsing the three-million mark not only in 1978, but also in 1980, 1982-1983, 1990, 1991, 1993 and 1996. By the end of the 1998 season, more than 100 million fans may have crossed the Dodger Stadium gates.

From Koufax to Drysdale, Sutton to Messersmith, Valenzuela to Hershiser, Ramon Martinez to Nomo, the Dodgers have been known for their pitching. Dodger Stadium helps pitchers by allowing the worst batting average, the fewest homers, the fewest runs and basically no triples. The power alleys are flyball cemeteries.

Dodger Stadium. Photo courtesy of Los Angeles Dodgers.

Park Factors

Year	Avg	R	H	2B	3B	HR	L-Avg	R-Avg	L-HR	R-HR
1992	99	89	100	89	103	62	98	102	75	51
1993	104	94	103	87	42	97	115	97	97	97
1994	89	78	87	72	40	97	89	89	103	94
1995	92	81	89	67	47	74	91	92	78	72
1996	89	79	85	71	46	70	91	87	55	78
1997	93	84	91	81	59	90	93	94	90	91

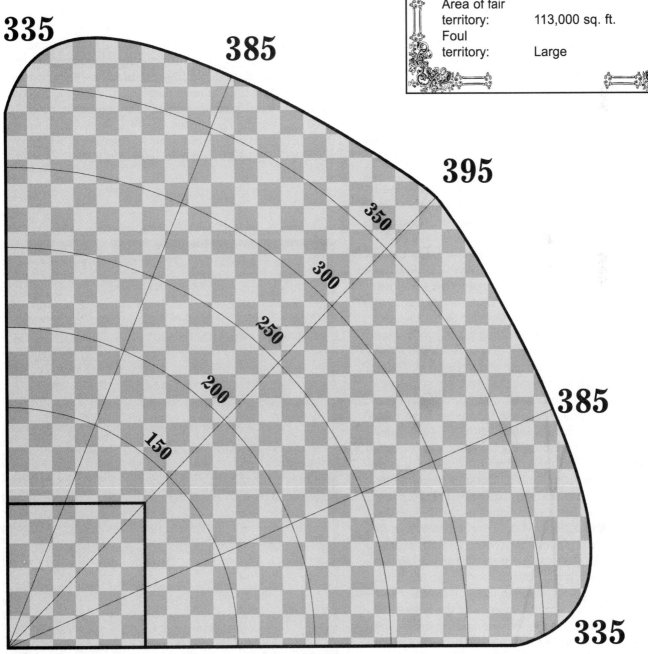

335

385

395

385

335

350

300

250

200

150

MEMORIAL COLISEUM
HOME OF LOS ANGELES DODGERS

Even Brooklyn politicians thought it was inconceivable for the Dodgers to move. But move they did before the 1958 season. Before the Dodgers left town, people used to cheer their teams with a degree of fanaticism presently displayed only by children aficionados. Nowadays, losing the nationalist-like passion for one's team has become a rite of passage to adulthood. If adults still possess loyalties like those previously given to baseball teams, that fervor has been transferred to their alma mater's teams. After all, college teams never move.

The Dodgers used Los Angeles Memorial Coliseum as their temporary home between 1958 and 1961. Walter O'Malley was ridiculed because of the bizarre dimensions. The Coliseum was anything but a baseball stadium. Team officials were able to fit a diamond on the field, but the result was an incredibly short left field line, a humongous foul territory down the third base line, a fairly big right field, and no foul territory down the first base line.

Memorial Coliseum was really two stadiums fitted together. The area from center field to the right field foul line was large, about 58,000 square feet. Meanwhile, the area from center field to the left field foul line was tiny, measuring only 45,000 square feet of fair territory. Wally Moon, a lefthanded hitting Dodger outfielder, mastered the art of looping pop flies the other way for easy home runs, "Moon Shots," as they were popularly called.

The field dimensions were ridiculed, but there was no ridiculing the attendance figures. May 7, 1959, was Roy Campanella Night, and the attendance of the game was 93,103. In 1958, the San Francisco Giants earned $329,000 (in 1996 dollars) after playing a series at the Coliseum. That was a huge payoff for a visiting team.

The large attendance figures show that O'Malley was not the villain in LA that he was in Brooklyn. In fact, it was O'Malley who made the Dodgers into something Charles Ebbets or his successors could not: O'Malley made them consistent winners. In 1959, the Dodgers won their first World Series in LA by defeating the Go-Go White Sox. In addition to being winners, the Dodgers also cemented a strong relationship with the community, as strong as the one they had with Brooklyn. The Dodgers reached out to their multi-ethnic patrons, signing the best players available, regardless of their race or ethnicity. In 1997, the Dodgers were still leading Major League Baseball as they signed the first two players from South Africa. Fernando Valenzuela, the Dodger camps in the Dominican Republic and their Latin America outreach efforts have made this team one of the most followed in the world. When Hideo Nomo repeated after Tommy LaSorda in the 1995 All-Star Game "I bleed Dodger Blue," he was voicing the feelings of all the newly acquired Asian fans. The baton was picked

up by Chan Ho Park after Nomo was released in the middle of the 1998 season.

The move of the Dodgers and Giants to the West Coast destroyed the Pacific Coast League. For a long time, the PCL was given a 4-A level, admitting that its talent level was close to the major league level. Unfortunately, the PCL never made its move to become a major league. It politely asked once to be a third major league, but there are some things in life that you just take, and don't ask for. The PCL's leadership was weak in this respect, and never made the financial commitment needed to establish itself a major league. Instead of venturing on its own, it valued the safe relationship it had with the majors. Instead of rocking the boat, the PCL got thrown overboard. Baseball did not arrive to the West Coast with the Dodgers and Giants. It had a long, rich history. With seasons going over the 200-game mark due to the extended baseball weather, its players had time to hone their skills. Many local players would have much rather played near home than travel 3,000 miles to the East Coast. The PCL should have been the third major league, but its unwillingness to match salaries and invest in larger parks hurt it.

Homers by Direction at the Coliseum

The dimensions of the Coliseum resulted in a disproportionate amount of home runs to left field. Officials attempted to alter home run breakdown by changing the dimensions of the field. These are the dimensions of center field, right-center and right field as they changed through the years:

	CF	R-C	RF
1958	425	440	301
1959	420	375	300
1960	420	394	300
1961	420	380	300

	Homers to left field	Homers to center field	Homers to right field
1958	182	3	8
1959	132	1	39
1960	155	3	28
1961	147	7	38

Memorial Coliseum Park Factors		
Year	R	HR
1958	115	127
1959	103	129
1960	132	198
1961	104	145

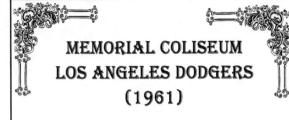

MEMORIAL COLISEUM
LOS ANGELES DODGERS
(1961)

Opened for MLB in 1958

Fences:	LF: 42 feet
	CF to RF corner: 6 feet
	RF corner: 4 feet
Altitude:	340 feet
Capacity:	94,600
Area of fair territory:	103,000 sq. ft.
Foul territory:	Tiny down first base
	Huge down third base

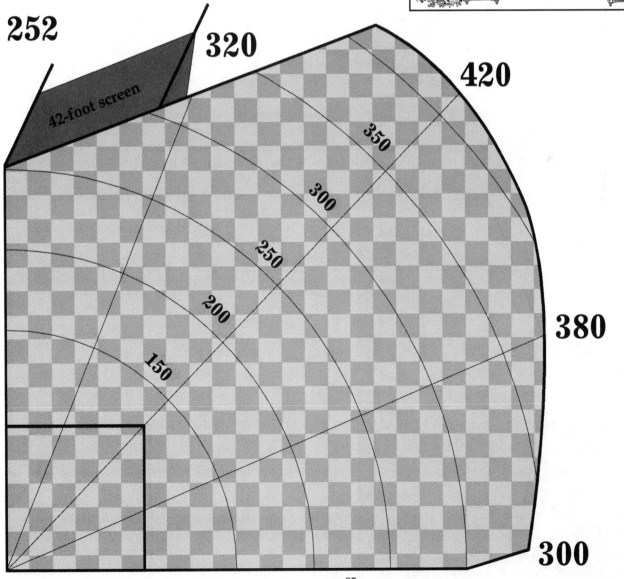

42-foot screen

252 320 420 350 300 250 200 150 380 300

Many have wondered what would happen if a regular fan took over a team and ran things for a while. Charles Ebbets was a regular guy who took over a team, and the result was the greatest love affair in sports: Brooklyn and their Dodgers.

Harry von der Horst was the majority owner of the Brooklyn National team and its greatest fan. But when he became ill in 1902, he knew he had to sell the team. Knowing that Brooklyn manager Ned Hanlon intended to buy the team and move it to Baltimore, von der Horst sold his shares to Ebbets, making him the majority owner.

Ebbets joined the Brooklyn organization in its maiden season in 1883. Because of his loyalty and industriousness, Ebbets rose from ticket seller to business manager, and because of Hanlon's intentions, to team owner. Like many Dodgers to come, Ebbets' brain was wired differently. He became the Brooklyn owner without any money. Instead of solidifying the team's financial ground by selling his best ballplayers to wealthier teams, Ebbets concentrated on building Brooklyn fans a modern ballpark. The only land Ebbets could afford was a garbage dump surrounded by shanties in Pigtown. The area was called Pigtown because every morning, pigs left their owners'

homes to feast on the waste. Pigs and chickens walked up and down the dirt paths as if they were people. The unaccompanied animals somehow made it home before sunset every day. In addition to beasts running wild, the area smelled like sulfur and rotten fish. The shanties were made of wooden boards, metal sheets and cardboard. No area appeared to be worse for a baseball park.

Nevertheless, Ebbets proceeded to acquire the land by creating a phony company to purchase it. The operation had to be kept secret, or people would increase their asking price. By the fall on 1911, Ebbets had bought all the land except for one parcel, whose owner could not be found. Ebbets hired a detective who traced the owner from Brooklyn to California, then to Berlin and Paris, until finally finding him, out of all places, in Montclair, New Jersey. On March 4, 1912, three years after Ebbets began buying land, he broke ground. The park opened in 1913, and Brooklyn grew up around the park.

Originally, Ebbets Field was similar to its contemporary ballparks. The outfield was huge by today's standards: 419 ft. down the left field line and 450 ft. to center. However, the new park seated only 18,000 people. Because Ebbets Field was originally built on a small piece of land, the park became tiny when the capacity was increased. Wooden bleachers were added in the outfield. The foul territory was small. As a result, the fans were close to the action. Dodger management tried to increase capacity again in 1930 by replacing the wooden stands with concrete bleachers. When the new stands were fully usable in 1932, management received the agonizing news that the new bleachers sat as many people as the old ones did.

After these new bleachers were finished, Ebbets Field was ordained as the home run park many fans remember. Left field had lost 31 feet and center field almost 48 feet. Unlike the gargantuan Polo Grounds and Yankee Stadium, Ebbets Field thrived because it was small.

The fans at Ebbets Field were something else. There was Jack Pierce, who always bought three seats whenever he attended: one for himself, another for his bartender, and a third for a bunch of balloons he carried with him. The bartender's job was to blow the balloons during the game--that is until Jack discovered helium. Much to the dismay of fans trying to see around the balloons, Jack would fill them and let them go all game long.

In addition to Jack, Ebbets Field had an army of quirky personalities. There was the Dodger Sym-Phony, made of fans who thought of themselves as musicians. The unpaid fans played songs like Babe Herman fielded. The park had a crazed public announcer whose comments were more entertaining than informational. There was a game when the left field fans had tended their clothes on the fence. The batters complained that the light colored clothes were making it hard for them to see a pitched ball.

Charles Hercules Ebbets, Patron Saint of Baseball in Brooklyn.

Field officials asked Tex Rickard to do something about it. "Will the fans in left field please removed their clothes," he announced, making the crowd burst into laughter.

The loudest fan of all was Hilda Chester. When poor Hilda suffered a heart attack, her doctor forbade her to cheer. So Hilda grabbed a frying pan and metal spoon and banged. Even the players knew who she was because of the racket. They were fond of her, and in the late '40s, the players gave her the first of her famous cowbells, so she could bang away and not spray fellow fans with food.

One time, Hilda was sitting in the outfield bleachers when she called Pete Reiser over with her unique voice. "Hey, Reiser," she said. "Give this note to Leo." Reiser picked up the crumbled note and gave it to his manager, Leo Durocher, without reading it first. But before handing the note over, Reiser had a quick word about something else with Dodger GM Larry MacPhail. The note said: Get Hugh Casey hot, starter Whit Wyatt is losing it. Durocher, thinking the note was from MacPhail, removed Wyatt from the game, which he had pitched brilliantly up to that point. Casey proceeded to make a close game out of an easy win. Following the game, Durocher told Reiser never to give him notes from MacPhail during a game. After Reiser told him who sent the note, Durocher went into a screaming fit so energetic that people weren't able to make out the words. Hilda was a good cheerleader, but her managerial debut was a dubious one.

After Charles Ebbets died in 1925, the team fell into chaos. In order to save the franchise, the Dodgers hired Larry MacPhail, who had recently rescued the Reds by introducing night baseball, among other things. Despite the fact the team was practically bankrupt, the first thing he did was spend the owners' money to renovate Ebbets Field. He replaced the 15th Century bathrooms with modern ones, he cleaned up the park, and brought night baseball to Ebbets. In the first Brooklyn night game, Cincinnati Red Johnny Vander Meer pitched his second no-hitter in consecutive outings.

MacPhail also signed Babe Ruth as the first base coach, hoping that when Ruth replaced Dodger manager Burleigh Grimes, more fans would flock to the park. Many claimed that Ruth was hired as a gag, but Ruth told many he believed he was going to made manager. Until his death, Ruth waited for the phone to ring with a major league management offer. In addition to Ruth, MacPhail acquired several has-beens and castoffs. One of the castoffs was shortstop Leo Durocher.

Durocher had a turbulent life as a player. He had the habit of stealing money from fellow players. He gambled, drank, got into fights. But he also enjoyed managing amateur teams during the offseason. So when Durocher learned Ruth thought he was going to become the next Dodger manager, he did anything to humiliate him. Durocher played with the Yankees in the mid '20s and didn't like Ruth. Once, in the Dodger locker room, Durocher pushed Ruth against a locker and punched him repeatedly in the face. At the same time, MacPhail realized two things: his team of castoffs had a special chemistry, and Durocher, not Ruth, should be the next manager.

The relationship between Durocher and MacPhail was difficult to understand. Once Durocher slugged MacPhail in the face during a press conference to fire Durocher as manager. MacPhail reacted by getting up and hugging Durocher, reappointing him manager while in tears. Their relationship resulted in Durocher being fired over 60 times, but also resulted in the 1941 pennant, the first Dodger pennant since 1920.

The Dodger players were as quirky as their fans and managers. One time in Havana, Hugh Casey and other Dodgers were drinking with Ernest Hemingway. After shooting birds with the ballplayers, Hemingway sized up Casey and invited him to box. Casey roughed up Hemingway, who, being a sore loser, kicked Casey in the testicles. Hemingway tried to make it up to Casey, but the players drove away, fearing that what the writer really wanted to do was kill them. Years later, both Hemingway and Casey committed suicide in separate incidents.

MacPhail eventually left the Dodgers and was followed by Branch Rickey. The raunchy days of the Dodgers were replaced by the turbulent years of Jackie Robinson. Breaking the color barrier is one of the most significant events in sports history. The integration of baseball was a powerful event, but Robinson's lasting power is due to his personality. How many people remember that Chuck Cooper was the first black in the NBA, or that Kenny Washington and Woody Strode were the first blacks in the NFL? Even in baseball, there will be no 100th Anniversary Season for Colombian Luis Castro, the first Latino to play in the majors in 1902.

Jackie Robinson could have been easily forgotten, but his courage, his love for the Dodgers, his activism, and his personality make his legacy that much greater. In addition, his playing for the Dodgers, before the greatest fans, in the greatest stadium, cannot be overlooked for fueling his lasting power.

Fans buying hot dogs outside Ebbets Field.
Courtesy of the Library of Congress.

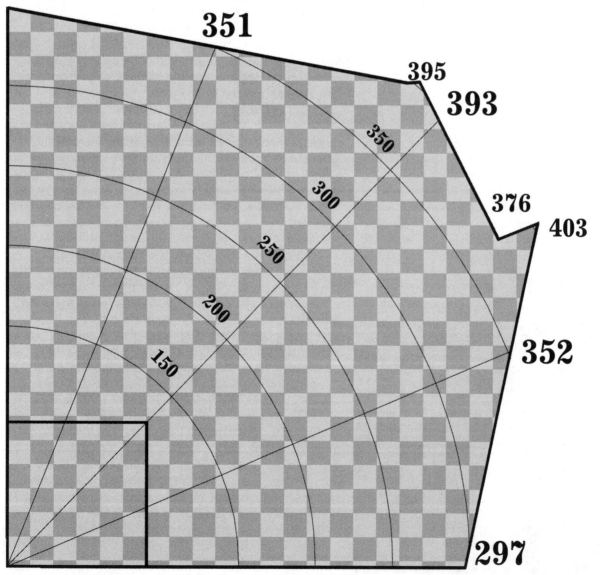

Ebbets Field
Park Factors

Year	R	HR
1955	106	122
1956	103	120
1957	133	145

EBBETS FIELD
BROOKLYN DODGERS
(1955-1957)

Opened for MLB in 1913

Fences:	LF to L-C: 9.87 feet
	CF: 20 feet
	R-C to RF: 38 feet
Altitude:	55 feet
Capacity:	31,902
Area of fair territory:	100,000 sq. ft.
Foul territory:	Small

348

351

395

393

350

300

376

403

250

200

352

150

297

**Ebbets Field
Park Factors**

Year	R	HR
1932	93	95
1933	99	120
1934	93	100
1935	90	106
1936	115	109
1937	114	95

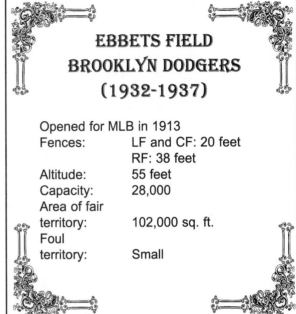

EBBETS FIELD
BROOKLYN DODGERS
(1932-1937)

Opened for MLB in 1913
Fences: LF and CF: 20 feet
                    RF: 38 feet
Altitude: 55 feet
Capacity: 28,000
Area of fair
territory: 102,000 sq. ft.
Foul
territory: Small

353 1932-33,
356 1934-37

356

365

20-foot wall from LF line past CF

399

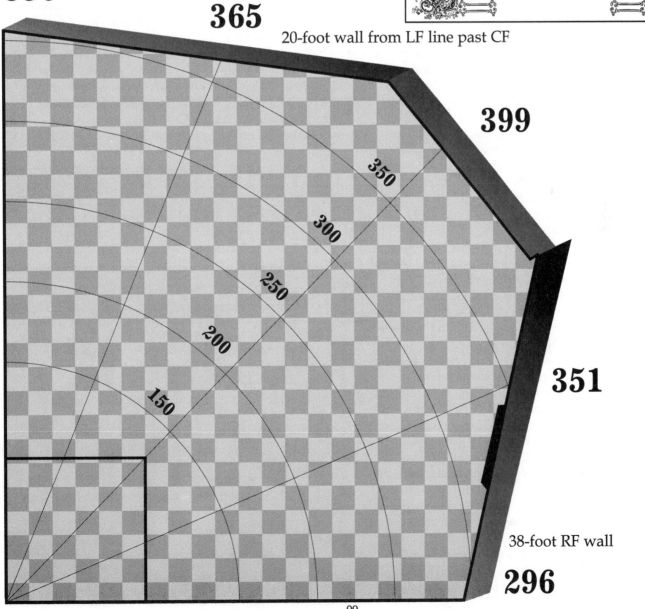

350

300

250

200

150

351

38-foot RF wall

296

BEFORE JACKIE ROBINSON
& THE LATINO RACIAL EXPERIENCE

Moses Fleetwood Walker was the first African-American to play in major league baseball in 1884. After he was banned from the league because of his color, baseball would not see another African-American player until Jackie Robinson in 1947.

There are some obvious questions that can be asked about this terrible period in the majors: Why did it have to happen? How harshly should we judge those who played a role? Could the color barrier have been broken earlier? You can write whole books about these questions, but we will tackle lightly the third one.

In 1911 the Cincinnati Reds signed two former Negro League players, Rafael Almeida and Armando Marsans. Almeida played in 1904 and 1905 with the All Cubans team. Marsans played in 1905 with the All Cubans team and with the Cuban Stars in 1923. Almeida was a white Cuban. Marsans was not white.

Whether Marsans was 75 percent of African descent or 50 percent is not relevant. He was a colored man, and the reaction to his playing is what should be interesting. The *Cincinnati Enquirer* assured the fans that both players were "two of the purest bars of Castillian soap to ever wash upon our shores." But the fact that Marsans was part black was not missed by the African-American media. The *New York Age* speculated, "Now that the first shock is over, it would not be surprising to see a Cuban a few shades darker... breaking into the professional ranks... It would then be easier for colored players who are citizens of this country to get into fast company."

In the next three years, four former Negro League players were signed by major league teams. They were all light-skinned: Mike Gonzalez, 1912; Jack Calvo, 1913; Alfredo Cabrera, 1913; and Dolf Luque, 1914. Though these players were not black, they could at least be used to measure the level of play of black baseball. In his first season, Almeida averaged .313--in the dead ball era. Marsans hit .317 in his second season and was a terror on the basepaths. Mike Gonzalez proved an excellent defensive catcher. His smarts would eventually allow him to become an interim manager in the majors. Cabrera played only one game in the majors. Jack Calvo hit .242 in his first season, but did not play again in the majors until seven years later. None of these players set the baseball world on fire, but they showed that there was major league talent in black baseball, contradicting white baseball's argument that blacks were not good enough to play. The shining example of the talent available in black baseball was Dolf Luque.

Luque has the most major league wins for a former Negro League player. He led the league in wins in 1923 with 27. His major league record of 193-179, 3.24 ERA, shows that there was indeed major league talent in the early Negro Leagues.

However, the early hopes of the Cubans paving the way for the U.S. blacks faded. Fans did not protest Marsans' playing in the majors. Marsans played for eight years in the majors. Marsans is evidence that if someone had pushed the envelope, integration may have happened much, much earlier. Instead, segregation became institutionalized for good during the Great Depression. In 1935, Red Barber reacted to the signing of Roberto Estalella by writing that he suspected "there was a Senegambian somewhere in the Cuban batpile where the Senatorial lumber was seasoned." This was 24 years removed from the hopes raised by Marsans. By that time, Black writers no longer viewed the Cuban signings as a good omen, but rather as a redefinition of the color barrier. Clark Griffith, who had brought many Cuban Negro League players to the majors, told black writer Sam Lacy in 1937 that "the climate wasn't right" to bring an African-American to the majors.

As it became clear to African-Americans that the signings of Cubans did not mean blacks were nearing integration, their feelings toward Latin America changed. First, every time a colored Latin was signed, it was another slap in the face of black America. Second, Latin American countries began raiding the Negro Leagues.

During a game, Effa Manley, the owner of the Brooklyn and later the Newark Eagles, saw a few foreign men talking to her ballplayers. She hopped out of her seat as if her hair was on fire and ran toward the men.

"What are you doing, talking to my players," she yelled. "Now, you fellows should be ashamed of your-

Effa Manley

Effa Manley could be the subject of a book all by herself. She was a white woman born from the affair of her white mother with her white father. Her mother later married a black man and had several mixed-race kids. Manley, raised by her black stepfather, like to pass herself as a light black woman. Manley was 100 percent ethnically black. She didn't let her white race interfere with who she wanted to be.

Manley owned the Eagles from 1935 to 1948. She had an awesome eye for talent. Among the talent that the major leagues drafted from her team were Larry Doby, Don Newcombe and Monte Irvin. She fought to receive just compensation for losing these players. Bill Veeck paid for Larry Doby.

selves, trying to steal my ballplayers right under my eyes... Aren't you ashamed of yourselves, you--you *chili con carnes*?" (From Jim Reisler's book *Black Writers/Black Baseball*.)

Players like Josh Gibson and Willie Wells had to explain to their black fans in the States why they had bolted their teams. Wells told writer Wendell Smith that in Mexico he was called "El Diablo." Smith responded, "Yeah, that's what they're calling you in Newark, too, but they don't mean it the same way."

But the relationship between Latin America and the Negro Leagues was not one-sided. Latin America took talent away, but it provided some benefits as well. Not all Cubans were allowed to play in the majors. Dark superstars like Martin Dihigo and Jose Mendez were left in the Negro Leagues despite having clearly evident Hall-of-Fame talent.

Negro League leader, player and manager, Dick Lundy believed that what was best for the Negro Leagues was to become a solid organization, not only in the front offices, but on the field as well. Cuba provided the talent to make the Negro Leagues more respectable, as Lundy desired. Also, the Cubans taught young African-American players the kind of baseball knowledge that can only be passed down from generation to generation.

"In Cuba I saw Martin Dihigo, Silvio Garcia, 'Walla Walla' Oms, and some of the other great Cuban players," Monte Irvin said. "And you would learn a lot just by watching them. And the same thing applied when you played in Mexico, Puerto Rico, Santo Domingo or Venezuela." (From James A. Riley's *Biographical Encyclopedia of the Negro Baseball Leagues*.)

Up to 15 percent of all the players who ever played in the Negro Leagues were Latinos. (Though their invasion of the majors appears to be a recent phenomenon, Latino players have been a force in American baseball for decades.) By 1938, the talent level had increased in the Negro Leagues, partly due to the additional Latino talent, to the point that the following decade could be considered the Golden Age of the Negro Leagues. Wendell Smith wrote that in the decade before 1938, black baseball had evolved from players carrying knives and razors into the field. They no longer played games in costumes. "Now [1938] their rosters are filled with brilliant, colorful, dazzling players who know the game from top to bottom," Smith wrote. "Negro teams now have everything the white clubs have."

Though the signing of Latino Negro League players by major league clubs did not end the color barrier, it did prove two things: 1. There was major league talent in the Negro Leagues. 2. Fan opposition to these colored players was minimal. The fans would not have stormed the Major League Baseball offices if blacks were allowed to play. Major League Baseball had the power to end segregation unilaterally before the Great Depression. Major

Martin Dihigo

Martin Dihigo is the only player to be inducted in the Hall of Fames of three countries: The United States, Cuba and Mexico. He is considered by many to have been the most versatile player in the history of baseball. He toiled in the Negro Leagues from 1923 to 1945, playing every position and pitching as well. Hall-of-Famer Johnny Mize thought he was having an incredible campaign in the Dominican Republic because he always came on with men on base. He then realized that they kept intentionally walking Dihigo to get to him. Mize said Dihigo was the best player he ever saw in his life.

After his playing career was over, he served as the minister of sports for Fidel Castro. This highly politicized position strained his relations with other Cuban players who decided to flee communism. However, as much as they disliked his ideologies, the Cuban exiles still take pride when they talk about *El Inmortal*.

League Baseball simply decided not to do it. The Latino impact was two-fold. It added general talent to the Negro Leagues, but often took away the top stars.

Now, you may ask yourself, Why in the world would colored Latinos come to the United States? Especially, when African-American people claimed to be treated like human beings in Latin America?

Well, Latin America is a very complex place. When you think of Cuba before World War II, consider it another state of the Union. Cuba was a protectoriate of the United States, a political and cultural satellite of the U.S. Americans brought with them American-style racial prejudice. When Jackie Robinson and the Dodgers held their spring training in Cuba in 1947 (to avoid a Spring Training controversy in the South), Robinson had to stay in a hotel for blacks only. In a conversation with Minnie Miñoso last year, he said that he faced as much discrimination in Cuba as he faced in the States.

Discrimination exists in Latin America, but it is different than the discrimination found in the United States. In Bolivia, the last thing some people want to be is Native American. They will even get afros, as they would rather be black than be thought of as Indians. In the Dominican Republic, the last thing some people want to be associated with is being black. They gladly pass as Indians if they can. Latin America is large and most countries are different from one another. The discrimination toward black people there ended at the level that they may not marry you because of your race. This is a very real and serious discrimination, but it is different from the lynching

discrimination of the United States.

"[Black] players on teams in the Mexican league live just like big leaguers," Willie Wells told Wendell Smith. "We have everything first class, plus the fact that people here are much more considerate than the American Baseball fan... Don't let anyone tell you that the owners in the Negro Leagues in the States can match salaries paid in the Mexican league... One of the main reasons I came back to Mexico is because I've found freedom and democracy here, something I never found in the United States. I was branded a Negro in the States, and had to act accordingly. Everything I did, including my playing ball, was regulated by my color. They wouldn't even give me a chance in the big leagues because I was a Negro, yet they accepted every other nationality under the sun... Here in Mexico, I am a man. ...I can live where I please and will encounter no restrictions of any kind because of my race." (James Reisler's *Black Writers/Black Baseball*.)

Adolfo Luque

Dolf Luque was one of the few former Negro League players to cross to the majors before Jackie Robinson. Unlike Robinson, who managed his temper in his fight for integration, Luque could not manage his temper for anything. After a wonderful major league career, Luque managed in Mexico. The way he motivated his players was by carrying a gun with him under his baseball uniform. Not one of his players ever doubted that he would use it if they didn't obey him. One time, he and Cool Papa Bell got into a fight. The gun went off, but neither was hurt. Luque also managed in the Negro Leagues.

These are Luque's major league numbers:

YR	TEAM	W	L	SV	IP	ERA
1914	Bos	0	1	0	8.2	4.15
1915	Bos	0	0	0	5	3.60
1918	Cin	6	3	0	83	3.80
1919	Cin	9	3	3	106	2.63
1920	Cin	13	9	1	207.2	2.51
1921	Cin	17	19	3	304	3.38
1922	Cin	13	23	0	261	3.31
1923	Cin	27	8	2	322	1.93
1924	Cin	10	15	0	219.1	3.16
1925	Cin	16	18	0	291	2.63
1926	Cin	13	16	0	233.2	3.43
1927	Cin	13	12	0	230.2	3.20
1928	Cin	11	10	1	234.1	3.57
1929	Cin	5	16	0	176	4.50
1930	Bro	14	8	2	199	4.30
1931	Bro	7	6	0	102.2	4.56
1932	NYG	6	7	5	110	4.01
1933	NYG	8	2	4	80.1	2.69
1934	NYG	4	3	7	42.1	3.83
1935	NYG	1	0	0	3.2	0.00
TOTALS		193	179	28	3220.1	3.24

However, Wells was a little gung ho about Mexico. Here is another, less militant account of Mexico: "I'll be sorry to leave Mexico. I got a little sick from the food or the water, but they say everybody does... The good things about Mexico are 1) the hotels, 2)the crowds--they know their baseball down here and if they razz you, you can't understand them, 3) the good level of competition and 4) no bullshit stuff about sitting in the back or not being served or just being thought as a no-account nigger. The bad things are 1) some of the food is too spicy for my taste, 2) my stomach is tender, 3) the women aren't really accessible. They look nice but they are definitely off limits except for the whores and I ain't messin' with foreign whores." (From the *National Pastime* Number 17, p. 27-28.)

If you were a black player from any country other than Cuba, you must have been crazy to play in the United States before Jackie Robinson. Non-Cuban Latinos simply did not come to the United States. Jackie Robinson also opened the doors to these players.

The Dominican Invasion, as the influx of Dominican players was referred to, would have happened much earlier had it not been for a catastrophe in 1948. The delay in the arrival of Dominican players may give the idea that the dark-skinned Latinos had to blaze their own path in the 1960s. This was not the case. The path was open to them as well, except that most of the Dominican major league talent disappeared in one night.

"The Santiago plane leaving for home ran into one of the evening storms that plunge the [Dominican-Haitian] island in darkness in an instant. At Santiago, the storm had knocked out the airport lights, and the pilot turned back south trying to reach Santo Domingo. The wreckage was found on a peak in the wild Rio Verde country, miles from anywhere. The 32 dead included almost all the top-ranking players in the country. Loro Escalante, the brothers Pepe and Pepito Lucas, Bombo Ramos and Grillo-A were alone the nucleus of a big league team." (Sports Illustrated, Feb. 25, 1963.)

This plane crash was what delayed the non-Cuban Latino integration of the majors. Jackie Robinson opened the doors for everyone. It was just too late for these 1948 players. After Jackie Robinson, the doors opened for all Latinos willing to relocate to a new country. Unfortunately for the Cuban players, who fought in the trenches with the African-Americans in the Negro Leagues, the doors would stay open for only 13 more years after Robinson. Fidel Castro shut the door to the majors shortly after his 1959 take over of the country.

Armando Marsans, a former Negro League player and colored Cuban, threatened the color barrier by playing in the majors from 1911 to 1918. Photo courtesy of the Library of Congress.

Washington Park was constructed at a time when baseball was young. There were Ichthyosaurs swimming in the Gowanus swamps. The world of baseball was so new that not everything had names yet. If you went up to a player and asked him what a "save," a "platoon" or a "screwball" meant, you might get a completely unexpected answer. In fact, the Brooklyn team wasn't even called the Dodgers, yet. Instead they went with names such as the Bridegrooms, the Trolley Dodgers or the Superbas, the latter after a group of actors touring the Vaudeville circuit as Hanlon's Superbas. Coincidentally, the Brooklyn manager was Ned Hanlon, so the nickname stuck.

Washington Park was built in 1883, when Brooklyn was still its own city. It was built on the site where George Washington fought the real first battle of the War of Independence. On August 27, 1776, Washington's troops suffered a terrible defeat in the battle, but eventually won the war because the remaining troops were able to escape the British army by crossing the swamps of the Gowanus. After the defeat, Tom Paine wrote on the head of a drum next to a campfire in the snow, "These are the times that try men's souls..." Oh, how Brooklynite those words sound.

Six years after the park opened, it burned down. It was rebuilt, and the National League Bridegrooms used it as their home park for the 1890 season. The Bridegrooms left Washington Park and played their games at Eastern Park between 1891 and 1897. It was at Eastern Park that the Brooklyn team got the nickname the Trolley Dodgers because of the fans having to dodge the trolleys to get to the park.

There was much change in 1898. Despite the objections of the cities of New York and Brooklyn, Albany ordered both cities to join into one, and New York City as we now know it took its present form. The same year, Charles Ebbets moved the Superbas, as they were known by this time, back to Washington Park.

The park was not Ebbets' first choice. The stench from the Gowanus Canal and nearby factories made this an unpleasant recreation site. The park had a peculiar center field scoreboard. It stood on stilts, so when balls would roll under the fence, players had to crawl underneath to get it.

The park was antiquated and seated few people. Ebbets did everything he could to increase capacity. He took as much of the foul territory as possible and converted it to seating area. The 90-foot backstop in 1898 was reduced to 15 feet by 1908 (the average distance from home plate to the backstop wall is about 60 feet). Shaquille O'Neal could have probably touched the first row of seats with one hand and third base with the other. Basically, there was no foul territory. When Ebbets ran out of room, the former architecture student began looking for a plot of land where to build the new home of the Dodgers.

Eventually, Ebbets would construct Ebbets Field in the Flatbush area. Unfortunately for him, Ebbets Field's seating capacity also became obsolete quickly.

Why weren't the Brooklyn Dodgers called the New York Dodgers?

Several old towns make up what is known now as the borough of Brooklyn, including Breuckelen (Brooklyn), New Amersfoort (Flatlands), Midwout (Flatbush), New Utrecht, and Boswick (Bushwick). Brooklyn became a city in 1834 and annexed all of its neighbors by 1894. The city was made mostly of German immigrants, who were proud of their town. In 1898, Brooklyn was annexed to New York, but Brooklyn residents resisted the annexation by defending their own identity in every issue they could, including the name of their baseball team.

Washington Park Park Factors		
Year	R	HR
1899	105	102
1900	119	112
1901	110	61
1902	84	63
1903	99	92
1904	92	52
1905	99	152
1906	76	68
1907	86	123

WASHINGTON PARK
BROOKLYN SUPERBAS
(1899-1907)

Opened for MLB in 1883

Fences:	LF and CF: 12 feet
	RF: 42 feet
Altitude:	55 feet
Capacity:	N/A
Area of fair territory:	N/A
Foul territory:	Small

500

335

445

400

350

300

250

200

150

300

295

Imagine if you were the manager of a team barnstorming through time. Before every game, you would meet with your team and fill them in on what team you were going to play, but you would also remind them of the different set of rules they would encounter as they played in different parks and different eras. Before playing at Eclipse Park, you would give the team a summary on the different type of baseball they would play in 1884:

--The mound is 50 feet from home plate.

--A batter is awarded a base after seven balls in the American Association.

--A batter is called out after the umpire calls four strikes.

--Foul balls caught after only one bounce are outs.

--Pitchers cannot raise their arms above shoulder level while delivering a pitch.

These rules made playing in Eclipse quite different than playing in today's parks. The equipment used also affected the game. Many gloves were fingerless, with barely more padding than a winter glove. The ball was deader. The players concentrated on ball placement because the ball did not travel far. The bats' handles were thicker to maximize accurate placement of the ball, not power like today. The bats of today have thin handles, with the most weight centered on the barrel. These bats maximize bat speed and power. They are perfect for driving a live ball 380 feet for homers. However, long flyballs were long outs in Eclipse. The correct way to slug in Eclipse was to hit line drives and then run.

Out-of-the-park homers were rare in Eclipse. Fences were in place to keep people from watching for free, and to prevent balls from getting lost. In 1889, A.G. Spalding's Official Baseball Guide sold baseballs for $1.50 each. Sam Crawford said when he was 17 years old, barnstorming through Nebraska, he could buy 12 pounds of round steak for a dollar. Today's owners would probably not want to lose baseballs either if each one cost as much

The Louisville Slugger

Pete Browning of the Louisville Colonels was in the midst of a slump when he broke his good luck bat in 1884. Browning looked so depressed and pathetic that a woodworker watching him felt moved to help the out-of-luck slugger. The worker took Browning to his shop where the two spent all night trying to make the perfect bat. The next day, Browning went 3-for-3, and the first Louisville Slugger became a hit.

In 1905 Honus Wagner signed a contract giving permission to have his autograph printed on each bat. Thus Wagner became the first athlete to endorse a retail product.

During a slump, the Cincinnati Reds called the makers of the Sluggers asking for advice on how to pull out of a slump they were having. The advice given to the Reds was to let the bats lie in the sun. The Reds caught fire following the instructions; however, the "advice" was pulled out of the air by a Louisville Slugger employee.

as 16 pounds of round steak. (A pound is currently going for $2.50.)

Because owners did not want to lose baseballs, the fences were distant from the plate, resulting in few homers. Between 1884 and 1891, the most homers hit by the Colonels was 27. Eclipse Park was unforgiving to hitters. Fewer runs were scored, and fewer homers were hit at Eclipse than at the average park of its time.

The Colonels began in the American Association. The AA came to existence in 1882 and was recognized by the National League in 1884. The winners of the two leagues met in the first World Series until the AA collapsed following the 1891 season. The Colonels were admitted into the NL in 1892 and merged with Pittsburgh before the 1900 campaign.

Revisions to the rules:	
1885	--A foul ball had to be caught on the fly for it to be an out.
	--The AA allowed overhand deliveries by pitchers.
1887	--A base on balls was awarded after five balls.
1888	--A batter was out after three strikes.
1889	--A base on balls was awarded after four balls.

Eclipse Park Park Factors		
Year	R	HR
1884	71	29
1885	105	167
1886	123	360
1887	112	97
1888	92	18
1889	98	85
1890	114	83
1891	79	33

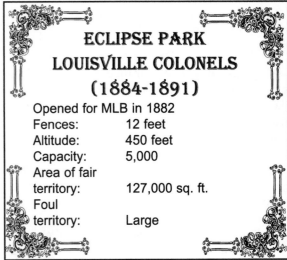

405

360

498

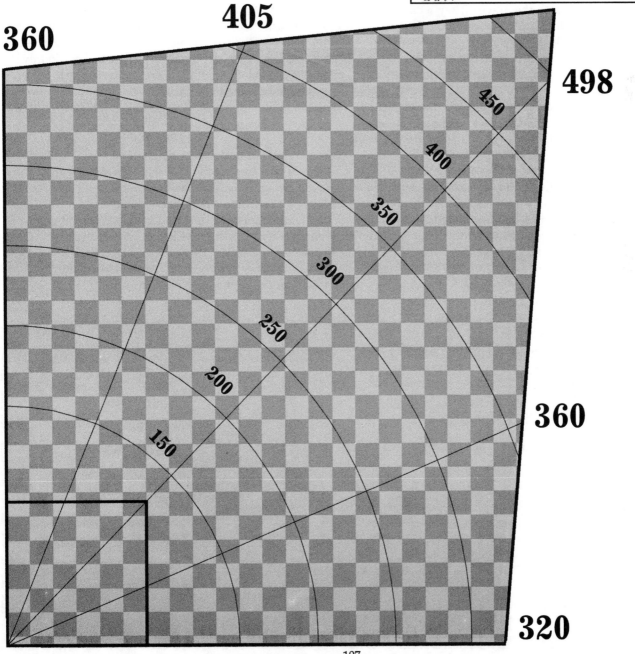

450

400

350

300

250

200

150

360

320

COUNTY STADIUM
HOME OF THE MILWAUKEE BREWERS

One day in the spring of 1953, John Quinn, the general manager of the Boston Braves, handed his players hats with the letter "M" on them. That's how the players learned the team had left Boston. Milwaukee was told a few weeks before Opening Day that it was getting a major league team.

Warren Spahn started the first game at County Stadium. He was working to the second batter of the first inning when the crowd, for no particular reason other than to celebrate that baseball had arrived in Milwaukee, began standing and cheering all around the park.

Fans poured in from all of Wisconsin and its neighboring states to watch the Braves. They set a National League record for attendance in 1954. The parking lot was jammed with people barbecuing. Fans would roll kegs of beer off the train and into the park. But the crowds decreased with time, and in 1966, the Braves moved to Atlanta.

In 1970, Milwaukee struck gold again when a group led by Bud Selig bought the Seattle Pilots. The team was renamed the Milwaukee Brewers. The first Brew Crew won 65 games against 97 losses.

County Stadium is the northern-most park in the majors without a dome. Team officials have lost much money because of the inclement April weather. Milwaukee, being a small market, cannot afford to lose revenue from the April games. In addition, many fans are unwilling to travel three hours if there is the risk of a game being canceled. The Brewers depend on out-of-town fans to help boost the attendance.

County Stadium's days are numbered. Ground was broken for Miller Park on November 9, 1996, before a crowd of 20,000. The new park will have a retractable dome and will be asymmetrical. Officials hope the new park will mark the end of Opening Days like the latest one in 1997, when the game time conditions were 35 degrees and winds at 30 mph. Gov. Tommy Thompson said at the groundbreaking ceremony that he hopes this new park, like Lambeau Field in Green Bay, will unite the state for a few hours each day. George Petak, the former state senator who cast the deciding vote for the $250 million park in October

1995, was present at the ceremony. The resulting anger surrounding his vote cost him his office when he lost his next election.

The best thing about the groundbreaking ceremony was the smell of the bratwursts being cooked. County Stadium may be passing on, but its legacy will remain evident around the waist of happily fed Brewer fans.

The location of Miller Park is questionable. It is directly East of County Stadium. If you threw a baseball from the right field bleachers, you could probably hit the new park. The County Stadium area is not bad, but it isn't great. The park is easy accessible by highway, which is important if they want to draw from Chicago's far northern suburbs. There's a big cemetery to the north and a veterans center to the west, which are full of green because of their abundant trees and grass fields. However, County Stadium sits in an indentation in the city--almost like in a dry riverbed. Its area is very industrial, with the Breweries within smelling distance. Train tracks and highways dominate the landscape near the stadium.

The best area for the new Miller Park would have been on the lake front to the north of downtown. The beauty of that area rivals any other city in the Midwest. Though being in that area would have helped walk-up traffic, that area was out of reach financially.

Hopefully, the new park and the new museum of contemporary art will provide two huge buildings to revitalize Milwaukee. Both huge buildings will have state-of-the-art architecture and technology. Their aesthetic impact remains to be seen.

County Stadium with Miller Park going up behind center field. Photo by Oscar Palacios.

				Park Factors					
Year	Avg	R	H	2B	3B	HR	L-Avg	R-Avg	L-HR	R-HR
1992	93	79	87	79	74	74	90	94	54	85
1993	103	97	103	96	114	74	100	105	113	56
1994	103	113	106	104	94	99	108	99	76	119
1995	111	122	116	116	110	83	119	106	97	76
1996	101	103	100	96	106	91	96	104	96	109
1997	102	101	104	112	119	90	96	107	81	98

COUNTY STADIUM
MILWAUKEE BREWERS
(1992-1998)

Opened for MLB in 1953

Fences:	10 feet
Altitude:	635 feet
Capacity:	53,192
Area of fair territory:	107,000 sq. ft.
Foul territory:	Above average

376

315

402

350

300

250

200

150

376

315

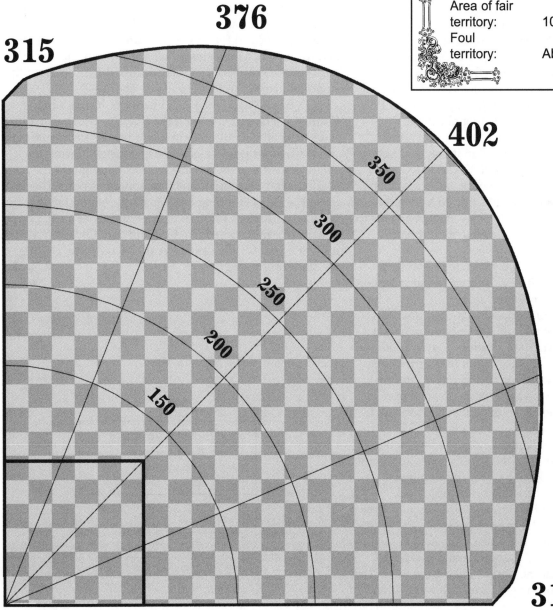

SICKS' STADIUM
HOME OF THE SEATTLE PILOTS

The 1969 expansion Seattle Pilots got off on the wrong foot in Sicks' Stadium. The minor league ballpark was supposed to be rehabilitated to major league standards, but by Opening Day, 7,000 seats and the left-field fence still had to be completed. The ballpark didn't even have lights. No night games were played that season at Sicks'. The Pilots needed all the help they could get, and not having lights was another straw that broke the camel's back. The team floundered, losing 98 games, and they drew poorly, less than 700,000 fans. After their first, dismal season, owner Dewey Soriano sold the team to Bud Selig, who promptly moved the Pilots to Milwaukee. During the winter, Selig renamed the team the Brewers. In 1972, the Brewers switched divisions with another expansion team, the second-generation Washington Senators. That expansion team also left its original town and moved to Texas, becoming the Rangers. The Brewers were now in the American League East and the Rangers in the West. The Brewers are still on the move. When the divisions were realigned one more time in 1994, the Brewers were placed in the AL Central. But they weren't done, yet. For the 1998 season, the Brewers moved to the National League Central. For having such a relatively short history, the Brewers have been in more motion than if they had been doing the Chicken Dance for the past 30 years. Nonetheless, the move to the NL Central was a smart one because they were able to draw Cubs fans to Milwaukee in 1998. The Brewers were not able to draw White Sox fans to Milwaukee. (Heck, the White Sox are having problems drawing to their own stadium right now.) The White Sox play in the South Side of Chicago. Chicago is 20 miles long, which means that White Sox fans had a much longer drive than the Northside Cubs fans do.

Back to where it all started. Sicks' Stadium didn't give the Pilots a chance. It was an ancient minor league park built back in 1913. The 1969 Opening Day capacity was a meager 18,000 fans. It wasn't until June of that season that the attendance was increased to 25,420, and by that time no one wanted to watch a losing team. For a major league stadium, the park wasn't much to look at. It was basically a group of seats bunched together. There was a small one-deck grandstand whose shadows tended to cover home plate every time the Pilots needed to mount a comeback. However, Sicks', like many other minor league stadiums, had a feature that beats triple-deck grandstands and solid-gold water fountains any day: proximity to the action. The foul territory was small. Except for the home plate seats behind the posts, every seat in the stadium was awesome. Only the grandstand had a roof, the rest of the stadium had no posts blocking the view. The only seats where you couldn't get a foul ball were behind the home plate. A great seat is one where you can catch a foul ball.

Sicks' was a tiny stadium. At 100,000 square feet of fair territory, the stadium was smaller than any current park. The power alleys were barely more than 340 feet from home plate. This park was a home run haven. The Pilots and their opponents hit 167 home runs at Sicks' in 1969. On the road, the Pilots and their opponents hit 130 homers. That means it was about 28 percent easier to homer at Sicks' than at its contemporary ballparks in the 1969 season.

Just because it was easy to homer in Sicks' doesn't mean it was a hitters' park. When it came to scoring runs, the ultimate measure of offense, the park was close to neutral. The short fences allowed outfielders to play closer to infield and to catch balls before them that would have normally dropped for hits. Also, lumbering baserunners had to stop with long singles off the wall. In addition, the park cut the number of triples because the throw from the right-field corner to third base was short.

Seattle had had a rich history of baseball in the Pacific Coast League. Losing the Pilots was just a small setback. Seattle would regain major league status just eight years after losing the Pilots. The expansion Mariners claimed Seattle as their home in 1977. Though the Mariners have struggled the past couple of years, baseball in Seattle looks as strong as it ever has. A brand new retractable dome stadium will open in July of 1999. The new park will be called SafeCo Field. SafeCo will pay $1.8 million a year for the next 20 years for rights to the stadium's name.

Sicks' Stadium Park Factors		
Year	R	HR
1969	103	128

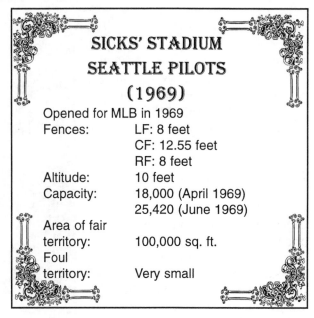

SICKS' STADIUM

SEATTLE PILOTS

(1969)

Opened for MLB in 1969

Fences:	LF: 8 feet
	CF: 12.55 feet
	RF: 8 feet
Altitude:	10 feet
Capacity:	18,000 (April 1969)
	25,420 (June 1969)
Area of fair territory:	100,000 sq. ft.
Foul territory:	Very small

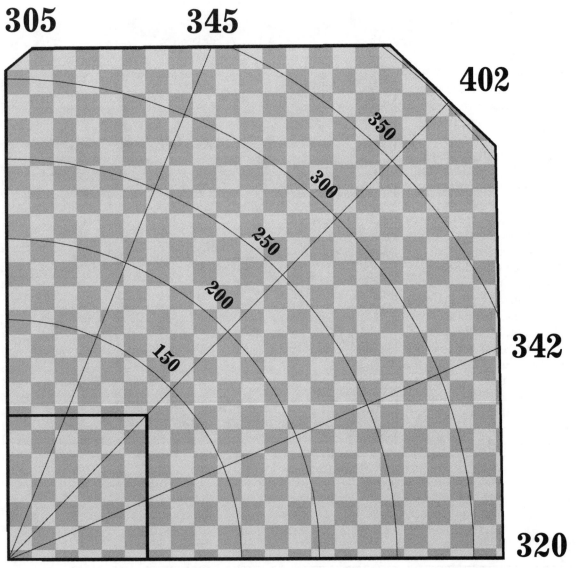

305   345   402

350

300

250

200

150

342

320

There is no other experience in Major League Baseball like entering the Metrodome. Fans risk getting blown away as they make their way into the stadium through revolving doors. The roof of the dome is kept inflated by 250,000 cubic feet of air pressure per minute. This method of keeping the roof up by using air pressure has caused much speculation among fans and players alike.

The suspicion is that the air flows aid long flyballs. The Metrodome outfield is five percent larger than the Astrodome's outfield, yet an atypical number of homers are hit at the Metrodome, about 10 percent more than at other American League parks. In addition, an above-average number of hits, doubles and triples makes this dome a nightmare for pitchers. The air pressure may not be the culprit as suspected, because the extra pressure increases drag and friction on the ball. The park is fairly dry, but contrary to popular belief, humid air is actually lighter than dry air.

Minneapolis is almost as high as Atlanta, but not high enough to blame the altitude for the number of home runs. One thing the dome does have going for it is an awesome hitting background. Perhaps because it is an easier place to see a pitch, batters can move their bats ever so slightly to put more of their sweet spots on the ball.

Though the Metrodome outfield background provides great contrast for hitting, it is almost wasted material, especially right field. There are areas where you can see the folded football seats, much like a high school basketball court with its seats folded. These and other short-comings of the Metrodome were used as an excuse to force the city to build a new stadium. The team threatened to sell and move the franchise for the 1998 season. So far there's no new stadium, and the franchise is still is in Minnesota. The future of the franchise, however, remains unclear.

The Metrodome has the magic that makes parks fun: uniqueness. The bouncy artificial turf can turn pop-fly singles into doubles as fielders have to wait a long time before the ball comes down from its bounce. The Metrodome is a fun place to cheer because the crowd noise reverberates as loud as a jet or a jackhammer, earning the park the nickname the Thuderdome. Photos courtesy of the Twins.

Park Factors										
Year	Avg	R	H	2B	3B	HR	L-Avg	R-Avg	L-HR	R-HR
1992	103	100	104	111	184	98	104	102	111	93
1993	100	109	102	121	104	86	99	100	95	82
1994	99	97	98	100	88	105	99	99	89	111
1995	99	105	99	98	128	119	96	101	132	113
1996	102	108	103	114	116	104	101	104	106	102
1997	101	101	103	100	91	86	105	99	99	78

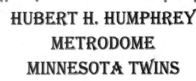

HUBERT H. HUMPHREY
METRODOME
MINNESOTA TWINS
(1992-1998)

Opened for MLB in 1982
Artificial turf

Fences:	LF-CF: 13 feet
	RF: 23 feet
Altitude:	815 feet
Capacity:	55,883 (baseball)
Area of fair territory:	111,000 sq. ft.
Foul territory:	Very small

343   **385**

408

367

327

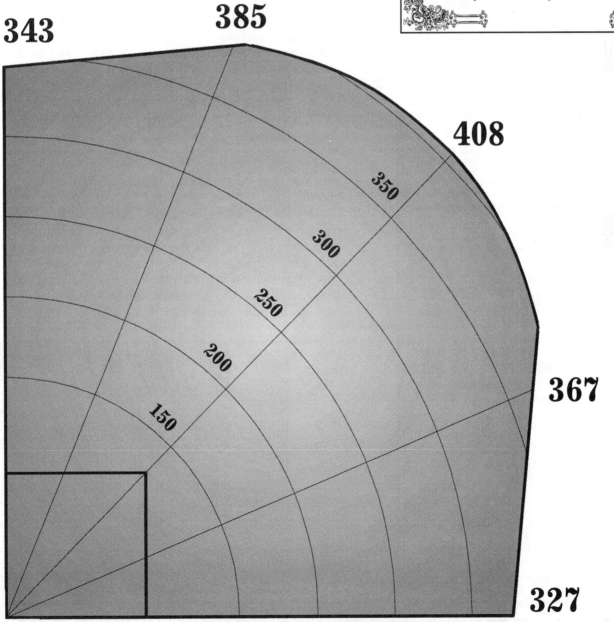

METROPOLITAN STADIUM
HOME OF THE MINNESOTA TWINS

In 1953, a Minneapolis committee called the Minute Men began work on bringing a major league team to the city. The committee started by selecting Bloomington, a suburb located halfway between St. Paul and Minneapolis, as a site for a new ballpark. The Met, as fans referred to Metropolitan Stadium, was completed in the spring of 1956. The park had a triple-deck grandstand behind home plate, but nothing else. It looked as if someone had sliced the grandstand of a major league stadium and dropped it in a Minnesota corn field. The committee had in mind a park that could be converted easily into a big league stadium if a team showed interest in the area.

Between 1956 and 1960, the stadium was the home of the American Association Minneapolis Millers. However, things were about to happen amidst the cornfields of Minnesota. Just like Joe Jackson appeared to Ray Kinsella in the movie "Field of Dreams," the Washington Senators appeared on the field, willing to make it their home for the 1961 season. Before signing the dotted line, Senator owner Calvin Griffith demanded the capacity of the stadium be increased and for the committee to guarantee him a 2.5 million attendance in the first three years. The committee accepted his requests, and in 1961 the Washington Senators became the Minnesota Twins.

The park's sole purpose was to bring a major league team to the area. Once that was accomplished, the park became expendable. Unfortunately, the Met didn't have an Astrodome to replace it like Colt Stadium had. Instead, the park was changed yearly to make it more suitable for the majors. In 1961 temporary bleachers were added along the left field line, and the grandstand was permanently extended down the lines. In 1965, the Minnesota Vikings paid to have a second deck added to the left field bleachers. Later on, Harmon Killebrew launched a gargantuan homer that dented one of the new bleacher seats. To honor his muscle, the seat was painted red.

The changes did not improve the appearance of the stadium. Though downtown Minneapolis was visible 20 miles behind the third base line, what were overwhelmingly visible were the parking lots. Fans came to the park to see the team. The ballpark itself was not a draw. At least there was a great team to watch. The 1965 Twins made it to the World Series and battled Los Angeles Dodgers in a tremendous seven-game series. The Dodger pitching proved too strong as they held the Twins to a .195 batting average and won the series.

Though the park was tasteless in the summers, it became magical in the winters. The awesome Minnesota Vikings defense fed on the inclement weather to trash their opponents. The Viking players were not allowed to have heaters on the sidelines in order to commune with the cold. But these same Vikings pushed for an indoor stadium, leaving behind an intimidating arena matched today only by Lambeau Field. The Twins went along with the Vikings because they could not afford to play at the Met by themselves. By the end of the Met's life, it had become the worst kept park in the majors. It was literally falling apart.

Both teams moved to downtown Minneapolis after 1981, hurting the feelings of some St. Paul fans. Metropolitan was demolished and the Mall of America now stands on the former baseball grounds. At first losing the stadium was a huge blow to the city of Bloomington, but after opening in 1992, the Mall of America has more than made it up. Over 35 million people visit it annually, over 10 times more than the attendance of the Vikings and Twins combined. The mall employs over 11,000 workers, far more than the Met ever could.

This is a list of all the stores at the Mall of America

Metropolitan Stadium Park Factors		
Year	R	HR
1977	107	106
1978	88	82
1979	118	114
1980	119	110
1981	115	109

METROPOLITAN STADIUM
MINNESOTA TWINS
(1977-1981)

Opened for MLB in 1961

Fences:	LF:12 feet
	CF: 8 feet
	RF: 5 feet
Altitude:	815 feet
Capacity:	45,919
Area of fair territory:	109,000 sq. ft.
Foul territory:	Average

343

360

402

350

300

250

200

150

370

330

GRIFFITH STADIUM
HOME OF THE WASHINGTON SENATORS

Once upon a time, there was a big man sitting on a chair watching a baseball game. The seat was small and the man kept shifting his weight from left to right, right to left, until he'd had enough. Oh, no. He did not leave the baseball game. He was a big fan. What he did was stand up to try to wake up his legs which had been asleep since the third inning. When he stood up, every one around him did the same in respect, for the big man was none other than the president of the United States, Mr. William H. Taft. Ever since, baseball crowds have imitated what the big man did in Griffith Stadium, doing what is now known as the seventh inning stretch.

President Taft invented the 7th Inning Stretch.
Photo courtesy of the Library of Congress

Taft also started the tradition of the president throwing the first pitch of the season in 1910. Now, the non-aficionado public gave Taft a bad reputation. We, as baseball fans, have the duty to do him justice. Taft got little respect because Teddy Roosevelt decided not to run for president in 1908. Roosevelt was so strong politically as to be able to choose Taft as his successor. Roosevelt was a charismatic leader who is credited for doing much progressive work. However, if Roosevelt did the groundbreaking, Taft did the real digging. Roosevelt, known as the trustbuster, noisily dissolved 44 trusts in seven-plus years. Taft, with a Lou Gehrig-like steadiness, busted 90 trusts in his four-year term. Taft also opposed big government and the institution of the Federal Income Tax. In 1912 Roosevelt turned against Taft, calling him a "fathead" with a brain of a "guinea pig." Roosevelt split the Republican vote when he ran as a Progressive Party candidate, allowing Woodrow Wilson to win the 1912 election. Wilson provided the leadership needed for Congress to ratify the Income Tax Amendment in 1913. In 1921 Taft was appointed Chief Justice of the Supreme Court by President Harding.

After the president had thrown the first pitch in Griffith Stadium, the festivities for the year were usually over. The Senators were horrible, except for the 1924 season. Walter Johnson posted a 23-7 record that year, but ran into problems in the World Series, losing both of his starts against the Giants. Johnson found redemption when he was called to relieve Game 7. Johnson shut out the Giants from the ninth through the 12th innings, when the Senators scored the winning run.

Griffith Stadium was a pitchers' park and the second-hardest park in which to homer in the 20th Century. Nevertheless, two players were able to clear the left field bleachers: Mickey Mantle with a 500-foot shot and Josh Gibson, who did it twice.

Griffith Stadium Park Factors		
Year	R	HR
1911	95	45
1912	92	125
1913	111	231
1914	104	81
1915	95	27
1916	100	36
1917	85	32
1918	104	75
1919	93	18
1920	94	16

Income Tax Collected per U.S. resident (in 1996 dollars):

Taft's presidency	$0.00
1915	$14.00
1935	$47.50
1955	$1,131.51
1975	$1,618.87
1995	$2,309.49

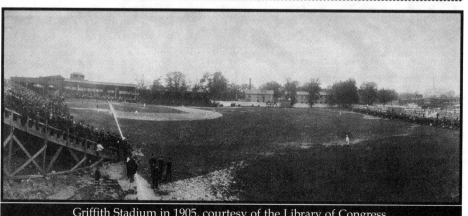

Griffith Stadium in 1905, courtesy of the Library of Congress.

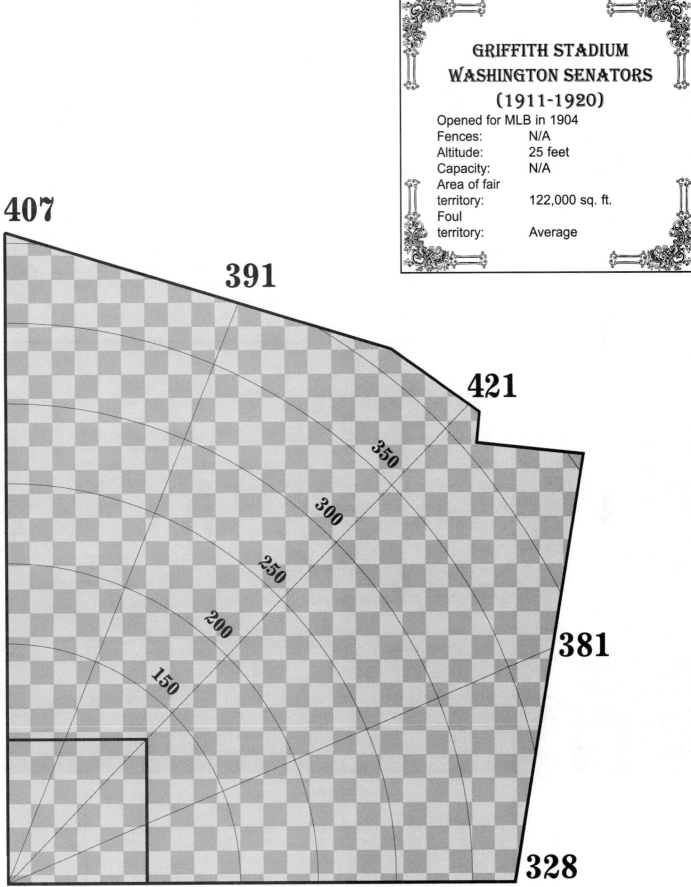

407

391

GRIFFITH STADIUM
WASHINGTON SENATORS
(1911-1920)

Opened for MLB in 1904
Fences: N/A
Altitude: 25 feet
Capacity: N/A
Area of fair
territory: 122,000 sq. ft.
Foul
territory: Average

421

350

300

250

200

150

381

328

OLYMPIC STADIUM (LE STADE OLYMPIQUE)
HOME OF THE MONTREAL EXPOS

Olympic Stadium (Le Stade Olympique) opened as an outdoor venue in 1977. Ever since then, the park has been Montreal's Vietnam War. The behemoth's total cost is $1 billion. The 552-foot tower that now stands remained half-finished between 1976 and 1987. For two years, a dome was in place but could not retract. After more millions were sprinkled over the stadium, it finally had a retractable dome in 1989. In 1991 Montreal was forced to play its final 13 home games on the road because of a collapsing park.

Originally built for the 1976 Olympic Games, the park was supposed to have a retractable dome, but strikes and out-of-control expenses resulted in a park that was always about to be completed. The canvas roof is suspended by steel cables wiring down from the tower. The cables connect to 26 cone-shaped supporting fixtures, giving the park the look of the inside of a golf ball. The tower makes the stadium easy to find because it is visible from as far as 50 miles away on clear days.

Fans welcomed the new stadium in 1977 with a season attendance of over a million. At the time the team was beginning to develop some stars like Gary Carter, Ron LeFlore, Tim Raines, Andre Dawson, Bill Gullickson and Tim Wallach. In 1981, they almost made it to the World Series after winning the second half of the strike-torn season. In 1983 a franchise-high 2,321,000 people attended the stadium, but by 1991, the number had sunk to 978,000.

The mascot of the team is called Youppi!--an expression used by children similar meaning to "Oh, Goodie!" in English. Like the Creature from the Black Lagoon, Youppi! appears to have risen from a decrepit pile of artificial turf. Nonetheless, the mascot is popular with fans.

Olympic Stadium, courtesy of the Montreal Expos.

Park Factors

Year	Avg	R	H	2B	3B	HR	L-Avg	R-Avg	L-HR	R-HR
1992	103	118	100	126	126	105	102	104	115	98
1993	97	94	96	118	85	89	108	90	102	81
1994	109	108	108	132	108	90	110	108	97	86
1995	99	97	98	110	123	67	96	100	76	100
1996	100	111	100	110	172	110	109	96	134	99
1997	104	104	106	118	131	86	104	105	92	82

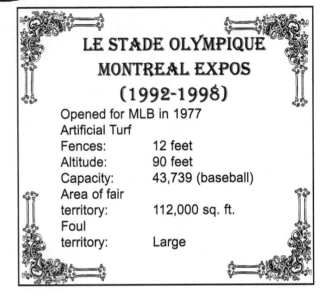

LE STADE OLYMPIQUE
MONTREAL EXPOS
(1992-1998)

Opened for MLB in 1977
Artificial Turf
Fences: 12 feet
Altitude: 90 feet
Capacity: 43,739 (baseball)
Area of fair
territory: 112,000 sq. ft.
Foul
territory: Large

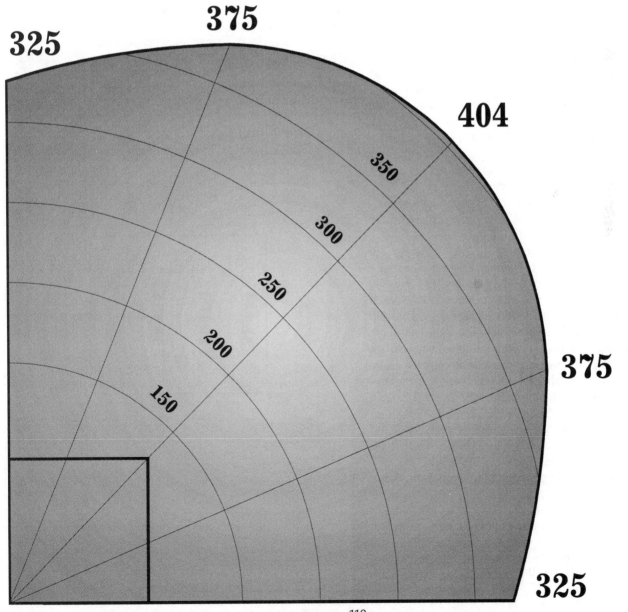

325

375

404

350

300

250

200

150

375

325

PARC JARRY
HOME OF THE MONTREAL EXPOS

Major League Baseball officially became an international sport when the expansion Montreal Expos played their first season in 1969 at Parc Jarry. Originally, the Expos wanted to play at the 25,000-seat Autostade, but city officials refused to raise the $7 million necessary to place a cover on the stadium and add 12,000 seats. The National League president traveled to Montreal and told the mayor they would lose their expansion team unless they found a new site soon. The mayor and the NL president agreed on an easily accessible recreational area.

At first Parc Jarry sat 3,000 people, but the city expanded it to sit 28,456. The park was supposed to be only a temporary home for the Expos until a new park was built. It looked very similar to another temporary park, Colt Stadium. Parc Jarry had the appearance of an overgrown high school stadium, with an uncovered grandstand and eight towering light posts. Despite the relatively uncomfortable conditions, people came to watch baseball. The attendance figures were so good that Parc Jarry became obsolete quickly. However, year after year, the plans for a new covered stadium fell through. It would not be until 1977 that the Expos would finally have a covered stadium, the billion-dollar escargot of Olympic Stadium.

While playing at Parc Jarry, officials had a difficult time calling games. They didn't want to disappoint the fans that were packing the stands year after year, but they had to protect the fans that were mercilessly exposed to the weather. One day in April of 1971, plows created monumental mounds of snow behind the outfield walls. Instead of going home because of the cold conditions, fans hiked to the top of the hills and watched a game for free.

Despite the simplicity of the park and the few amenities it offered fans, it was a fun place to play baseball. A stiff breeze usually helped balls clear the right field wall where they would land in a pool. The grandstand and the bleachers were low, taking away the usual background of white shirts that fielders have to battle to catch flyballs. However, the lower grandstand did not block the afternoon sun, giving right fielders a hard time when flyballs lined up with the sun.

Despite a 420-foot center field, Parc Jarry had smaller power alleys than average. The result was that Parc Jarry allowed a higher number of home runs and runs scored than the average National League park. After the Expos moved on to their next stadium, Parc Jarry was converted back to a civic area. Professional tennis matches as well as large outdoor gatherings now take place on the former baseball grounds.

Despite its temporary appearance, Parc Jarry may have been the apex of baseball in Montreal, a city with a rich baseball history. Montreal welcomed Jackie Robinson to its bosom as he prepared to shake the major leagues by honing his skills with the Triple-A Montreal Royals. Without Montreal, integration would have taken much longer. Perhaps the majors would have never seen the likes of Larry Doby, Willie Mays, Hank Aaron or Ernie Banks.

Montreal's love of the game dates back almost as far as baseball itself. The reigning queen of Montreal's young baseball days was the Delorimier Downs Stadium. Constructed in 1928, it was the home of eight minor league pennant winners.

Despite having the lowest ticket, parking and concession prices in the majors, Montreal continues to have attendance problems. Memories of the packed stands of Parc Jarry are fading quickly. The old park appeared innocent in its simplicity, especially compared to Olympic Stadium.

Parc Jarry Park Factors		
Year	R	HR
1969	107	145
1970	103	132
1971	100	116
1972	105	120
1973	110	111
1974	109	117
1975	119	122
1976	105	91

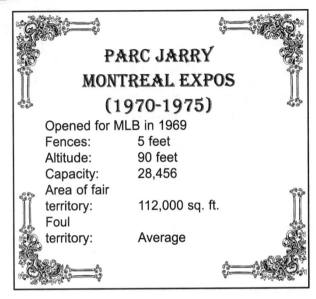

PARC JARRY
MONTREAL EXPOS
(1970-1975)

Opened for MLB in 1969
Fences: 5 feet
Altitude: 90 feet
Capacity: 28,456
Area of fair
territory: 112,000 sq. ft.
Foul
territory: Average

340   **368**

417

CF was 415 in 1970,
417 in 1971-1973,
420 in 1974-1975

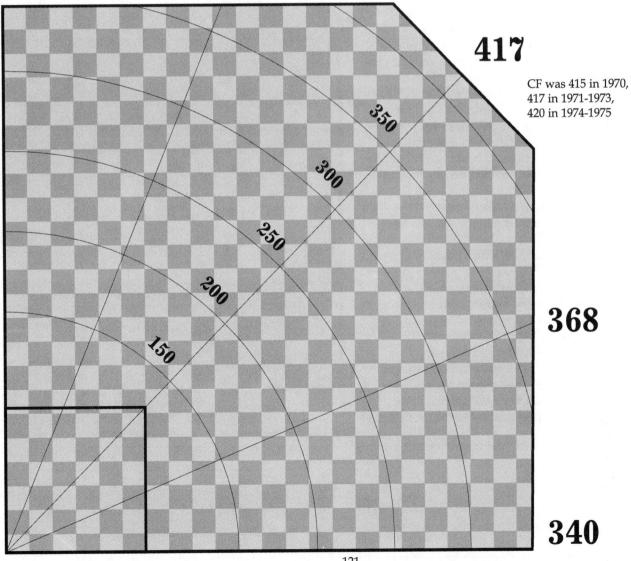

368

340

SHEA STADIUM
HOME OF THE NEW YORK METS

After two years of watching ball at the old Polo Grounds, Mets fans were treated to a sparkling-new Shea Stadium. Some of the inauguration festivities included Bill Shea pouring water from the Gowanus Canal with his right hand and water from the Harlem River with his left. Bill Shea was a popular lawyer who had been instrumental in bringing a National League team back to New York. Mayor Robert F. Wagner insisted the new facility be named after Shea, and so it was. That April day in the spring of 1964, fans were given Mets helmets, which they raised during the National Anthem in salute of the new stadium. The stands were jammed with 48,736 fans, but just in case the Mets could draw more people, the stadium was built with the plan that someday capacity may be increased to 90,000. Shea had that pleasant new park smell, but the 1964 Mets had a different sort of smell. That season, they lost more than 100 games for their third straight season.

From the outset, Shea was tough on hitters. They complained of poor visibility. The swirling winds were supposed to conspire against extra-base hits. Airplanes disrupted hitters with their roaring engines. And, players said, the ball didn't carry at all at the new facility, an expression often misused in baseball. One of the reasons the ball doesn't carry at Shea is because the stadium is near sea level. But the real reason the ball doesn't "carry" well in Shea Stadium is because it is was a big park. At 113,000 square feet of fair territory, it is a difficult park for hitters. The dimensions down the line don't look menacing to hitters. But the wall very quickly drops back to 371 feet. In many parks, the increase in distances between the lines and the power alley is more gradual. In Shea, it is like an abyss.

Unlike the Polo Grounds, which shattered the confidence of many pitchers, Shea is a good place to groom a young pitching staff. That is what happened in the 1969 season, when Tom Seaver, Jerry Koosman and Nolan Ryan matured to bring the Mets their first World Championship. Beginning on August 16, the Mets won 38 of their last 49 games to overcome the Chicago Cubs and finish with a 100-win season. The Mets proceeded to sweep the Atlanta Braves in the NLCS. They topped that performance by casually defeating the powerhouse Baltimore Orioles in five games. The fans celebrated the World Series win by storming Shea Stadium and taking anything they could remove as a souvenir. Cleon Jones and Tommie Agee ran for their lives toward the outfield bullpen instead of heading for the dugout and the celebration. Fans tore off pieces of the players' uniforms and vandalized the field, taking pieces of sod as mementos. The field looked like it had been hit by a meteor shower because of the holes in the grass left by fans.

The Continental League

Following the Giants' and Dodgers' departures from New York, the city created a committee to bring another baseball stadium to the Big Apple. The head of the committee was William Shea. After failing to gain an expansion team for the city, Shea went to work on creating a third major league. The Continental League, as he named it, was the first serious challenge to Major League Baseball since the Federal League back in 1914 and 1915. What made the Continental League a formidable foe was that it had big money behind it. In addition, the league recruited the support of Branch Rickey and Senator Estes Kefauver.

The Continental League proceeded to establish franchises in areas neglected by MLB: New York, Houston, Dallas-Ft. Worth, Minneapolis, Toronto, Atlanta, Denver and Buffalo. The Continental League offered to buy MLB minor league teams in those cities, but MLB did not want a friendly relationship with the upstart league. When Congress passed a ruling saying that MLB would not be breaking antitrust rules by opposing the establishment of the new league, the Continental League was forced to compromise. MLB and the organizers of the new league reached the agreement that New York would get an expansion team. As a result, William Shea was finally successful in bringing a team to New York, and so the stadium was named after him. Eventually, all the Continental League cities, except for Buffalo, were home to major league teams.

Park Factors										
Year	Avg	R	H	2B	3B	HR	L-Avg	R-Avg	L-HR	R-HR
1992	97	90	97	98	97	91	96	98	96	86
1993	97	96	98	85	88	98	93	101	96	99
1994	103	109	104	86	112	105	104	102	118	97
1995	99	89	99	90	130	102	104	94	124	88
1996	94	82	94	79	73	79	91	96	89	73
1997	101	101	100	107	100	88	101	102	112	77

SHEA STADIUM
NEW YORK METS
(1992-1998)

Opened for MLB in 1964
Fences: 8 feet
Altitude: 55 feet
Capacity: 55,775
Area of fair
territory: 113,000 sq. ft.
Foul
territory: Above average

338

378

410

378

338

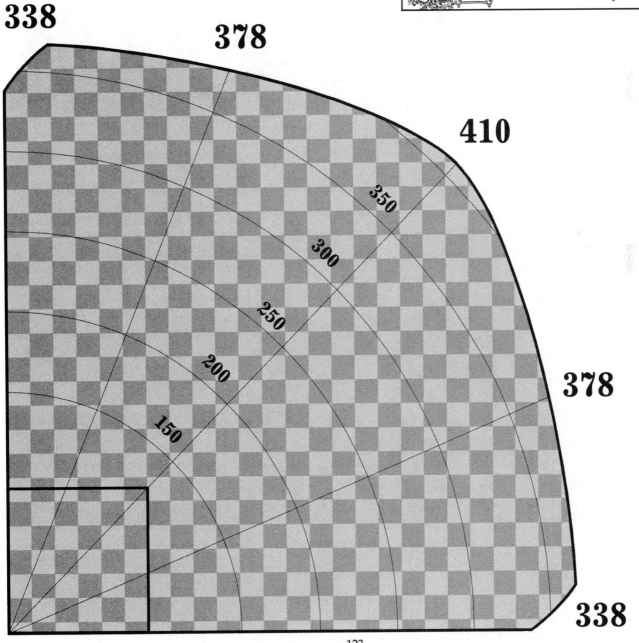

YANKEE STADIUM (NEW)
HOME OF THE NEW YORK YANKEES

Yankee Stadium has become the incredible shrinking park. Left-center field once extended as far back as 460 feet from home plate, and center field was a majestic 490 feet when the park opened. Slowly, these dimensions have been reduced to 399 to left center and 408 to center field. The monuments of Babe Ruth, Lou Gehrig and Miller Huggins were taken out of the playing field after the 1974-75 renovation. They still stand, but behind the outfield wall.

The old facade of Yankee Stadium was taken down for the renovation. Part of it was saved, and it is now on display behind the outfield bleachers. Another aspect of old Yankee Stadium that was saved was the sloping outfield. Left field is three feet higher than right field. During the renovation, the Yankees played their home games at Shea Stadium. In the early part of the 1998 season, a beam fell crushing a seat. Suddenly, there was news about the collapsing Yankee Stadium in every media outlet. The incident gave momentum to the Yankees, who are asking for taxpayers to fund a new billion-dollar stadium.

The beam fell when the stadium was closed, forcing the Yankees to again borrow Shea Stadium for a rare four-team doubleheader. The Yanks also had to make special arrangements with the Detroit Tigers to swap homestands.

The short distance toward the right field pole gives lefthanded pull hitters a tremendous home run advantage. Left field has no foul territory, and this hurts the number of triples hit at the park. Righthanded batters have a harder time than normal at this park because of the depth of left-center field. Overall, the park favors pitchers more than offense.

Photos courtesy of the New York Yankees.

Park Factors

Year	Avg	R	H	2B	3B	HR	L-Avg	R-Avg	L-HR	R-HR
1992	101	109	102	96	81	115	103	100	175	89
1993	94	86	89	73	62	104	99	89	109	102
1994	96	83	92	91	83	95	105	90	102	92
1995	106	103	105	106	87	105	110	101	126	94
1996	104	101	103	93	56	103	105	103	117	91
1997	99	92	96	92	142	98	93	103	87	111

318

399

YANKEE STADIUM
NEW YORK YANKEES
(1992-1998)

Opened for MLB in 1923

Fences:	
	LF: 8 feet
	L-C: 7 feet
	CF: 7 feet
	R-C: 9 feet
	RF: 10 feet
Altitude:	55 feet
Capacity:	57,545
Area of fair territory:	113,000 sq. ft.
Foul territory:	Large behind home, small down the lines

408

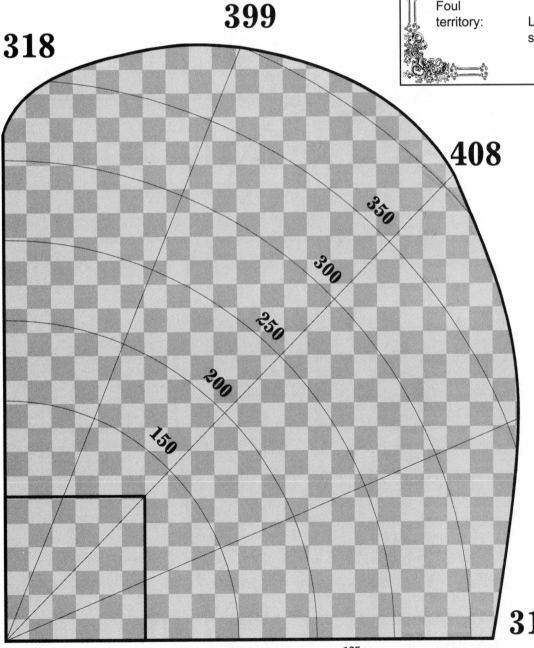

350

300

250

200

150

314

YANKEE STADIUM
NEW YORK YANKEES
(1976-1984)

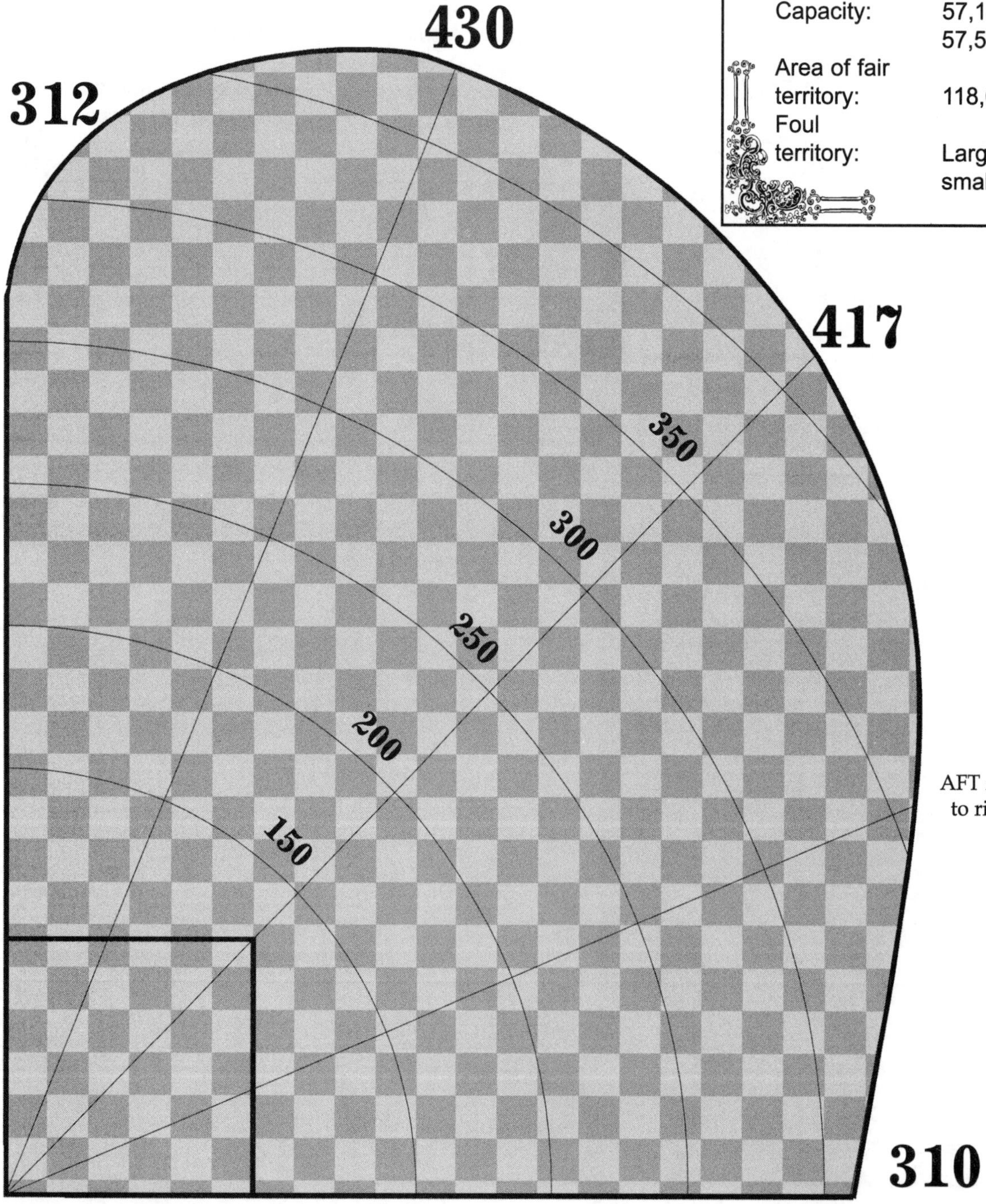

Opened for MLB in 1923

Fences:	LF: 8 feet L-C: 3.58-7 feet CF: 7 feet R-C: 8 feet (1976-78) R-C: 7 feet (1979-84) RF: 10 feet
Altitude:	55 feet
Capacity:	57,145 (1976-79) 57,545 (1980-84)
Area of fair territory:	118,000 sq. ft.
Foul territory:	Large behind home, small down the lines

AFT from LF pole
to dead center field: 66,500

430
312
417
350
300
250
200
150
310

AFT from dead center field
to right field pole: 51,400

The cure was worse than the disease, but it seemed like a good plan at the time. The Yankees shared the Polo Grounds with the Giants from 1913 until 1922. The Giants were the fan favorites, with the Yankees normally lagging behind in attendance--that is until Babe Ruth arrived in New York City in 1920. That year, Babe Ruth hit a record 54 home runs and slugged .847. The Yankees set an attendance record, topping the one-million mark for the first time in history. Giants owner and manager John McGraw was green with envy. He couldn't stand to play second banana in his own home town. He told the Yankees after the 1921 season that they could no longer play at the Polo Grounds. McGraw knew that it would be nearly impossible for the Yankees to build a stadium in Manhattan. He thought that the Yankees would stop drawing well outside of Manhattan and the Giants would once again be kings. However, the Yankees built a new park across the river from the Polo Grounds. And the park was not just any park, it was the first to be called a "stadium" because of its large capacity, 58,000 people. Powerful people gathered at the opening. John Philip Sousa provided fitting music with a military band. Babe Ruth homered in the fourth inning of the game. McGraw could not believe what he had done when he heard the attendance for the first game had topped the 74,000 mark. The era of super-stadiums had arrived. Yankee Stadium felt as large as the Grand Canyon.

Yankee Stadium was the result of changes in society. The urban workweek had been reduced from 66 hours in 1860 to 60 in 1890, down to 47 in 1920. The last 30 years marked the first time in the history of the world that the urban masses had leisure time, and the masses were hungry to use it. Baseball, along with recreational sports and theater, became the recipient of the newfound leisure time. Meanwhile, another great pastime had been made harder to obtain: alcohol. Billy Sunday, an average outfielder with the Cubs, Pirates and Phillies in the 1880s became a powerful evangelist--as powerful as his disciple, Billy Graham, is now. Sunday led the war against alcohol, and in 1920, his dream came true when the 18th Amendment, banning alcohol, was passed. For 13 years major league owners had to make up for that loss of revenue. Yankee Stadium showed it was possible to make up for the lost revenue with large attendance numbers.

Many say that Babe Ruth, here in this stadium, saved baseball when it had been mortally wounded by the Black Sox Scandal. However, the Babe was already defying the imagination of fans by the time the scandal broke out. Baseball pretty much saved itself from the scandal. The game was just too much fun for the first large generation with a disposable income. The crowds would have kept coming despite the scandal, even if Ruth had not

appeared. Perhaps Prohibition deserves some merit. Once alcohol was banned, there weren't enough crooks to keep the supply coming. In 1927 alone, Al Capone made $963 million (in 1996 dollars). With that kind of money, well, gambling was child's play. The same year, Ruth hit 60 home runs.

Ruth was getting paid well. In 1928, Ruth made the unheard of sum for a ball player of $70,000 ($648,000 in 1996). The "House that Ruth Built" was making much more money for its owners. These were the good times, but in a year, it all came crashing down in the Depression.

The Yankee Stadium before 1928 was about grandeur. Huge crowds, the Babe, the Yankees. It was still a place without monuments and made with as much beautiful wood as solid concrete. Yankee Stadium was a pitchers' park, despite Ruth's numbers. Center field stretched as far as a Dakota prairie, 490 feet. Left-center was death valley for flyballs. The distance down the right-field line was only 295 feet, but it quickly receded to 429. The park was made more Babe-friendly after 1927.

Yankee Stadium Park Factors		
Year	R	HR
1923	104	184
1924	94	186
1925	90	137
1926	96	111
1927	92	133

Yankee Stadium Park Factors					
Year	R	HR	1950	93	87
			1951	76	96
			1952	90	101
			1953	78	76
1937	98	103	1954	94	101
1938	104	145	1955	89	89
1939	70	107	1956	92	81
1940	91	117	1957	80	77
1941	90	107	1958	104	100
1942	90	129	1959	81	65
1943	87	139	1960	83	84
1944	114	134	1961	85	83
1945	117	270	1962	84	88
1946	96	102	1963	96	90
1947	87	96	1964	100	75
1948	96	114	1965	101	99
1949	97	142	1966	87	89

Yankee Stadium Park Factors		
Year	R	HR
1976	96	118
1977	94	84
1978	94	118
1979	88	97
1980	96	90
1981	96	84
1982	92	88
1983	96	83
1984	86	80

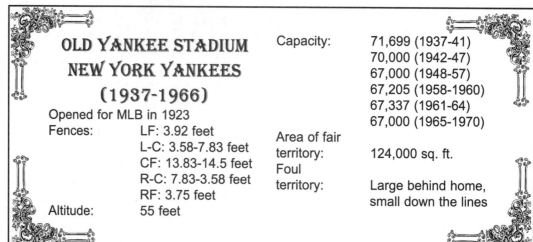

OLD YANKEE STADIUM
NEW YORK YANKEES
(1937-1966)

Opened for MLB in 1923

Fences:
- LF: 3.92 feet
- L-C: 3.58-7.83 feet
- CF: 13.83-14.5 feet
- R-C: 7.83-3.58 feet
- RF: 3.75 feet

Altitude: 55 feet

Capacity:
- 71,699 (1937-41)
- 70,000 (1942-47)
- 67,000 (1948-57)
- 67,205 (1958-1960)
- 67,337 (1961-64)
- 67,000 (1965-1970)

Area of fair territory: 124,000 sq. ft.

Foul territory: Large behind home, small down the lines

457

301

461

407

400

350

300

250

200

150

344

296 (295 from 1937-38)

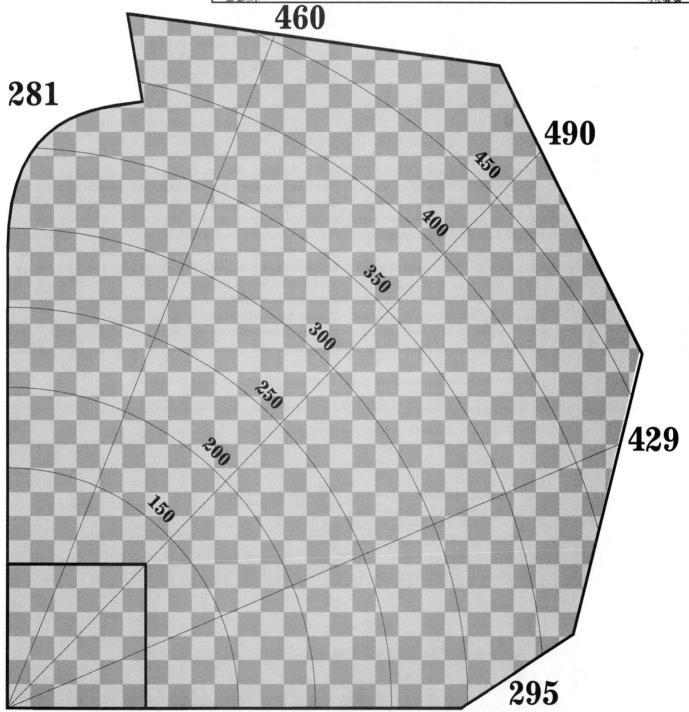

OLD YANKEE STADIUM
NEW YORK YANKEES
(1923-1927)

Opened for MLB in 1923
Fences: LF: 3.92 feet
                 L-C: 3.58-13.83 feet
                 CF: 13.83-14.5 feet

R-C: 7.83 feet
RF: 3.75 feet
Altitude: 55 feet
Capacity: 58,000 (1923-25)
                  62,000 (1926-27)

Area of fair
territory: 151,000 sq. ft.
Foul
territory: Large

460

281

490

450

400

350

300

250

200

150

429

295

HILLTOP PARK
HOME OF THE NEW YORK HIGHLANDERS

Like many other early American League parks, Hilltop Park had a makeshift look. The single-decked wooden park was built in just six weeks. A covered grandstand hugged the diamond from first base to third base. Uncovered seats continued from the bases to the outfield parallel to the foul lines. Over 16,000 people fit into the stands, but often room for more people was made by allowing up to 15,000 more on the immense field.

The Highlanders, who later became the Yankees, were a chartered member of the new American League; however, their first city was Baltimore. The Baltimore Orioles, as the team was originally called, moved to New York City for the 1903 season. No other major league club moved for the next 50 years, giving baseball fans the feeling that baseball teams were as much a part of their cities as the fans themselves.

Hilltop Park was built on the highest point of Manhattan. The land was acquired by Ban Johnson, who considered it essential that his AL have a team in New York. Johnson was forced to deal with shady mob characters to obtain the land. The site was not ideal for a park because of the hard bedrock that had to be blasted in order to level the field and construct the stands. The park was built on a shoestring budget. As a result, most of the outfield lacked grass. There was a marshy area in right field that was inaccessible to outfielders. A rope was placed before the wet area. Any balls that rolled past the rope were doubles. When the rope proved an unsatisfying solution, an extremely short fence was placed before the depression until the marsh was filled with dirt and rocks. The year of 1903 was filled with great advances for humanity such as powered flight; the first modern film,

the "Great Train Robbery"; the Flatiron Building; and even peace between the AL and the NL. The ragged Hilltop Park, however, was not one of those great achievements. Perhaps the lowest point for New York ballparks came when the Polo Grounds burned down, and both the Highlanders and the Giants used Hilltop Park as their home park in 1911.

Team owner Joseph Gordon insisted his team be called the Gordon Highlanders after the best known regiment in the British army. However, people liked to call the team the Hilltoppers, after the big mound on which their park was built. The team officially became known as the Yankees in 1913, the same season it moved to the Polo Grounds. Yankees shared the Giants' home park until Yankee Stadium was ready in 1923.

Although the Yankees are now almost synonymous with the word "winner," that was hardly the case in their humble beginnings. When John McGraw left Baltimore, he took other good players with him. When the Orioles moved to New York, they came with little talent. Clark Griffith was the manager of the team between 1903 and 1908. The team sank to last in 1908. Between 1908 and 1915, the team went through eight managers, including proven winners such as Griffith, Frank Chance and Hal Chase. Nothing worked. It was not until 1921 that the team finally won a pennant. Then the team didn't stop winning. Babe Ruth and Yankee Stadium made the franchise rich. Wealth, luck and a ton of talent allowed the Yankees to win 34 pennants, almost a pennant every two years.

Hilltop Park was the Highlanders' (formerly known as the Baltimore Orioles and later known as the Yankees) first home in New York. Courtesy of the Library of Congress.

Hilltop Park
Park Factors

Year	R	HR
1903	98	76
1904	120	529
1905	104	156
1906	138	136
1907	127	159
1908	100	225
1909	103	84
1910	117	116
1911	127	96
1912	114	193

HILLTOP PARK
NEW YORK HIGHLANDERS
(1903-1912)

Opened for MLB in 1903
Fences: NA
Altitude: 55 feet
Capacity: 16,000
Area of fair
territory: 146,000 sq. ft.
Foul
territory: Large

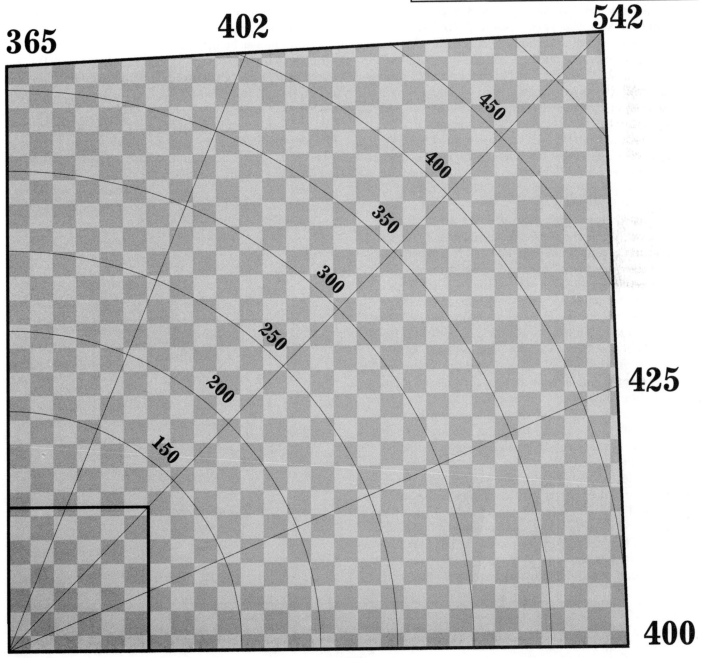

365   402   542

450

400

350

300

250

200

150

425

400

UMAX COLISEUM
HOME OF THE OAKLAND A'S

Football makes the Oakland Coliseum go 'round. This is true when it comes to shape and renovations. The Coliseum is such a football stadium that the stands behind home plate had to be cut out to make room for a backstop. The imposition of a baseball diamond onto the football field resulted in a huge foul territory, as the stands distance themselves from the foul line in a circular path.

Ironically, the stadium became more of a baseball place when the Raiders moved back to Oakland. Originally built for $123 million (1996 dollars), the Coliseum just underwent a $100-million renovation. The changes included reshaping the outfield fences. Straight walls and quirky angles have replaced the old round walls. The stadium's fair territory was also greatly reduced in size. The chances for hitting a home run are still well below average at the Coliseum, but the chances of hitting a double and triple have increased from well below average to slightly above average. In fact, the chances to hit a triple are now almost 10 percent better than average. As a result, the park is now neutral when it comes to runs scored or hits allowed. The number of outfield errors has skyrocketed. The chances for outfield errors being committed are more than 40 percent greater at the Coliseum than at the average American League park.

The Coliseum deteriorated when the Raiders moved from Oakland to Los Angeles for their 1982 season. The stadium was revitalized in the late 1980s when the new management began making changes to create a better baseball ambience. Ivy was planted on the outer slopes of the bowl. A manual scoreboard was installed in 1986.

Baseball has been played in Oakland since before the 20th Century, but the city had to wait until 1968 for a taste of the major league variety. Of all people, Charlie Finley brought baseball to Oakland after uprooting the A's franchise for the second time in its history, taking it on a trek from the rolling hills of Kansas City, across the plains, mountains and desert before making their new home in the brand new Coliseum. By that time, the A's white elephant mascot of Connie Mack had been replaced with Finley's mule, Charlie O.

Finley was a lazy journalist's best friend, providing controversial, funny or brilliant quotes with equal ease. His colorful promotions made him a fan favorite. Among his attempted innovations were an orange ball and a successful push for the designated hitter (the DH idea had floated for decades before it was put into practice). When Marvin Miller was fighting for free agency, Finley scared him by suggesting all players should be free agents at the end of each season. Miller knew that limiting the free agent pool at the end of each year would increase the players' salaries, but making all players free agents at the end of every season would lower demand and keep salaries down. Finley's idea was dismissed by the other owners.

Finley was two cups George Steinbrenner, one cup Marge Schott and two tablespoons of Leona Helmsley. In the 1973 World Series, he tried to have second baseman Mike Andrews disqualified from the series after Andrews committed two errors in the 12th inning of an A's loss. Finley's attempt to replace Andrews' World Series roster spot with another player is an example of the type of unpopular moves he made toward players. When Ken Harrelson left the Kansas City A's, he called Finley the worst enemy of baseball. In 1997, with Finley freshly buried, Harrelson still could not forgive him, saying Finley was the most vicious man he ever met.

The Coliseum was renovated in the middle of the 1996 season, forcing the A's to play a few games in Las Vegas. The construction changed the Coliseum's shape from that of a normal cookie-cutter stadium, to a spaceship-like shape. Below is the Coliseum before the renovations.

Coliseum Park Factors

Year	R	HR
1986	87	86
1987	81	77
1988	86	72
1989	103	102
1990	77	73
1991	86	84
1992	95	122
1993	86	98
1994	82	80

Park Factors

Year	Avg	R	H	2B	3B	HR	L-Avg	R-Avg	L-HR	R-HR
1996	101	99	100	105	109	88	105	99	74	95
1997	105	108	108	103	53	107	101	108	131	93

Oakland-Alameda County Coliseum,
A.K.A. Umax Coliseum.
Photo taken in 1993 by
the United States Geological Survey

UMAX COLISEUM
OAKLAND A'S
(1996-1998)

Opened for MLB in 1968

Fences:	8 feet, except power alleys: 15 feet
Altitude:	25 feet
Capacity:	45,177 (baseball)
Area of fair territory:	108,000 sq. ft.
Foul territory:	Large

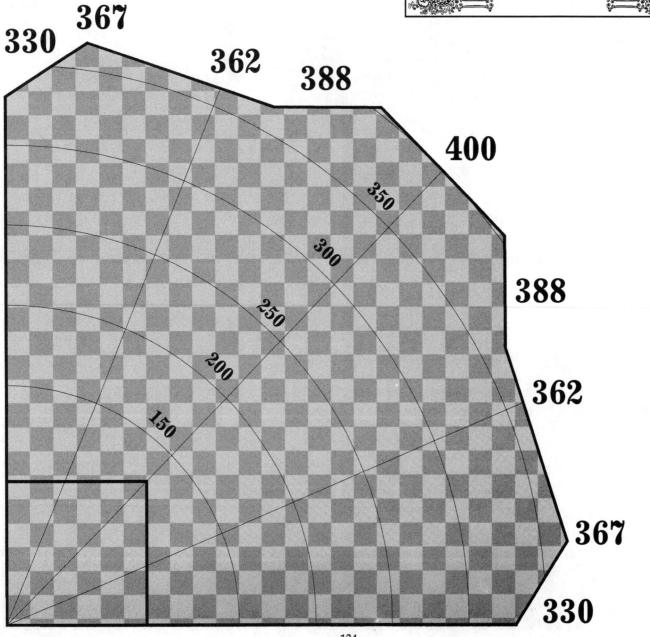

330 **367** **362** **388** **400** **388** **362** **367** **330**

350 **300** **250** **200** **150**

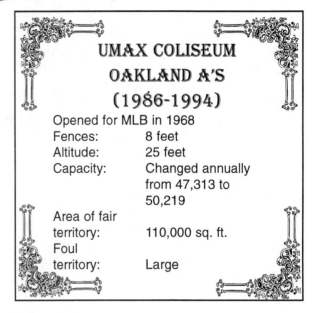

330   **375**

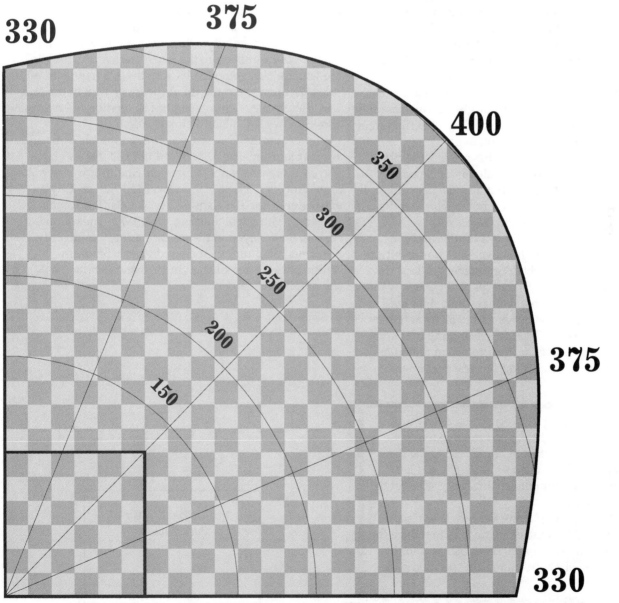

400

350

300

250

200

150

375

330

MUNICIPAL STADIUM
HOME OF THE KANSAS CITY A'S

The first version of Municipal Stadium was called Muehlebach Field. Built in 1923, Muehlebach was the home of the Yankees minor league team the Kansas City Blues and of the Negro League Kansas City Monarchs. By 1955, the park was completely rebuilt and renamed Municipal Stadium. The capacity was increased from 17,476 in 1923 to 30,296 in 1955, mainly by adding a second deck to the grandstand. In 1955, Charles Finley moved the Philadelphia A's to Kansas City.

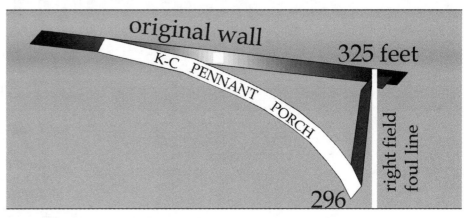

Finley brought many eccentricities with him, such as a children's petting zoo he set up behind the left field foul line. The zoo had pheasants, monkeys, rabbits and the A's traveling mascot, "Charlie O.," a Missouri mule. One of his biggest eccentricities was his thinking that the New York Yankees won often because of the short distance down the right field line in Yankee Stadium. He built a plywood wall that curved from the original away from the original wall and reduced the distance down the right field line to 296 feet in Municipal Stadium, too.

There were two flaws with his project. The first flaw was that his "K-C Pennant Porch," as he called it, would not only benefit his team, but also the opposition. If the Yankees were successful at their home with that distance, they were going to be mighty successful in Municipal Stadium, too. Also, the A's of 1963 and 1964, when this crazy idea came to him, were not power-hitting teams. Only two A's hit double-digit homers in 1963. In 1964 the team had more power, but lost 105 games. What Finley needed was a better team, not a short right field fence. In 1963, his team was out-homered 52-87 at home. In 1964, the margin was 107-132. The last thing his team needed was an easier place for the opposition to homer.

The second flaw in his design was that it was against the rules:

Commissioner Ford Frick shot down Finley's Pennant Porch after a couple of exhibition games. So, Finley responded by building a "Half-Pennant Porch." The tip of the new fence was only 296 feet from home, like Finley wanted, but right before the fence reached the foul line, the wall quickly retreated back to the 325 feet required by rules. To the right of the tip of the inner wall to the foul line, there were only two feet of fair territory. The drawing above shows K-C's Half Pennant Porch.

After the 1967 season, Finley took his team on another journey. The A's arrived in Oakland and have played there ever since. Municipal Stadium was not abandoned for long as the league awarded Kansas City an expansion team, the Kansas City Royals. The Royals played in Municipal Stadium until 1972. The following season, they played in their new stadium, Ewing M. Kauffman Stadium, then named Royals Stadium. Municipal was demolished in 1976 and is now the site of a public garden.

1.04   (a) Any playing field constructed by a professional club after June 1, 1958, shall provide a minimum distance of 325 feet from home base to the nearest fence, stand or obstruction on the right and left field foul lines, and a minimum distance of 400 feet to the center field fence.

      (b) No existing playing field shall be remodeled after June 1, 1958, in such manner as to reduce the distance from home base to the foul poles and to the center field fence below the minimum specified paragraph (a) above.

Municipal Stadium Park Factors		
Year	R	HR
1959	108	109
1960	103	103

MUNICIPAL STADIUM
OAKLAND A'S
(1959-1960)

Opened for MLB in 1923
Fences: LF: 38.5
                 CF - RF: 14 feet

Altitude: 750 feet
Capacity: 30,611
Area of fair
territory: 116,000 sq. ft.
Foul
territory: Average

330   **375**

421

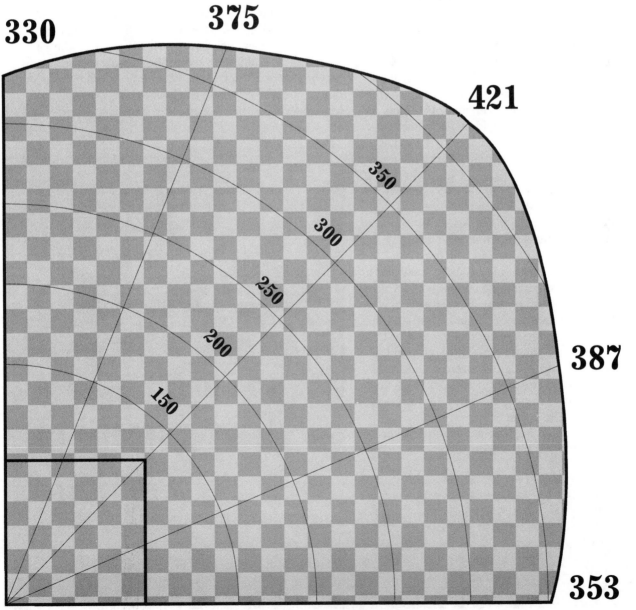

350

300

250

200

150

387

353

SHIBE PARK
HOME OF THE PHILADELPHIA ATHLETICS
&
THE PHILADELPHIA PHILLIES

Shibe Park, also known as Connie Mack Stadium, is the common ancestor of all of the current major league parks. At first, people doubted the wisdom of Philadelphia A's owners Ben Shibe and Connie Mack when they decided to build a park with a capacity of 20,000 that could easily be expanded to hold over 30,000. The park, which opened in 1909, was the first made of concrete and steel. This was in response to the number of wooden ballpark fires, which had risen to epidemic levels. The old ballparks were disasters waiting to happen.

The facade and the interior of Shibe Park were so beautiful that instantly every owner in the majors wanted one just like it. When the owners saw that the attendance for the first game at Shibe was over 30,000, they all rushed to replace their wooden parks with concrete and steel parks. Almost immediately, Braves Field, Comiskey Park, Ebbets Field, Fenway Park, Forbes Field and Wrigley Field were built. Also, concrete and steel versions of League Park, the Polo Grounds, Redland Field and Navin Field replaced their wooden predecessors. Other parks would join this crop such as the last Sportsman's Park and Yankee Stadium. All these ballparks comprise the group known as the classic ballparks. The effects of Shibe Park can only be compared to the effect Babe Ruth had on the game.

So many people wanted to see baseball at Shibe Park, that homeowners across the street used to charge people for sitting on their rooftops and watching the games, much like Wrigley Field today. Management put an end to that practice when they built a 50-foot wall in right field. The A's were losing real money. A ticket in 1926 was worth $20.15 (in 1996 dollars). Forget about the myth that going to ballparks was cheap. It never really was. But in the past, teams didn't earn more money through parking fees, and between 1920 and 1933, there were no beer sales. A's ticket prices were held steady from 1927 to 1950, meaning that by 1949, the cost of going to Shibe had decreased from $20.15 to $14.75 (1996 dollars).

The Phillies played their last game at the Baker Bowl in 1938 and shared Shibe Park with the A's until the latter moved to Kansas City in 1955. Sharing ballparks with other baseball teams was not uncommon, but by the time Shibe was abandoned by the Phillies in 1960, there was only one city with two major league franchises, Chicago, so sharing parks became harder then. The last Major League Baseball teams to share a stadium were the New York Mets and Yankees in early 1998, when a beam fell from Yankee Stadium and crushed a seat. The Yankees and Mets also shared Shea in 1974 and 1975, when Yankee Stadium was being renovated. The St. Louis Browns and Cardinals shared Sportsman's Park. The Yankees and Giants shared the Polo Grounds. So the sharing of Shibe was not really as uncommon as it may seem today.

The Phillies moved to Veterans Stadium in 1961, leaving Shibe vacant. Shibe was demolished in 1976, and now a church sits where the ballpark used to stand. Many stadiumphiles believe this is very appropriate.

Exterior of Shibe in 1913. Courtesy of the Library of Congress.

Shibe Park in 1910, one year after its inaugural season. The right field wall was still short, which allowed fans to sit on the houses behind right field and watch the game. Homeowners began charging for these seats. Shibe Park officials reacted by increasing the height of the wall from 12 feet in 1909 to 50 feet in 1949. Photo courtesy of the Library of Congress.

Shibe Park AL Park Factors			Shibe Park NL Park Factors		
Year	R	HR	Year	R	HR
1943	112	99	1943	90	62
1944	98	98	1944	102	63
1945	92	75	1945	101	77
1946	116	92	1946	95	89
1947	99	103	1947	101	76
1948	103	108	1948	88	71

SHIBE PARK/ CONNIE MACK STADIUM PHILADELPHIA PHILLIES & ATHLETICS (1943-1948)

Opened for MLB in 1909

Fences:	LF - CF: 12 feet
	CF - RF: 20 - 30 feet
Altitude:	12 feet
Capacity:	30,611
Area of fair territory:	111,000 sq. ft.
Foul territory:	Large

Batting cage stored in deep CF during games.

334   **361** 367   **468**

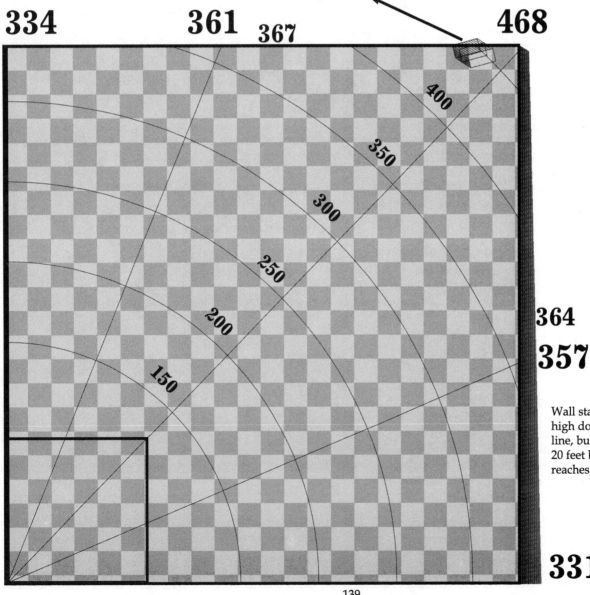

400

350

300

250

200

150

364

357

Wall starts out 30 feet high down the right field line, but slopes down to 20 feet by the time it reaches center field.

331

VETERANS STADIUM
HOME OF THE PHILADELPHIA PHILLIES

About the nicest thing anyone in Philadelphia would say about Veterans Stadium is that from above, it looks like a concrete doughnut. The Vet's circular form sits on the Southern tip of the city, isolated from just about anything save the tuna can that is the CoreStates Spectrum and the new-fangled CoreStates Center. No skyline over the outfield backdrop. No bright lights of Center City to sparkle during night games.

To a youngster seeing the inside of the Vet for the first time, the most striking aspect of the park is the colors. From the synthetic green turf and matching fences, to the yellow foul screens and numbers on the outfield walls, to the brightly painted seats--an assortment of red, orange, yellow and blue at various stages of the stadium's history-- the Vet is a virtual rainbow. A rainbow of fake, synthetic colors.

To make matters worse, many of those colorful seats are seemingly a thousand miles from the action on the field. You see, the Vet was built hastily by the city of Philadelphia, in a time when multi-purpose stadiums were the wave of the future. The circular configuration may work for football viewers, but it leaves the baseball fan too far from the field--so far that off the bat, pop-ups to second base and home runs to dead center field are indistinguishable.

On humid summer afternoons in South Philadelphia, the unforgiving sun lights up the green-painted carpet to an almost fluorescent shine, and bakes the turf rock solid. Thus the notorious "Sunday hops," as balls routinely hit the turf and bound over outfielders' heads. Infielders don't exactly have a picnic, either, as ground balls have a knack for finding the seams, the boundaries between two chunks of carpet. Isn't AstroTurf supposed to eliminate bad hops?

As hard and unforgiving as the Vet Stadium turf, the fans who inhabit the stadium are likewise merciless--towards the team, towards the umpires, even towards the innocent fan who misplays a foul ball. Phillies fans are born resentful--resentful that their city isn't New York, resentful that their team plays in a concrete monstrosity that lacks the appeal of Baltimore's Oriole Park at Camden Yards, just 90 minutes to the southeast.

Oddly, though, there is one feature of the Vet that has won the hard hearts of those fans for two decades. The Phillie Phanatic mascot, with his furry green costume matching the Turf and his slapstick routines, has earned the affection of youngsters and some of the older fans as well. He takes root atop the dugout and jinxes opposing hurlers. He zooms out on his motorcycle as groundskeepers touch up the field after the fifth inning, then dances with fans during the seventh-inning stretch. NL umpire Eric Gregg, a Philadelphia native, was once asked how he would have handled a controversial play that had occurred in a Phillies game some years earlier. "I would've called time out," Gregg answered without hesitation, "and boogied with the Phillie Phanatic."

Veterans Stadium, courtesy of the United States Geological Survey.

Park Factors

Year	Avg	R	H	2B	3B	HR	L-Avg	R-Avg	L-HR	R-HR
1992	98	100	98	96	137	101	100	97	138	78
1993	99	101	101	107	103	91	99	100	99	84
1994	98	92	97	114	87	84	101	95	84	84
1995	100	120	103	125	87	127	100	112	148	112
1996	99	93	102	108	103	86	95	102	80	89
1997	100	99	103	125	89	96	96	105	78	109

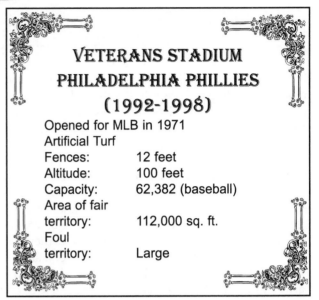

VETERANS STADIUM
PHILADELPHIA PHILLIES
(1992-1998)

Opened for MLB in 1971
Artificial Turf
Fences: 12 feet
Altitude: 100 feet
Capacity: 62,382 (baseball)
Area of fair
territory: 112,000 sq. ft.
Foul
territory: Large

330   **371**

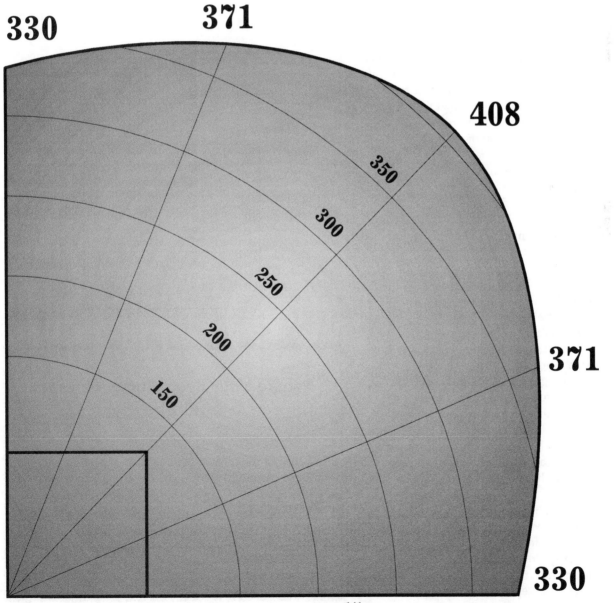

408

350

300

250

371

200

150

330

Before the 37-foot Green Monster in Fenway, there was a larger dinosaur standing as the right field wall of Baker Bowl. Despite a skyscraping height of 60 feet, left-handed batters loved the oversized edifice because it stood only 281 feet from home plate down the line.

The wall and the park are now only memories from when baseball was young. Baker Bowl opened its gates to fans in 1887. Originally a wooden stadium, the park caught fire on August 6, 1894. A spark from a plumber's torch is suspected of starting the blaze. The park was rebuilt with a facade in the style of a medieval castle.

The Baker Bowl fire was only one of a series of fires that tormented baseball owners. The dangerous regularity of ballpark fires eventually led to the use of reinforced concrete instead of wood. Reinforced concrete was first pioneered in Major League Baseball by Baker Bowl's crosstown rival, Shibe Park. The new design allowed for greater seating capacity and safer parks.

Unfortunately, the reinforced concrete design was not used until 1909. In 1903, a gallery overhanging the left-field bleachers in Baker Bowl collapsed, killing 12 fans and injuring over 200. Shockingly, the Baker Bowl was not condemned. Disaster struck again in 1927; miraculously, only one person was killed when a section of the right field stands collapsed.

In 1923, Baker Bowl left a different sort of baseball legacy. In the early days of baseball, ball clubs forced fans to return foul balls. There were even ugly incidents of fights between fans and ushers. But one day during the '23 season, a brave 11 year old named Reuben Berman refused to return a foul ball. The Phillies filed charges against the lad, who was held in a house of detention overnight. A judge reviewed the case and handed down a ruling that was legally weak, but divinely inspired with regards to baseball. The judge said that the child could not be blamed for wanting to keep the ball. The child, he continued, was just following his innocent instincts when he tried to keep the ball as a "souvenir," and should not be compelled to return it. The larceny charges were dropped, and baseball fans have been happier ever since.

This case might have provided a defense for the gym teacher who recently "interfered" with Mark McGwire's would-be 66th homer. County Stadium park officials claimed the fan reached over the wall and interfered with the ball. The police arrested him, charging him with trespassing and fining him over $500. Numerous replays showed that the ball was indeed a home run and that the fan did not reach over the fence at all. It was a bad situation for everyone. The fan got in trouble, McGwire lost a homer and the umps looked bad. To make matters worse, the gym teacher didn't get to keep the ball. A young man from New York kept it after a struggle with a dozen other fans. In the melee, a man in a wheelchair got pushed onto the ground. But back to Baker Bowl...

When the Orioles were building Oriole Park at Camden Yards, they had the option to demolish the B&O Warehouse in right field, but they chose to keep it because the warehouse gave Camden Yards an old-time feeling. To be more concrete, they wanted Camden Yards to look like Baker Bowl, which had the Reading Railroad warehouse behind left field (*B&O* and *Reading*, the same railroads as in Monopoly).

Baker Bowl continued to deteriorate, but Phillies officials decided against improving the ballpark. Instead, in the middle of the 1938 season, the Phillies moved to Shibe Park, sharing the stadium with the A's until 1954, when the A's left town. The Phillies used Shibe until 1970.

Baker Bowl Park Factors		
Year	R	HR
1930	124	116
1931	120	120
1932	133	218
1933	153	181
1934	126	134
1935	137	148
1936	128	187
1937	125	168

Where Your Beer Money Goes in Philly

According to the *Philadelphia Daily News*, the Phillies sold the most expensive cup of beer in the National League in 1997: $5.00 for an 18-ounce beer. Of that $5.00, $2.70 went to City Hall. The estimated number of beer cups sold in 1997 was 750,000 for $3.75 million, or $2.03 million to City Hall.

Source: *Philadelphia Daily News*, April 13, 1998.

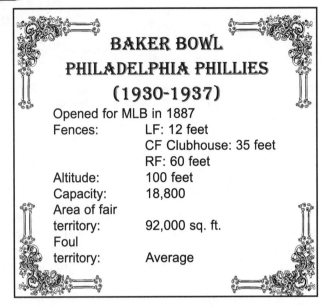

BAKER BOWL
PHILADELPHIA PHILLIES
(1930-1937)

Opened for MLB in 1887
Fences: LF: 12 feet
               CF Clubhouse: 35 feet
               RF: 60 feet
Altitude: 100 feet
Capacity: 18,800
Area of fair
territory: 92,000 sq. ft.
Foul
territory: Average

342

359

408

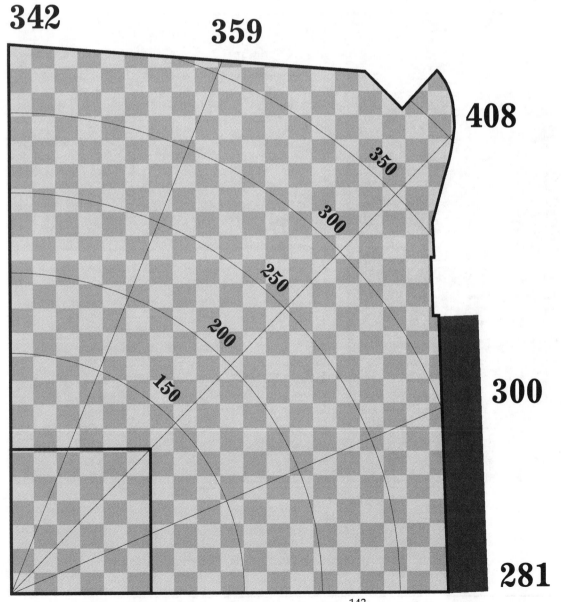

350

300

250

200

150

300

281

THREE RIVERS STADIUM
HOME OF THE PITTSBURGH PIRATES

Three Rivers Stadium gets its name because it is situated where the Allegheny and Monongahela Rivers merge to form the Ohio. The park is built on the site where Exposition Park stood. The Pirates used Exposition Park until 1909, moving to Forbes Field in July of 1909 and finally arriving at Three Rivers in 1970.

Three Rivers, originally conceived as a multi-purpose stadium, has been the site of several great events in football and baseball history, including Roberto Clemente's 3000th and final hit, and Franco Harris' "Immaculate Reception" of a Terry Bradshaw pass in the Pittsburgh Steelers' 1973 playoff win over the Oakland Raiders. The Steelers clinched three of their four AFC championships at Three Rivers between 1975 and 1980, but since the Super Bowl is normally played in warmer climates or indoors, there are no Super Bowl memories in the stadium. This Super Bowl policy makes it a little harder for the NFL to get public funds for their stadiums. A Super Bowl would bring much tourist money to a city, yet the NFL denies this money to cold-weather, non-dome cities.

However, there are plenty of World Series memories in this park, including Jim Rooker starting the 1979 Pirates World Series comeback by earning a much needed 7-1 win over the Orioles. The win marked the beginning of the Bucs' comeback from a 3-games-to-1 deficit to win the World Championship.

Three Rivers is one of the so-called "cookie-cutter" stadiums, meaning it's symmetrical (in the shape of a bowl), has an artificial surface and was built as a multi-purpose stadium. Despite the artificial turf, the park contributes to fielding errors, resulting in a few more runs scored in this park than normal.

Photos by David Arrigo, courtesy of the Pittsburgh Pirates.

Park Factors

Year	Avg	R	H	2B	3B	HR	L-Avg	R-Avg	L-HR	R-HR
1992	104	99	103	114	111	75	108	102	74	76
1993	96	101	97	102	112	98	94	98	132	81
1994	102	101	104	103	79	99	98	104	124	87
1995	102	113	103	124	87	113	102	102	104	119
1996	101	105	101	114	115	96	104	100	94	98
1997	100	107	99	108	147	112	98	103	156	90

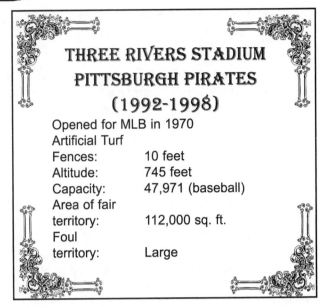

THREE RIVERS STADIUM
PITTSBURGH PIRATES
(1992-1998)

Opened for MLB in 1970
Artificial Turf
Fences: 10 feet
Altitude: 745 feet
Capacity: 47,971 (baseball)
Area of fair
territory: 112,000 sq. ft.
Foul
territory: Large

335   **375**

400

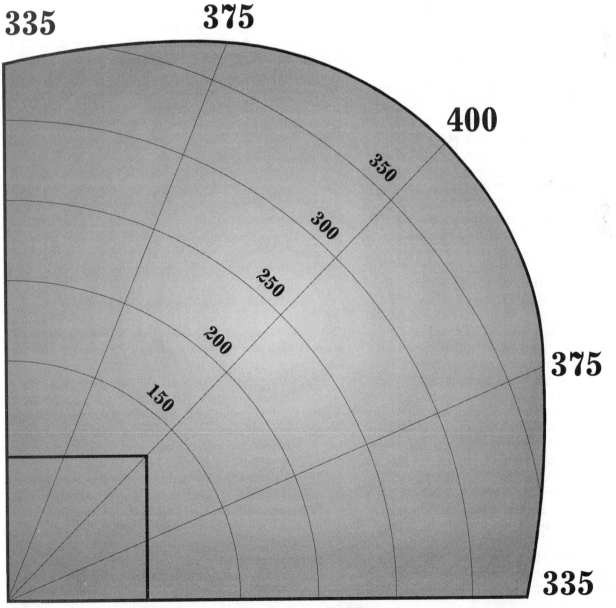

350

300

250

200

150

375

335

THE MAN IN RIGHT FIELD
ROBERTO CLEMENTE

On August 7, 1973, Vera Clemente spoke at her husband's induction into Major League Baseball's Hall of Fame in Cooperstown. The Hall's rule is that a player must wait five years after his last game to be inducted, but an exception was made for Roberto Clemente, who died on a mercy flight to Nicaragua on December 31, 1972. Clemente's career numbers more than justified his induction, but his heroic death shed light on the character of a great man. The reasons for his death are not fully understood, however. This essay will attempt to show why this man who had health, wealth and a good family gave up his life for the people of a foreign country.

The Puerto Rican Clemente played in Nicaragua for the first time in 1964. He arrived with the Los Senadores de Santurce baseball team. Among Clemente's teammates were Orlando Cepeda, Jose Pagan, Bob Oliver and Jerry McNertney. Back then, the Nicaraguans were unanimous in their unrestrained hatred of Clemente; in other words, he was treated no differently than any other opposing ballplayer.

The outfield fans in Nicaragua made the Wrigley Bleacher Bums look like a Poor Clares group of nuns. In one of the games, a few rowdy fans in the right field bleachers hurled a giant four-foot iguana at Clemente. "He couldn't settle down after that," his wife Vera said. "He thought it was some sort of flying prehistoric creature attacking him." Clemente's team lost the series to the Nicaraguan team, the Cinco Estrellas, and the Nicaraguans' home-field advantage had much to do with it. How can you play baseball when the fans in the stands have iguanas, snakes, or even goats with your name on them?

Just as in the United States, Clemente didn't hit it off with the media in Nicaragua. During one interview, he admonished one of the most popular and influential sports writers in the country, Edgar Tijerino. "[Edgar,] how can you write that Capira made a Clemente-like throw from left field yesterday?" Clemente asked. "I make my throws with intentions to make outs from the depths of the right field corner in Forbes Field -- with Pete Rose diving head first into third base. You should be more careful."

Clemente antagonized the Nicaraguan writers as no one else could. He used to get into silly arguments with them. In another conversation with Tijerino, Clemente contested that Juan Marichal was better than Sandy Koufax and that Marichal didn't get his due because he was Latino. Tijerino, as much Latino as Clemente, disagreed with him, but there was no way to make Clemente concede.

Clemente returned to Nicaragua in 1972 to manage the Puerto Rican team in El Mundial. Nicaragua won the whole thing that year, beating the unbeatable Cuban team for the title. The victory is still celebrated to this day. Legend has it that the Nicaraguan team was incredibly strong -- so strong that the manager of the team was said to have called his starters toward the mound where he threw a baseball on the ground. "Whoever picks up that ball will pitch the first game of the Series," he said.

After winning the Mundial, Nicaraguan fans embraced everything baseball, even the enemy -- Clemente, who had loved Nicaragua more than she loved him at first. He loved playing before the mad fans, although the flying reptiles were a distraction.

But this was not a relationship with a happy ending. All around Managua, Nicaragua, there are clues that the earth is different. Twenty miles from the capital is the Masaya Volcano National Park. Tourists drive to the top of this volcano to look inside the crater. About 2,000 feet down in the mouth of the crater, the tourists see waves of red-glowing lava crashing against the sulfur-stained cliffs. The volcano releases tons of corrosive gases, some times pausing to take in air. The gasping volcano reminds people that the earth beneath them is different. It is alive.

Within the city limits of Managua are tracks over 4,000 years old that were preserved on what was once soft mud. The tracks are of people and animals, all running in the same direction, toward Lake Managua. The tracks are about 25 feet below the modern surface. When you get out of the hole and look at what the people and animals were running from, you'll see a large mountain -- an extinct volcano to be more precise. Scientists believe the tracks were preserved when a mantle of burning ash landed on the soft mud. It is unknown what happened to those who were fleeing, but one can guess.

Shortly before 10 P.M. on December 22, 1972, a minor earthquake shook Managua. The people were preparing for Christmas and the New Year's celebrations. The quake was small, and the people dismissed it as they dismiss dozens of tiny earthquakes each year. But minutes later a second, stronger earthquake got the attention of the people in the capital. People ran out of their homes. The earthquake was short and people began joking with their neighbors, who had rushed to the street in various stages of undress. Their nervousness over the quake quickly gave way to joking conversation. They went back to their homes to continue doing whatever they were doing.

At 12:27 A.M., December 23, the world came to an end in Managua. A giant earthquake rippled through the sandy grounds below Managua. Over 90 percent of the buildings were leveled. Fires started on every city block. Unfortunately, all the fire stations were destroyed, and the fire trucks were crushed under the rubble. All the hospitals were destroyed. The blood bank sunk below ground level, swallowed by the earth. There was no power. There was

146

no water. All the TV stations, radio stations, and communications were gone. From one ham radio, an amateur operator began calling to the world for help.

In Honduras, whiskey for the holidays was poured down the drain so the bottles could be filled with water to send by a 40-minute flight to Managua. A convoy of ambulances left Costa Rica, only to find the streets of Managua impassable.

The doctors in Managua, instead of going out to find victims, had to begin rescue operations in their own hospitals. In one of those hospitals, the first two floors were crushed under the weight of the floors above. Paramedics had to crawl their way to the top floors where the newborn babies were kept. Their they found the babies, safe, but on the floors because their bassinets had toppled over.

Because no ambulances were going out to the streets, people made their own way to the hospitals to ask for help. The few doctors who were at the hospitals past midnight had to help over 20,000 people. One woman

The Managuan Blood Bank was completely destroyed in the earthquake. Photo by Noé Palacios U.

Downtown Managua after the 1972 earthquake.
Photo by Noé Palacios U.

Photo by Noé Palacios U.

Somoza's wife began touring a hospital. Someone came to ask her what to do with the hospital workers who had no place to work couldn't support their families. "Fire them all," she responded. "There's nothing left anyway. Fire the doctors, nurses, everyone." But the doctors and nurses continued to work for the next three months -- without pay.

Clemente flew to Nicaragua with aid, three times. To the Nicaraguan people, he seemed like the only powerful person in the world who cared for the country. Managua had been abandoned by the government. Clemente was the only one who stood up. Although Clemente had initially planned only three flights to Managua, he ultimately decided to keep on flying. On December 31, 1972, he departed on his fourth and final flight. Shortly after leaving the airport, his plane crashed. Clemente knew that the plane was in very bad shape. He knew the plane was overloaded. But he knew he had to take the chance because there were dying people who needed him.

When the sun rose over the waters of Puerto Rico, his best friend, Manny Sanguillen, had to be restrained. Five times he ran into the ocean, saying he was going to

begged a doctor to help her with the bundle she had in her arms. The doctor was too busy amputating the leg of a man and told her to wait. The man was not under anesthesia, but didn't utter a sound during the procedure. When the doctor was done, he went back to the woman. "Please help me doctor, he's all I have left," she said. The doctor looked into the bundle and found an infant not breathing. He opened the baby's mouth and took a hand-full of dust out of him. The baby was dead. The woman took her bundle and sat against a wall, where the bodies of her four other children lay lifeless.

The doctors, nurses and paramedics worked around the clock for three days. On the third day, the wounds they were treating began to change. They were no longer the type of wounds caused by the quake, but rather gunshot wounds. The government had put out its armed forces to guard the ruins from looters. Instead, the corrupt soldiers pillaged the ruins, and shot at anyone who came near. With the government shooting those who were returning to their own homes, and with medical care unavailable, thousands of people began walking away from Managua to another city 20 miles away. Behind them they saw a burning city. There was simply nothing left.

Clemente knew the dictatorship of Anastasio Somoza was one of the most brutal in the Western Hemisphere. He knew that its purpose was not to care for its citizens. Clemente heard reports of people being shot. He heard that the international aid was being stolen by people in Somoza's government and was not reaching the victims. He had no reason to doubt these reports. Clemente knew that if he took the aid himself, Somoza and his officials would not dare steal it from him. Clemente was right.

While Clemente was organizing a mercy mission,

The first floor of this building was completely crushed under the weight of the floors above. Photo by Ronald R. Espinal.

148

find his friend's body. No one ever did.

Between 10,000 and 20,000 people died in the earthquake. Almost every Nicaraguan family has someone to mourn, yet Clemente is mourned there as well.

Six and a half years later, there was another march by thousands of people, but instead of leaving a burning Managua, they came back to burn Managua. Instead of leaving the city with dying infants in their arms, they came back holding automatic rifles, and ousted Somoza. The episode resulted in the Sandinista Revolution, and later in the Contra war. Over 100,000 people died fighting. Had there been more people like Clemente at the time of the earthquake, those 100,000 lives might have been saved. That is why to this day Clemente is honored. The Hall of Fame is a much better place since his plaque joined its ranks.

Clemente died in service to humanity. He spent the last week of his life without sleep, collecting funds, clothes, food and medicine for the survivors of the earthquake, personally coordinating three air-lifts and boat shipments of aid. He renounced, for love of humanity, the joys and parties of a New Year's spent with his family. Without press conferences or boasting, Clemente was a hero. Like El Cid Campeador, Roberto Clemente will continue to win battles after his death.
--Managua's La Prensa, December 23, 1973.

Robert Clemente Jr. strikes a batting pose in front of his late father's memorabilia in San Juan on December 11, 1979. The Pittsburgh Pirates superstar died on December 31, 1972 while on a mercy flight to Nicaragua to aid earthquake victims. (AP Photo)

FORBES FIELD
HOME OF THE PITTSBURGH PIRATES

The year of 1909 was a watershed season for the development of the modern baseball stadium. Two months after the Athletics opened Shibe Park in Philadelphia, the National League boasted of its first concrete and steel ballpark in Pittsburgh. Forbes Field debuted on June 30 amid much praise for its architectural beauty, its attention to the comfort of the fans, and the aesthetics of the hilly surroundings. Pirates owner Barney Dreyfuss searched for the perfect setting for his new ballpark, and selected a site away from downtown Pittsburgh on the outskirts of town, conveniently accessible by a nearby train terminal. The result was magnificent.

Several new ballpark features made their first appearance at Forbes. Inclined ramps and a wide promenade replaced stairs as a means of access to all levels of the triple-tiered pavilion. The third level, accessible by elevators, was dedicated to press accommodations and numerous private boxes, precursors to today's skyboxes. Contemporary accounts marveled over the excellent sight lines afforded by the stadium's layout, although there was a section in the corner of the left field bleachers that had an obstructed view of home plate.

The ballfield was laid over a stratum of bedrock, covered by clay, soil and sod, making for unpredictable hops on sharply hit grounders. It was no coincidence that the most successful Pirates clubs featured infielders with quick hands and shotgun arms, like Honus Wagner, Bill Mazeroski, Glenn Wright and Pie Traynor. Some World Series lore was spawned by the unforgiving surface. The bouncer that struck Tony Kubek's Adam's apple in Game 7 in 1960 opened the door for Mazeroski's Series-ending home run heroics, while six of Roger Peckinpaugh's eight

Like many of the old ballparks, the young Forbes Fields lacked a warning track. Instead, the park had an outfield incline to slow down outfielders heading straight toward the concrete walls. On sellouts, this incline could be used to seat extra fans in fair territory, which was a common practice at the time.
Photo courtesy of the Library of Congress.

errors in the 1925 Fall Classic were committed at Forbes Field. The final two came in Game 7, when a steady downpour transformed the infield into slop, contributing to both the Senators' loss and to the cancellation of a postseason ceremonial dinner in Washington to celebrate Peckinpaugh's AL MVP award.

The playing area was expansive. The backstop was located 120 feet from home plate, creating a huge foul territory. The extreme distances to the outfield fences demanded fleet, strong-armed outfielders throughout the history of Forbes Field. Fred Clarke, Max Carey and Roberto Clemente carved out Hall-of-Fame careers while earning reputations for defensive prowess.

The park's dimensions also dictated the team's offensive approach. Home runs (of the over-the-fence variety) were rare until the dimensions were altered in later years. The wide gaps in the outfield produced doubles and triples by the bushel, punctuated by Owen "Chief" Wilson's record 36 triples in 1912. Paul Waner perfected the art of driving shots for extra bases down the foul lines. A quick glance at the all-time leader boards in doubles and triples reveals names familiar to veteran Pirates fans. The fact that a no-hitter was never witnessed in 61 years of play at Forbes Field is testament to the acreage outfielders had to patrol. Speed, both on offense and defense, was essential.

The opening of Forbes Field turned out to be a fruitful venture for Dreyfuss from the start, as the Pirates captured the NL pennant and went on to take the World

Entrance to Forbes Field in 1909.
Photo courtesy of the Library of Congress.

150

Series in seven games from the Detroit Tigers. Attendance records were smashed; Forbes Field attracted 81,885 fans in the three games played there. The year-long success of the park, along with the postseason plum Dreyfuss plucked in the way of gate receipts, no doubt spurred other owners to build parks along the lines of Shibe Park and Forbes Field, or to update their existing facilities.

Forbes Field itself underwent a few facelifts in the years that followed. In 1925, the stands were extended around right field in the form of a double-decked pavilion, shortening the right field foul line to 300 feet, although the fence angled sharply out to 375 feet midway to right-center. A screen erected in front of these new seats further hampered longball hitters. An alteration in left field in 1947 produced more dramatic results. Having acquired AL home run champ Hank Greenberg in the offseason and already boasting NL leader Ralph Kiner, the front office decided it was an opportune time to relocate the bullpen areas from foul territory to deep left field. This entailed building a wire fence 30 feet closer to home plate than the ivy-covered brick wall, shortening the distance down the line to a more accessible 335 feet for the two righthanded sluggers. The change was made by order of new co-owner John Galbreath in deference to Greenberg. Hammerin' Hank had announced his retirement after learning that he had been waived out of the AL and picked up by the Pirates. In negotiating his return, Galbreath made several concessions, including baseball's first six-figure salary and a promise to make Forbes Field more Hammer-friendly. While Greenberg played one last season there, his protégé Kiner went on an unprecedented home run binge, extending his string of consecutive league titles to seven through 1952. When he was traded the next year, the temporary fence came down and the bullpens were restored to their original positions. The era of Kiner's Korner, née Greenberg Gardens, was over.

The Pirates regrouped and pieced together one last winner at Forbes in 1960. Manning the field with stellar glove men like Clemente, Mazeroski, Bill Virdon and Don Hoak, they resembled championship Pittsburgh teams of the past, although first baseman Dick "Dr. Strangeglove" Stuart was an aberration who flailed away with both bat and glove. Avenging a four-game sweep in 1927, they took the World Series from the Yankees in seven, despite being outscored 27-55. In most un-Forbes- like fashion, the see-saw seventh game ended with Mazeroski's ninth-inning home run, the most famous moment in the park's history. Even at that high point, the demise of Forbes Field was already in sight. The sale of the ballpark to the University of Pittsburgh had been announced after the 1958 season, although the Pirates were allowed to play there until Three Rivers Stadium was completed in 1970. The move benefited future Hall-of-Famer Willie Stargell most of all; even he found the cavernous alleys difficult to surmount.

Forbes Field Park Factors					
Year	R	HR	Year	R	HR
1910	122	90	1959	105	68
1911	97	70	1960	96	63
1912	88	55	1961	98	71
1913	88	43	1962	101	84
1914	79	26	1963	96	75
1915	97	45	1964	102	68
1916	112	47	1965	97	60
1917	101	34	1966	100	51
1918	112	73	1967	101	86
1919	108	59	1968	100	70
1920	99	32	1969	88	52

Opening Day at Forbes Field.
Photo courtesy of the Library of Congress.

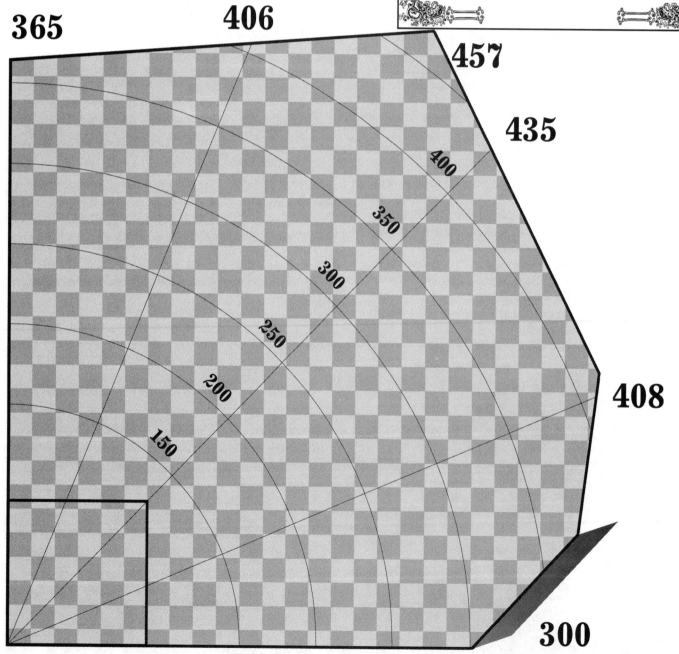

365 **406** **457** **435** **400** **350** **300** **250** **200** **150** **408** **300**

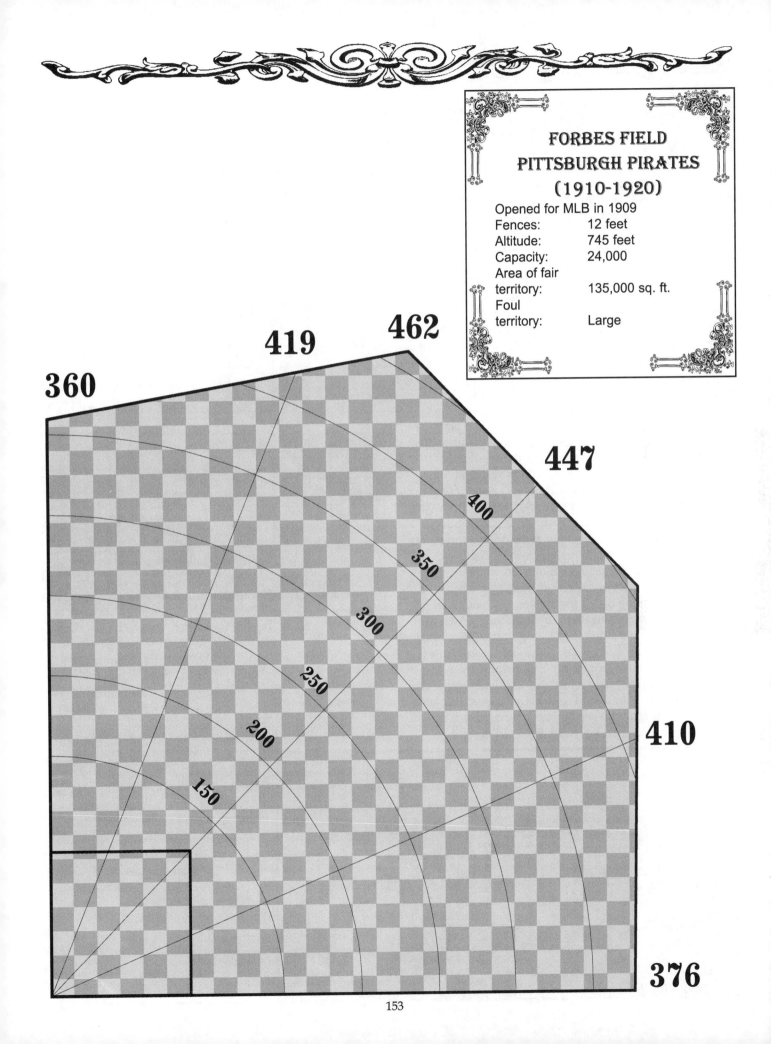

360

419

462

FORBES FIELD
PITTSBURGH PIRATES
(1910-1920)

Opened for MLB in 1909
Fences: 12 feet
Altitude: 745 feet
Capacity: 24,000
Area of fair
territory: 135,000 sq. ft.
Foul
territory: Large

447

400

350

300

250

200

150

410

376

EXPOSITION PARK
HOME OF THE PITTSBURGH PIRATES

Exposition Park battled the flooding Allegheny River throughout its existence. The park opened at three different, adjacent locations in 1882, 1883 and 1890, yet none of the designs was able to avoid the rising waters. The Pittsburgh Pirates played at the third version of Exposition until 1909, when the park was replaced by Forbes Field.

Despite the encroaching river, the park's designers still managed to create a gargantuan outfield of 400 feet down the lines and 450 to center field. The dimensions resulted in few homers, and those that did occur were mainly of the inside-the-park variety. Contemporary parks allowed almost twice as many home runs. In the runs scored category, Exposition favored neither hitters nor pitchers. The park was quite different from the current manicured parks, resulting in more hits and/or errors. Right field sloped downward away from home plate. The foul territory was extensive and conducive to more foul outs. There were no barriers to block the winds.

When the park was built, it was not built in Pittsburgh. It was built in the City of Allegheny. "Old Allegheny" was annexed to Pittsburgh in 1907, but many Allegheny residents would rather call the annexation a theft. A vote deciding whether to annex the city was not just left to Allegheny residents, but also to Pittsburgh residents. Two-thirds of the North Siders voted down the merger, but the "theft" went ahead.

Before being called the Pirates, the team was called the Alleghenies and later the Innocents. Pittsburgh acquired the name Pirates after trying to steal second baseman Lou Bierbauer from his old American Association team. Bierbauer had jumped his Philadelphia team to join the Players League. The AA and the National League had agreed that each team could protect their defected players. Philadelphia forgot to write Bierbauer's name as a keeper, and although everyone knew he belonged to them,

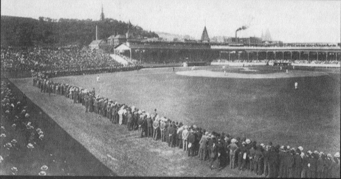

A flooded Exposition Park on top & drier crowds watching a ball game on fair territory--a common practice on sellouts back then. All three photos courtesy of the Library of Congress.

Pittsburgh tried pulling a fast one by claiming Bierbauer after the PL folded. An arbitrator referred to that deed as "piratical." Team officials liked the moniker and changed the team name to the Pirates.

Pirate Jake Beckley was perfectly suited for Exposition Park. He led the league in triples in 1890 with 22. He followed that accomplishment by hitting 19 triples in four of the next five seasons-- the season in which he failed to collect 19, he legged out only 18.

Exposition Park Park Factors		
Year	R	HR
1891	100	65
1892	86	179
1893	107	77
1894	88	56
1895	93	40
1896	82	18
1897	92	48
1898	91	49
1899	92	47

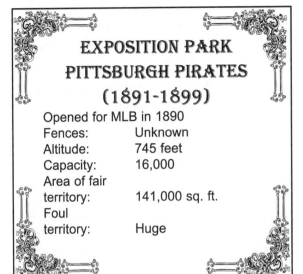

EXPOSITION PARK
PITTSBURGH PIRATES
(1891-1899)

Opened for MLB in 1890
Fences: Unknown
Altitude: 745 feet
Capacity: 16,000
Area of fair
territory: 141,000 sq. ft.
Foul
territory: Huge

400

413

450

413

400

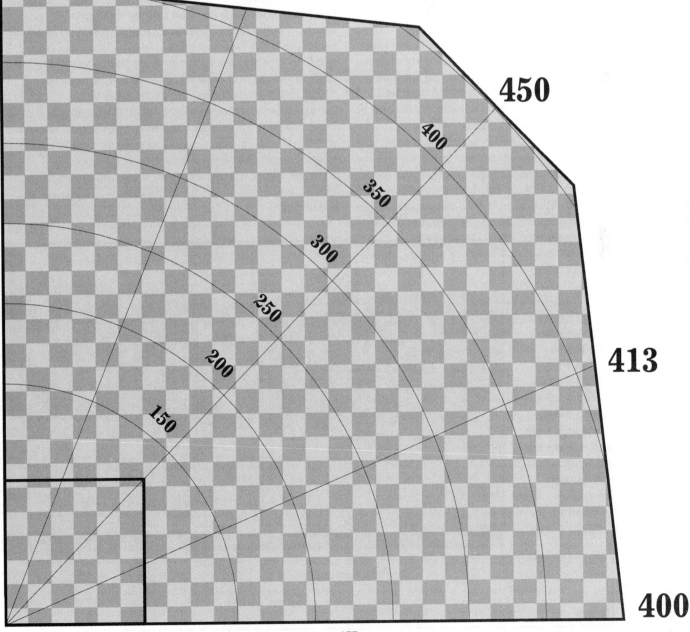

BUSCH STADIUM
HOME OF THE ST. LOUIS CARDINALS

At a time when it was not fashionable to build sports arenas downtown, the Cardinals built Busch Stadium in the heart of St. Louis. Since 1966, the stadium has brought over 65 million people to downtown St. Louis and is credited for reviving the once decaying area.

The stadium is as close to a perfect circle as humanly possible. The top of the stadium is crowned with a series of arches, imitating the Gateway Arch, which is a few blocks from the stadium. The idea of a round stadium with arches goes back quite a few years--over 2,067 years, in fact, back to Emperor Vaspasian's Roman Colosseum. The circular design became the formula used by the builders of the multi-purpose stadiums: RFK, Cinergy, Veterans, Three Rivers and Atlanta-Fulton County. Like the other "cookie-cutter" stadiums, Busch's facade is a series of plain columns intersected by meandering pedestrian ramps. The older baseball parks encased their structural columns and pedestrian ramps, shielding them from the view of passers-by. Except for the crown of the stadium, which cannot be appreciated from the ground level, the facade of Busch is more practical than aesthetic, almost like a round, multi-story parking garage.

Inside Busch, the magic of baseball takes over. The fans love their team like a mother loves a newborn. All the seats were changed and replaced with Cardinal Red seats before the 1987 season. For the 1996 season, the state-of-the-art artificial turf was replaced with natural grass. The grass looks like a master pointillist painting compared to the artificial turf's appearance of a mass-produced cereal box cover. A manually operated scoreboard debuted in the 1997 season. The visitors bullpen was made visible to the fans. St. Louis football is now being played in a dome, leaving Busch to adjust itself to baseball. Even the capacity was reduced from 57,673 to 49,676 to better accommodate the fans. With the Cardinals' logo painted on grass, the red seats, the city's river and downtown area, and the rabid fans, Busch Stadium has been reborn. It has been transformed from a place where baseball can be played

into a true ballpark.

But the facelift of the stadium can only go so far. It would be somewhat sad to see Busch Stadium go, because when all the cookie-cutter stadiums are gone, we may wish that at least one was left behind to remind us of the times when America thought symmetry was beautiful in baseball parks.

If I had a vote, I would choose Busch Stadium as the only cookie-cutter stadium to preserve. The ballpark is already downtown, and this has great benefits. For example, in 1998 buildings around the stadium hung signs indicating the number of homers Mark McGwire had. The signs were visible from the stadium. All of downtown was in a Mark McGwire frenzy -- from comic books sellers to bars, where McGwire's 62nd homer was replayed as if it were a top-10 single. This atmosphere would be difficult to recapture if the stadium were moved. All the stadium needs is to shield those ramps from the viewers, and perhaps to get rid of the goofy Stan Musial statue in front. The statue's proportions don't make any sense, and they just unveiled another smaller Musial statue anyway.

The artificial turf used to cut down the number of errors, but the St. Louis' new sod reduced them even more. Visiting teams made only 37 errors in 81 games in 1996; when St. Louis was on the road, their opponents made 67. The St. Louis infield is one of the easiest to play in the majors.

Busch Stadium. Photo by Oscar Palacios.

Park Factors										
Year	Avg	R	H	2B	3B	HR	L-Avg	R-Avg	L-HR	R-HR
1996	100	96	98	107	87	93	100	99	89	96
1997	98	96	96	103	55	95	95	100	95	95

Opened for MLB in 1966
Fences: 8 feet
Altitude: 455 feet
Capacity: 49,676
Area of fair
territory: 110,000 sq. ft.
Foul
territory: Large

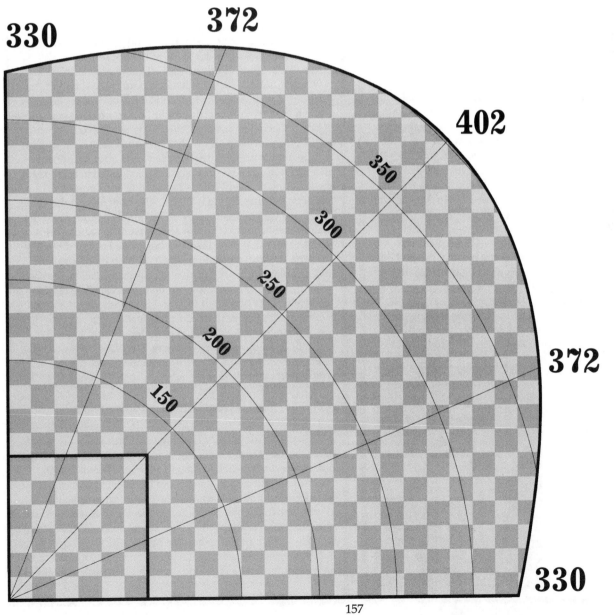

330   372

402

350

300

250

200

150

372

330

SPORTSMAN'S PARK
HOME OF THE ST. LOUIS CARDINALS
& THE ST. LOUIS BROWNS

The Browns were one of the original members of the American League. They played their first season in Milwaukee, but moved to St. Louis the following year. In St. Louis, the Browns played at a wooden Sportsman's Park, while the Cardinals played at Robison Field. In 1920, Sportsman's Park was rebuilt out of concrete and steel. From 1920 until the end of the 1953 season, the Browns and the Cardinals shared Sportsman's Park. While the Cardinals continued to draw well, the Browns fell on hard times. Bill Veeck was encouraged to sell the team after the 1953 season, and the new owners moved the team to Baltimore, where they became known as the Orioles.

Sportsman's Park fit naturally in its neighborhood because it used only one block. It wasn't buffered by a sea of parking spaces. Because it fit in only one block, its capacity was small.

Stan Musial, St. Louis Cardinals

Stan Musial was a good southpaw mound prospect, winning 18 games in the minors in 1940. An arm injury ended his pitching career in the spring of 1941, so he decided to become an full-time outfielder. He rose quickly through the St. Louis Cardinals' system, and by September of the same year, he had made the majors because the Cards had outfielders Terry Moore and Enos Slaughter hurt. Musial hit .426 in the 12 games he was in the show that season. The rest is history. Stan "the Man" terrorized the National League until 1963, collecting 3,630 hits in the process (1,815 at home and 1,815 on the road). For all those years, Musial did not get the credit he deserved, partially due to his humble nature. His character was best exemplified when he was tempted to jump to the Mexican League. In 1946, Musial was making $13,000 for the Cardinals, or $96,000 in 1996 dollars. The Mexican League approached him offering the 1996 equivalent of $369,000 to play for them. He declined the offer, saying he didn't want to break the heart of the St. Louis fans. He said that leaving St. Louis would have made it impossible for him to look his kids in the eyes.

In 1952, 11 years after becoming a major leaguer, Musial finally got to pitch in the bigs. He was leading the league in batting average, and was called to pitch to the man who was chasing him, Frankie Baumholtz. A lefthanded hitter, Baumholtz turned around and hit righthanded to even things out. Baumholtz reached base on an error, but Musial argued angrily it should have been a hit. He left the mound, saying he had been sorry to participate in a box office circus. Musial was probably alone thinking it was a hit, but that was Stan the Man.

A new Stan Musial statue outside Busch Stadium. Photo by Oscar Palacios.

Eddie Gaedel, St. Louis Browns

Bill Veeck owned a bad team in the St. Louis Browns. Yet, he thought he could make more money with gimmicks and a bad team than with no gimmicks and a good team. On August 19, 1951, Bill Veeck sent 3-foot-7 Eddie Gaedel to lead off the second game of a doubleheader, wearing number 1/8. Detroit's Bob Cain walked him on four pitches. As soon as Gaedel reached base, he was replaced by a pinch runner, the everyday right fielder, Jim Delsing.

Gaedel enjoyed the notoriety he received, appearing on several television shows, but his brush with fame began to fade almost immediately. Three weeks after his appearance, he was arrested for disorderly conduct. He worked for the Ringling Brothers Circus for a while and promoted Mercury Records. In 1961, Veeck, who now owned the White Sox, hired Gaedel to appear on Opening Day after fans complained they couldn't see the action over the regular sales people. Later that year, Gaedel's health deteriorated terribly. He suffered from constant headaches, high blood pressure and an enlarged heart. He also fell routinely. He was robbed in June of 1961 and was bruised on his face and knees. He managed to get home but died in his bed of a heart attack. He lived with his mother. After his death, a man approached the woman and asked if the Hall of Fame could have Gaedel's bat and uniform. Of course, he wasn't with the Hall of Fame, and she was left with no mementos of her son's major league appearance.

Pete Gray, St. Louis Browns

If Gaedel's story is a downer, Pete Gray's life was a great success. Gray lost his right arm when he was 6 years old. However, he reached deeper than any person has in baseball and hit .333 in the minors in 1944. He was called up in 1945 to help out during the player shortage caused by World War II. He had outstanding speed and instincts in the outfield, being perhaps the best Browns defender that season. He hit .218 in 234 at-bats that year, which was decent for a defensive specialist. Gray has been and will continue to be an inspiration and a role model for children with disabilities.

Sportsman's Park AL Park Factors			Sportsman's Park NL Park Factors		
Year	R	HR	Year	R	HR
1931	109	129	1931	110	87
1932	104	162	1932	103	97
1933	138	224	1933	103	62
1934	110	160	1934	125	119
1935	120	109	1935	103	75
1936	120	138	1936	92	87
1937	110	115	1937	104	117

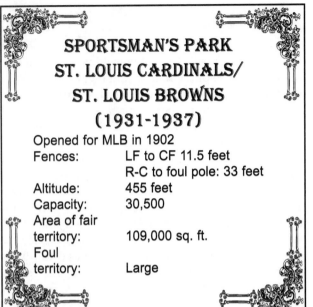

SPORTSMAN'S PARK
ST. LOUIS CARDINALS/ ST. LOUIS BROWNS
(1931-1937)

Opened for MLB in 1902

Fences:	LF to CF 11.5 feet
	R-C to foul pole: 33 feet
Altitude:	455 feet
Capacity:	30,500
Area of fair territory:	109,000 sq. ft.
Foul territory:	Large

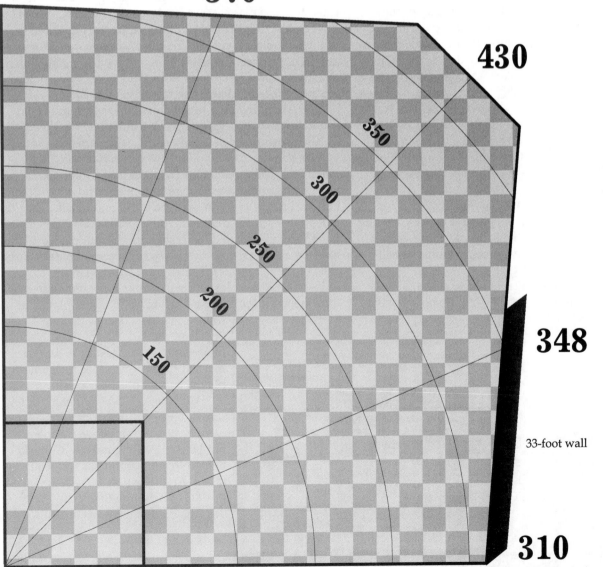

351

370

430

350

300

250

200

150

348

33-foot wall

310

ROBISON FIELD
HOME OF THE ST. LOUIS CARDINALS

The history of Robison Field is entwined with the rise and demise of the flamboyant owner of the St. Louis Browns, Chris Von der Ahe. A German immigrant and a prosperous saloon keeper, Von der Ahe knew little about baseball, yet he oversaw baseball's first dynasty. Von der Ahe was first introduced to baseball by Alfred Spink, later the founder of *The Sporting News*. Spink sponsored an independent ballclub in St. Louis, playing games on a field near Von der Ahe's saloon. Von der Ahe served as the concessionaire, and gained further proceeds when many of the crowd gathered in his saloon for postgame libations. When Spink helped organize the American Association late in 1881, Von der Ahe saw it as an opportunity to increase business, and bought controlling interest in the St. Louis franchise. Several of the AA clubs were backed by brewers and distillers; the Association was sneered at by the conservative National League as the "Beer and Whiskey League" because the sale of alcohol was allowed at games. Throughout Von der Ahe's ownership of the Browns, he always saw baseball as a means to promote his saloon business. Von der Ahe's success in baseball came in his early years with the Browns, chiefly due to the managerial genius of Charles Comiskey. The Browns won four consecutive league titles from 1885 through 1888. St. Louis played the NL champions in an early version of the World Series each of those years, defeating the Chicago White Stockings in 1886 in six games. The final game was the first extra-inning game in postseason history, and ended with a steal of home by Curt Welch, a play that became known as the "$15,000 slide."

Those years were the apex of Von der Ahe's fortunes, and ever the showman, he played it up by parading his players from his saloon to the ballpark before games, and afterward parading the day's receipts from the ballpark to the bank.

The formation of the Players League in 1890 and the defection of Comiskey to the new league began events that greased Von der Ahe's slide out of baseball. The AA folded after the 1891 season, but Von der Ahe helped facilitate the adoption of four AA franchises into the NL, including the Browns, the only AA franchise to survive to the present.

Chris Von der Ahe

To herald his entrance into the NL and to replace the original Sportsman's Park that had been lost to a fire, Von der Ahe built a new Sportsman's Park in 1892, seating 10,000. However, with Comiskey gone from St. Louis, the Browns lost 90 games or more in five of the next six years. Von der Ahe responded to shrinking crowds by selling his best players and investing in other entertainment attractions at the park. He had the grandstand truncated to build a horse race track within the park. "Shoot-the-Chutes," a rollercoaster/water slide, was installed in left field and right center. The rides continued even with games in progress. Sometimes before the ball game, Von der Ahe contracted Buffalo Bill's Wild West Show to perform on the field, damaging the playing surface.

Von der Ahe's antics drew criticism from his old friend Spink, whose *Sporting News* described the theatrics as "the prostitution of a ballpark." League officials plotted to oust Von der Ahe, and an 1898 fire in Robison Field aided their cause. Lawsuits from the fire, adulterous affairs, and a false arrest charge from an incident with the Players League left Von der Ahe broke and in jail. The NL agreed to settle his debts in return for Von der Ahe's resignation from baseball. Ownership of the team passed to the Robison brothers, who owned the Cleveland Spiders. They changed the name of the park from Sportsman's to Robison and the color of the uniforms from brown to red; thus the team became the Cardinals. The team played at Robison until a concrete and steel Sportsman's Park was built. Robison's final game was played in 1920, and marked the last major league game played in a wooden park.

Von der Ahe declared bankruptcy soon after his ouster from baseball. He went back into the saloon business, but began drinking heavily. Comiskey helped to support him as his health failed. An exhibition game was played in 1908 to help him financially. Von der Ahe died of cirrhosis in 1913.

Old Sportsman's Park before Von der Ahe turned it into an amusement park.

Robison Field Park Factors		
Year	R	HR
1893	99	69
1894	101	82
1895	101	147
1896	95	143
1897	97	310
1898	120	140

ROBISON FIELD
ST. LOUIS CARDINALS
(1893-1898)

Opened for MLB in 1893

Fences:	Unknown
Altitude:	455 feet
Capacity:	14,500
Area of fair territory:	159,000 sq. ft.
Foul territory:	Humongous

Shoot-the-Chutes Roller Coaster

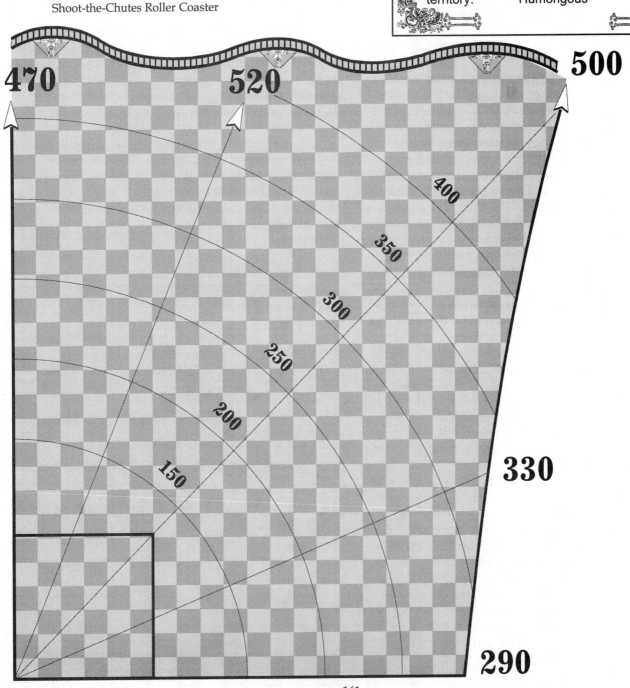

QUALCOMM STADIUM AT JACK MURPHY FIELD
HOME OF THE SAN DIEGO PADRES

Qualcomm Stadium is the prototype of the multi-purpose stadiums. When the seats are arranged for baseball, you'd say it is impossible that they could play football there, and vice-versa when the seats are arranged for football. The retractable seats leave two big corners down the foul lines where players can catch balls out of sight of the umpires.

Originally, the field was called San Diego Stadium, but was renamed Jack Murphy Stadium in 1980 after the sportswriter who drummed up public support for the park. The stadium was completed in 1967, in time for the NFL San Diego Chargers' season. After it was built, a baseball franchise did come. The city was awarded an expansion team that began play in 1969.

Qualcomm Stadium used to have more generous dimensions, but they were reduced for the 1982 season, making it more of a home-run stadium. For the 1996 season, right field was moved back three feet, and a nine-foot right-field wall section was replaced with a 17.5-foot wall and scoreboard. The changes in the wall reduced ever so slightly the chances for home runs being hit at this stadium. Righthanded batters still find this place much friendlier than lefthanded batters. Righthanded batters' chances of hitting a home run are nearly 15 percent better than for lefthanded batters. Righthanders enjoy a similar advantage over lefthanded batters in getting base hits.

Just because this is a home-run park, it doesn't mean it's a hitters' park. It is, in fact, a difficult place to score runs. Qualcomm is an awful place to hit doubles. Lately, the chances of hitting a triple in this park have improved to make this an average place for three-baggers. The stadium has a good infield, reducing the number of errors and runs.

The Padres' lease expires in 1999, and Padres management has begun talks with city officials about the construction of a new baseball-only stadium. The bizarre thing is that the Padres' management wants a stadium that would seat only 35,000 to 39,000 fans. This capacity would put the new park in the company of Wrigley Field and Fenway Park, in addition to dozens of bygone parks that were demolished due to their limited capacity.

I'm only speculating, but perhaps their thinking is that a small park may result in more tickets being sold. It's counterintuitive, but give me a chance to explain. There wouldn't be many tickets available, so fans would hoard as many tickets as possible as soon as possible. The threat of not being able to see a game all year long would drive fans to buy *more* tickets.

The same is true at Lambeau Field. Going to a Packers game is such an event that there is a waiting list for years into the future. If Lambeau Field held 150,000, fewer tickets would be bought in advance. If there were more seats than fans willing to go to a game, then several seats would be sold near to the date of the game. A bad weather forecast would hurt ticket sales. By reducing the number of seats in the new Padres stadium, people will have to buy tickets well in advance, and the threat of bad weather would not be a factor in their decision. The fans might buy September tickets in February. The Padres' urgency to field a contending team would then be reduced because so many tickets would be sold before the season had even begun. Also, the Padres wouldn't have to maintain seats for 40,000 to 50,000 when many of those seats would go unused for most of the year. Having a capacity under 40,000 is conservative, but one can argue that it might maximize profits.

The Padres are having great success selling tickets. Mexican tour buses regularly drop off hundreds of tourists. The Padres have done a good job cultivating fans south of the border. They even played the Mets in Monterrey, Mexico, in 1996 while the Republicans were kicking up their heels in their convention at Qualcomm.

Qualcomm Stadium is completely isolated from its surroundings by parking spaces. Photo courtesy of the United States Geological Survey.

Park Factors

Year	Avg	R	H	2B	3B	HR	L-Avg	R-Avg	L-HR	R-HR
1996	100	87	98	88	115	104	97	103	94	111
1997	95	92	96	86	59	122	94	96	114	131

QUALCOMM STADIUM
SAN DIEGO PADRES
(1996-1998)

Opened for MLB in 1969

Fences:	LF to R-C: 8.5 feet
	RF: 17.5 feet
Altitude:	20 feet
Capacity:	67,544 (baseball)
Area of fair territory:	110,000 sq. ft.
Foul territory:	Humongous

327

370

405

350

300

250

200

150

370

330

3COM PARK
HOME OF THE SAN FRANCISCO GIANTS

Before Willie Mays and Juan Marichal ruled the tiny peninsula, Candlestick Point was guarded by giant rock formations, which loosely resembled candlesticks. The rock columns, their tidelands, the small crabs, and the smell of the mud and bay water were covered and buried to create the parking lot for Candlestick Park, which is yards away from San Francisco Bay. The site was chosen because it was cheap. The idea of a downtown park was floated but local businesses opposed the proposal, protesting that the added traffic would deter customers.

The park was ready for use in 1960. Vice President Richard Nixon said, "This will be will be one of the greatest baseball parks of all time." Whether or not he honestly believed that is not known.

Fenway has the Monster, Wrigley had the vines, and Candlestick has the wind. Giants reliever Stu Miller was literally blown off the mound in 1961. In 1963, a batting cage was blown 60 feet and landed on the mound. However, fans across the nation, those who do not have to endure the freezing gusts, find the wind amusing. Routine outs become exciting.

Ever since the park opened, San Francisco fans and baseball players alike have hated the park. 3Com Park, as Candlestick was renamed in 1996, is still the most hated park in baseball. Keith Hernandez put a clause in his Mets contract, stipulating that he couldn't be traded to San Francisco. The park was double-decked and completely enclosed in 1971 to cut off the winds, but this didn't

3Com Park.
Top and bottom photos courtesy of the San Francisco Giants.

work, and they now swirl unpredictably.

Between 1971 and 1978, the park sported artificial turf in order to make it a better place for the NFL 49ers. The park returned to natural grass in 1979.

The park has a few aesthetic problems. For example, there's too much space behind the outfield wall in right field. If you look above the wall, there's a concrete monolith. Not only is the view behind the fence ugly, but it should be packed with fans close to the action. This is an example of the sacrifices that must be made in order for a ballpark to be a multipurpose stadium.

In 1989, before Game 3 of the World Series between the Giants and their cross-bay rival Oakland A's, a killer earthquake measuring 7.1 on the Richter scale hit the area. The 62,000 fans in the stands were not hurt, but the Series was delayed until 3Com was proven safe.

Before Game 3 finally began 12 days later, the fans gave a spontaneous standing standing ovation as if to tell the world, "The Bay Area survived, and it's still as strong as ever." It was a touching celebration of the enduring human spirit.

Year	Avg	R	H	2B	3B	HR	L-Avg	R-Avg	L-HR	R-HR
1993	96	99	100	79	115	119	94	99	119	118
1994	99	97	98	97	65	104	93	103	88	117
1995	89	88	89	85	69	90	89	89	66	104
1996	100	100	100	99	73	104	100	99	117	95
1997	96	95	96	92	91	93	99	93	104	85

3COM PARK
SAN FRANCISCO GIANTS
(1993-1998)

Opened for MLB in 1960

Fences:	8 feet
Altitude:	65 feet
Capacity:	58,000 (baseball)
Area of fair territory:	105,000 sq. ft.
Foul territory:	Very Large

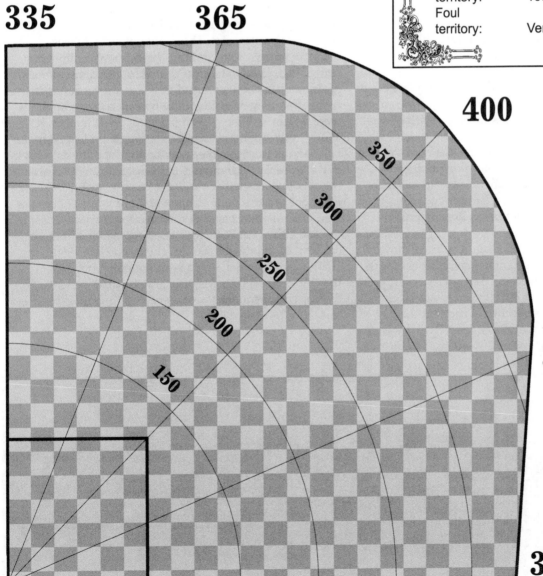

335 365

400

350

300

250

200

150

365

328

When the Giants left New York and the Polo Grounds, the first stadium they called home in San Francisco was Seals Stadium, the former home of the minor league San Francisco Seals. Although it broke many hearts, the 1958 move probably made more people happy than it saddened. San Francisco welcomed the team whole-heartedly and supported it more strongly than the fans had back in New York.

Though the move happened after the 1957 season, the wheels had been set in motion a few years earlier. Interstate highways wove together the United States in the 1950s. In 1950 and 1951, 3.5 percent of all Americans moved their residences to a different state. The population shift resulted in the West Coast gaining an incredible number of people. California went from 5.6 million to 6.9 million between 1930 and 1940 -- before the construction of interstate highways. Between 1950 and 1960, California gained over five million new inhabitants. In the same period, New York State gained less than two million. In the late 1960s, California surpassed New York as the most populous state in the union.

The demographic changes did not go unnoticed by the owners of major league teams. Unlike other industries which could truck their products elsewhere, baseball was static.

In 1953, the Braves left Boston for the huge crowds of Milwaukee, ending 50 years of continuity in major league baseball. No teams had changed cities in half a century, yet one year later the St. Louis Browns moved to Baltimore, and in 1955 the Athletics left Philadelphia for Kansas City.

In May of 1957, National League officials allowed both of their New York teams to move to California for the '58 season. The Dodgers moved to Los Angeles. In order to maintain their rivalry, the Giants followed the Dodgers out west. Chub Feeney, a Giants executive, said that the move was irreversible. He added that the Giants originally wanted to move to Minneapolis, one of their minor league cities, but San Francisco won out.

The move was a shock not only to New York fans, but to Giants hitters as well. The Giants' Polo Grounds was one of the most homer-friendly parks in the history of the majors. The Giants' new park, Seals Stadium, was a pitchers' park, however.

Seals Stadium was a handsome whitewashed park. It had one large grandstand that extended all the way down the lines. None of the seats were covered and all were open to the elements. There was a small set of bleachers in right field, creating a bizarre angle as the bleachers met the center field wall. Despite the park's small capacity, the 1958 Giants drew almost twice as many fans as the lame-duck New York Giants had drawn the previous year.

Nicknamed the "Queen in Concrete," the park was a solemn hunk of stone with both bad seats and good seats. The bad seats were very bad, and some of the good seats were pretty good. The Giants played at Seals Stadium for two years, while a brand-new facility was being built, Candlestick Park. In 1959, the dimensions of Seals Stadium were changed to make it more hitter-friendly. The San Francisco Giants' two years in Seals Stadium were decent, as they posted marks of 80-74 and 83-71.

Although the Giants brought major league baseball to San Francisco, the sport had thrived for decades in that city. Seals Stadium was built in 1931 for the Seals and the Missions of the Pacific Coast League. In 1914, Ewing Field opened to a major league-size crowd of 17,500 fans. Had major league baseball not invaded the West coast in the late 1950s, the PCL, with stronger leadership, may have become a third major league by the late 1960s. The Giants and Dodgers' move West benefited not only the clubs themselves. Major league baseball benefitted because the moves kept its baseball monopoly intact.

Ewing Field, San Francisco, courtesy of the Library of Congress.

Seals Stadium
Park Factors

Year	R	HR
1958	101	106

SEALS STADIUM
SAN FRANCISCO GIANTS
(1958)

Opened for MLB in 1958

Fences:	LF: 15 feet
	CF Scoreboard: 30.5 feet
	RF: 16 feet
Altitude:	65 feet
Capacity:	22,900 (baseball)
Area of fair territory:	112,000 sq. ft.
Foul territory:	Average

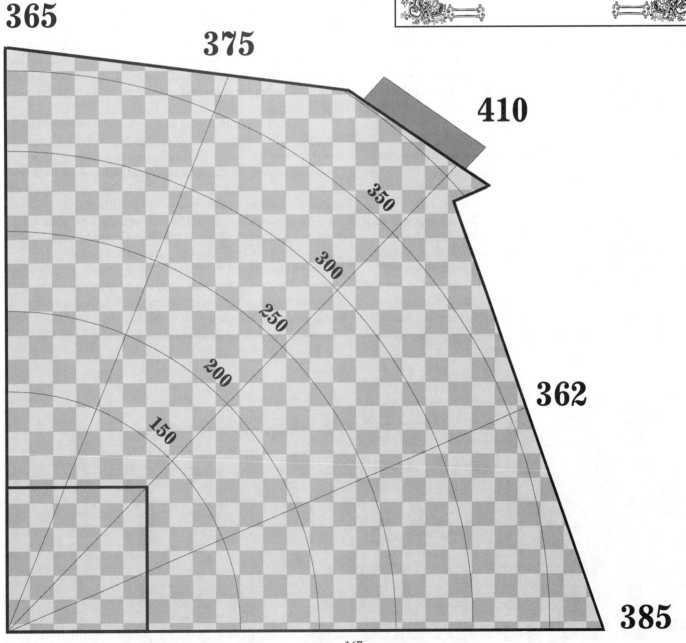

365

375

410

350

300

250

200

150

362

385

Baseball folklore has it that the idea of playing baseball at the Polo Grounds was originated by a boot-black. It all started back in 1880, when John B. Day owned an independent team called the Metropolitans. The "Mets" played their home games mostly at the Union Grounds and the Capitoline Grounds in Brooklyn. At the time, Brooklyn was a separate town, and not yet a borough of New York City. The Brooklyn Bridge had yet to be completed, so Mets fans had the arduous task of crossing the East River by ferry to see their team. Worst of all, the fields where the Mets played were disgraceful. The grass was cut irregularly if it was cut at all. The diamond shape was preserved not by a lawnmower, but by the constant stomping of feet.

This is when the shoeshiner joined baseball history. Day stopped to have his shoes shined and began conversing with the young lad performing the service. Shortly after, the shiner asked Day why his baseball team played his games so far away from home. Day, said he didn't know of a better place to play in Manhattan. Then the boy told him of a place where polo was played, at at 110th street and Sixth Avenue. Day obtained a lease from *New York Herald* publisher James Gordon Bennett, Jr. and played 24 games in the fall of 1880. Baseball in Manhattan proved to be a success, and Day fitted the grounds for baseball for the next season.

At the time, New York was without a major league baseball team. William A. Hulbert, the owner of the Chicago White Stockings (the present-day Cubs), restructured the National Association of Professional Base Ball Players at the end of the 1875 season. He helped create the National League in 1876 in an attempt to rid baseball of the problems that had plagued the earlier league: alcohol,

rowdyism, and players jumping teams for the highest bidder. Hulbert pulled off the coup, but at the end of the 1876 season, he faced some of the same lack of professionalism he wanted to put down. With the pennant race all but decided, the Philadelphia Athletics and New York Mutuals refused to undertake an expensive road trip that wouldn't have affected the standings. Hulbert then did the unthinkable: he kicked both teams out of the National League. Between 1877 and 1882, New York City did not have a major league team.

New York was the largest city in the states and a potentially valuable source of revenue. Day had his act together and was invited to join the American Association, the National League's main rival, in 1882. Surprisingly, Day refused and instead chose to remain independent. In 1883, the National League invited the Mets to join, but again, Day refused. This time, he allowed his Mets to join the American Association and created a whole new team for the NL. Day now owned franchises in each of the competing leagues.

Day had both teams play at the Polo Grounds. On the west side of the park, he constructed a shabby grandstand for the AA fans, who were a bit rowdier by nature. On the east side, he constructed a state-of-the-art facility for the more affluent NL fans. In 1885, Day closed his Mets operation, taking its best players and adding them to the New York Nationals. It would not be until 1962 that another Mets team would play at the Polo Grounds.

Around 1887, the team business manager, Jim Mutrie, loved to call his players "big fellows." Mutrie was supposed to be the the manager, but he was more like a cheerleader during games, leaving the baseball thinking to Buck Ewing, who acted as the real manager and team cap-

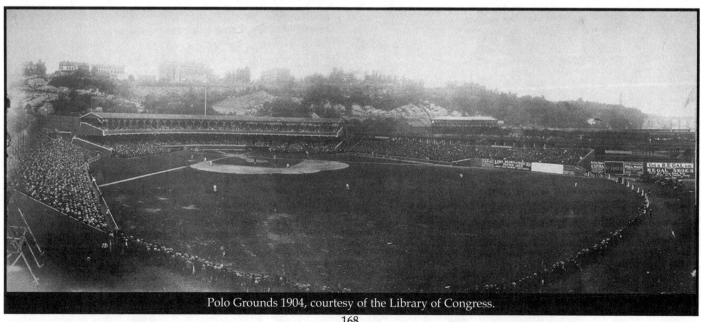

Polo Grounds 1904, courtesy of the Library of Congress.

Polo Grounds in 1905, courtesy of the Library of Congress.

tain. Mutrie then started calling the team "My Giants" because the team had a couple of big players like 6-foot-3, 220 pound Roger Connor. A sportswriter picked up Mutrie's cheer and the New York Nationals became the New York Giants.

John McGraw arrived in Baltimore at age 18 and established himself as a major league star by age 22. He helped the Orioles win three championships in the 1890s with his trademark aggressive baseball. In 1901, McGraw left the NL and joined Ban Johnson's new American

League, signing with the new Baltimore Orioles. In 1902, McGraw's fate changed drastically. Tiger outfielder Dick Harley slid into McGraw with spikes high, ripping McGraw's knee into a bloody mess. McGraw fought back. Ban Johnson's AL was supposed to play a cleaner baseball than the NL, and Johnson was not pleased with the incident. McGraw missed a month of play. In the first game back from injury, McGraw got into a savage argument with an umpire. The argument escalated to the point that McGraw's Orioles forfeited the game. Ban Johnson had had enough with McGraw and suspended him indefinitely.

McGraw, who was owed money by the Orioles, proceeded to buy out his contract from Baltimore and returned to the NL as the manager of the Giants. He inserted himself in 59 games for the Giants between 1902 and 1906, but his career as a player was mostly finished. McGraw proceeded to become one of the best managers of all time. One of his first moves was to raid players from his former AL Orioles and bring them to the Giants. Most importantly, he pulled the plug on a recent experiment where the Giants had been trying to convert one of their pitchers into a first baseman. McGraw took one look at Christy Mathewson and promptly sent him back to the mound.

Mathewson was the antithesis of the normal baseball player of his era. He was from an affluent family and attended a posh private school for boys. A deeply religious man, he did not pitch on Sundays. Mathewson, a smart pitcher, had something of a photographic memory. In 1903, Mathewson and "Iron Man" Joe McGinnity appeared in 100 of the Giants' 139 games.

On August 12, 1951, the Giants were 13.5 games back of the Dodgers. However, baseball magic was in the air. Between August 15 and the 28, the Giants won 16 games in a row, cutting the lead to 5.5 games. During the

John McGraw, Giants Manager (1902-1932).

WIN THE PENNANT! THE GIANTS WIN THE PENNANT! THE GIANTS WIN THE PENNANT! THE GIANTS WIN THE PENNANT! Bobby Thomson hits it into the lower deck of the left field stands. THE GIANTS WIN THE PENNANT! And they're going crazy, they're going crazy! Yeaaah! I don't believe it. I don't believe it. I cannot believe it.

Branca followed the flight of the homer, twisting his neck as if rigor mortis were setting in. Thomson proceeded toward home and was mugged by a jumping crowd of teammates. The rest of the Dodgers walked towards the clubhouse in right field. No one looked back toward home plate, except for Jackie Robinson, who stood motionless with his glove tucked between his right hand and his and hip. Thomson was carried off the field. He tried shaking as many hands as possible, but he couldn't shake them all. The fans had stormed the field. And so the Polo Grounds determined the race. The "long" drive landed 314 feet from home plate.

stretch run, the Giants won 37 games and lost seven. By the end of the regular season, the Giants and Dodgers were tied. A three-game playoff was set to settle the pennant. The first game was played at Ebbets Field. Bobby Thomson hit a two-run homer to win Game 1, 3-1. Game 2 was played at the Polo Grounds, and the Dodgers slugged out a 10-0 victory. In Game 3, Brooklyn was leading 4-2 with one out and two on in the bottom of the ninth. Ralph Branca was called in to face Bobby Thomson. Russ Hodges of WMCA Radio called the play:

Branca pitches. Bobby Thomson takes a strike called on the inside corner. Bobby hitting at .292. He's had a single and a double. Drove in the Giants' first run with a long fly to center. Brooklyn leads it 4-2. Hartung down the line at third not taking any chances. Lockman without too big a lead at second. He'll be running like the wind if Thomson hits one. Branca throws. There's a long drive! It's outta here I believe! THE GIANTS

Polo Grounds Park Factors		
Year	R	HR
1947	103	154
1948	99	149
1949	106	161
1950	92	127
1951	100	168
1952	105	186
1953	95	144
1954	103	171

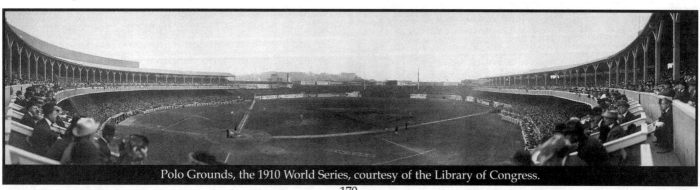

Polo Grounds, the 1910 World Series, courtesy of the Library of Congress.

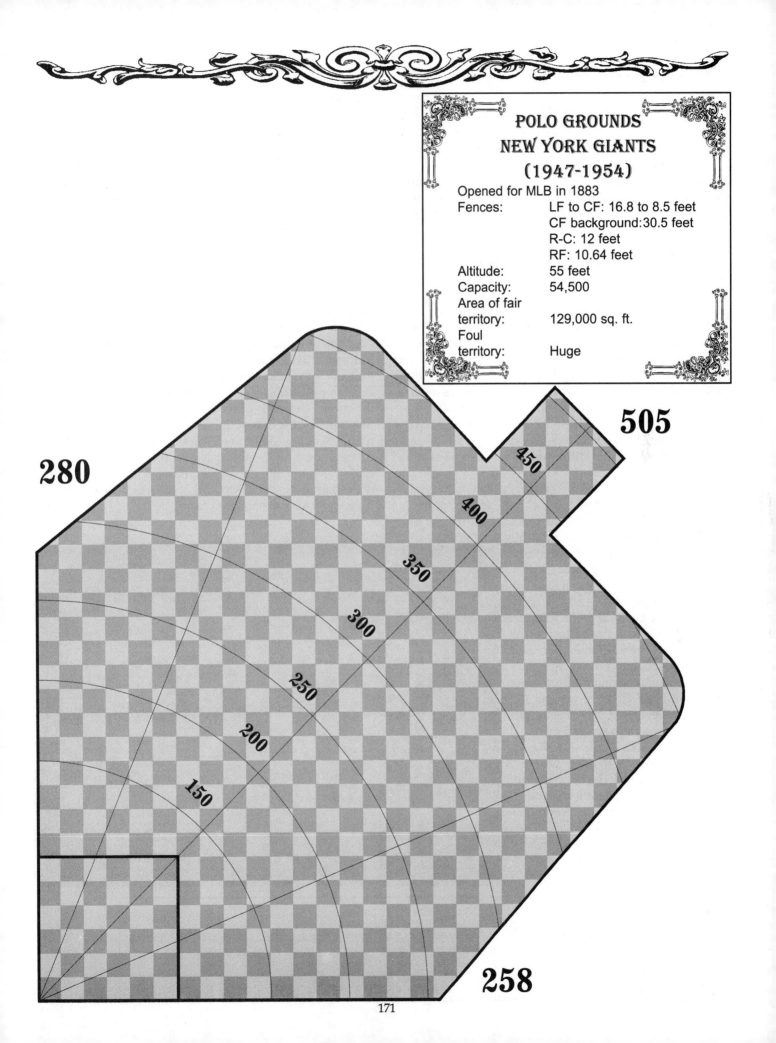

POLO GROUNDS
NEW YORK GIANTS
(1947-1954)

Opened for MLB in 1883
Fences: LF to CF: 16.8 to 8.5 feet
             CF background:30.5 feet
             R-C: 12 feet
             RF: 10.64 feet
Altitude: 55 feet
Capacity: 54,500
Area of fair
territory: 129,000 sq. ft.
Foul
territory: Huge

505

280

450

400

350

300

250

200

150

258

KINGDOME
HOME OF THE SEATTLE MARINERS

Twelve years after the Astrodome opened, Seattle's Kingdome became the second domed stadium in the majors. The cost of the Kingdome was almost identical to the Astrodome's cost ($177 million in 1996 dollars for the Astrodome and $183 million 1996 dollars for the Kingdome). The stage appeared set for domes to take over the majors, but the Kingdome and Montreal's Olympic Stadium may have killed this trend. The Kingdome illustrated the aesthetic problems with domes, and Olympic Stadium's construction delays and cost overruns presented further problems. The cost of Olympic Stadium in 1996 dollars was $2.1 billion.

The Kingdome has been criticized for its dull, gray appearance. It was nicknamed "The Tomb" in the 1980s. It looks somewhat like a granary. The place appears remarkably small from the outside, more like a basketball arena than a baseball stadium. The Kingdome is on the outskirts of downtown Seattle, and from a distance it looks like a cute budding volcano against the majestic Cascades in the background.

The top of the dome is not very high, and speakers hanging from it are within reach of high popups or fly-balls. The field is also quite small because the seating of the multi-purpose dome was originally designed for football (the Seattle Seahawks also call Kingdome their home). Because of the lack of space, the field of play is small.

In the beginning, the Kingdome and the Mariners did not attract many fans. The M's drew 1.3 million in their maiden season, but did not cross the one-million mark again until five seasons later. The Kingdome was not sold out until Opening Night in 1990. The 1990s proved to be a much better decade for the M's. Players like Ken Griffey Jr., Jay Buhner, Edgar Martinez, Alex Rodriguez and Tino Martinez provided plenty of excitement with offensive outbursts of historical proportions. In 1997, the M's set a new major league record with 264 homers, besting the record of 257 homers set by the Baltimore Orioles in 1996. When the offense was not providing the excitement, Randy Johnson used to provide fireworks of his own on the mound. Coming over from Montreal in 1989, the "Big Unit" established himself as an icon of Seattle. Beginning in 1991, he had more strikeouts than innings pitched for eight straight seasons.

The new generation of stars has sent baseball excitement in the Northwest to new levels. Attendance has not been a problem in Seattle, but after a few dome-rattling earthquakes, the Kingdome proved to be one itself. Ground was broken in March of 1997 for a retractable-roof stadium. Still, the sun may not shine on the M's, since Seattle has 250 cloudy days a year. Team officials predict the new SafeCo Stadium will embody everything that was good in past baseball stadiums, while still accommodating the special demands of the Pacific Northwest weather. At $414 million, the cost of the new stadium will be much higher than the Kingdome's original cost. However, much is being spent on the aesthetic quality of the new stadium -- something Puget Sound area fans sorely need after staring at the Kingdome's dull concrete walls for more than 20 years.

The Kingdome from above. Courtesy of the United States Geological Survey.

Park Factors

Year	Avg	R	H	2B	3B	HR	L-Avg	R-Avg	L-HR	R-HR
1995	100	103	99	123	62	110	100	100	131	100
1996	97	94	96	109	79	105	101	94	113	101
1997	98	98	97	109	83	106	91	102	89	122

KINGDOME
SEATTLE MARINERS
(1995-1998)

Opened for MLB in 1977
Artificial Turf

Fences:	LF 17.5 feet
	CF: 11.5 feet
	RF: 23.25 feet
Altitude:	10 feet
Capacity:	59,166
Area of fair territory:	108,000 sq. ft.
Foul territory:	Large

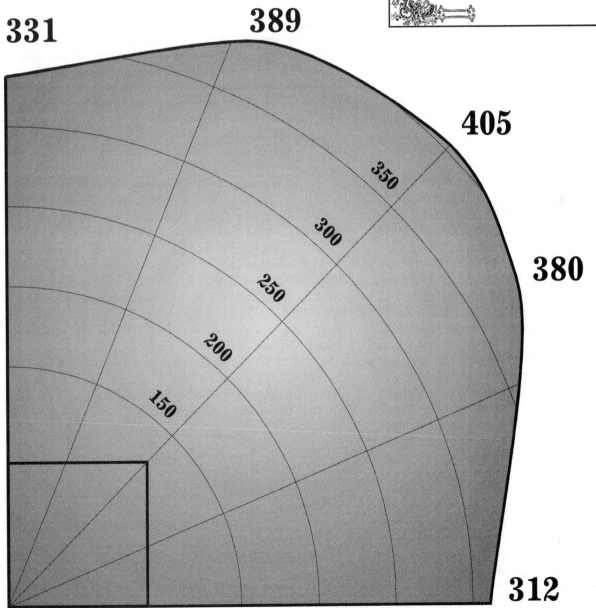

331   **389**   **405**   **380**   **312**

150 200 250 300 350

Before we say anything about Tropicana Field, let's say something to please the locals: Tropicana Field is not in Tampa. It is in St. Petersburg. The taxpayers of St. Petersburg paid for the park, and it doesn't seem quite fair that their city's name was excluded from the team's title.

It also is unfair that the stadium itself is less than wonderful. Let's forget about aesthetics for a moment, and concentrate instead on a few features that affect the way the game is played there:

1) It has artificial turf. They could have gotten away with this in the late 1980s, but times have changed. If you spend a lot of money on a stadium these days, it had better have grass--even in a dome. Either make the dome retractable or outfit it with grow-lights. Neither option is beyond the grasp of technology any longer.

2) As we just noted, the dome isn't retractable. The builders get a break here because the dome was completed in 1990, just as SkyDome began to demonstrate the feasibility of retractable domes. (Back then, the park was called the Florida Suncoast Dome. It was renamed the ThunderDome in 1993 before becoming Tropicana Field in 1996). The permanently closed dome made the Devil Rays' games less enticing for national broadcasts. The Arizona Diamondbacks enjoyed much more media attention because Bank One Ballpark grabs viewers' attention. The Trop lacks the same appeal.

3) The ceiling is too low. Above second base, the dome reaches a height of 225 feet. But the roof is slanted at a 6.5 degree angle. By the time the roof gets over center field, it is a mere 85 feet above the ground. It's a good thing that Sammy Sosa and Mark McGwire did not get to play at the dome this season. Their home run totals may have been lower. That is because the umpires didn't know quite what to do when a fair ball hit the catwalk. Balls starting hitting the catwalk almost as soon as baseball started being played in the dome. Frank Thomas and Jim Edmonds each hit the catwalk in the first 10 games played, alarming team officials who thought the walkways were out of the reach of hitters. People think that both balls should have been homers, but Edmonds' blast was ruled a ground-rule double. And the problems didn't end there. Before you knew it, pop flies were shattering the lights above, and glass was raining everywhere.

Let's hope the dome is insured because it isn't absolutely clear that it can withstand winds above 135 miles per hour. Hurricane Georges gave the community a little scare in September of 1998, when it approached the Dominican Republic with top winds in the range of 135 MPH. Luckily, the hurricane missed the Tampa Bay area.

So how long will the Devil Rays play in the Trop before they decide to ask for a new stadium? Attendance wasn't as good as it was in Colorado or Arizona. Attendance for the Marlins hasn't been good either. This may be a bad sign for the Rays. Part of the reason why attendance is bad in Florida is that many of the residents of the state moved to Florida after making a major league allegiance in another city. There are a lot of people who live in the Tampa-St. Pete area who were not born there. They still consider themselves from New York, Boston, Philadelphia, etc.

To make matters worse, the Devil Rays demanded to play in the American League East. The Brewers smiled and gladly moved to the National League, where they enjoyed larger crowds. The Rays got what they wanted, the chance to attract tourists from former American League East cities and Tampa area residents who used to live in American League East cities, but they got taken as well. The American League East is by far the most free-spending division in baseball. True, money doesn't guarantee wins, but it does make it easier. How are the Devil Rays going to compete with teams who collect double the revenue? Well, the answer that's in fashion these days is: They'll have to get a new stadium. To make things worse, the ballpark has already received a $62-million facelift. It was completed before the 1998 season started.

Not all the news is bad, though. Major league baseball has arrived to St. Petersburg. After near-misses with the White Sox in the late 1980s and the Giants in the early 1990s, the Tampa-St. Pete region can finally take its place among the country's elite urban centers.

Major League Baseball is like an engagement ring. Having a team means you're in. Losing a team is like a bitter break-up. The Tampa Bay Devil Rays may have problems drawing fans over the next few years because the honeymoon will end, and they'll still lack the revenue their competitors enjoy. Hopefully the area will retain the team it worked so hard to land.

The Trop is 13 percent larger from the left field pole to dead center, than from dead center to the right field pole. Overall, it is one of the smallest parks in the majors right now.

Tropicana Field Tampa Bay Devil Rays	
Average	100
Runs	108
Hits	103
Doubles	106
Triples	68
Home Runs	127
LHB-Average	99
LHB-Home Runs	152
RHB-Average	100
RHB-Home Runs	110

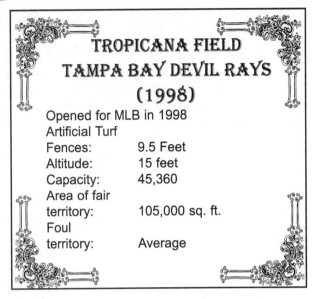
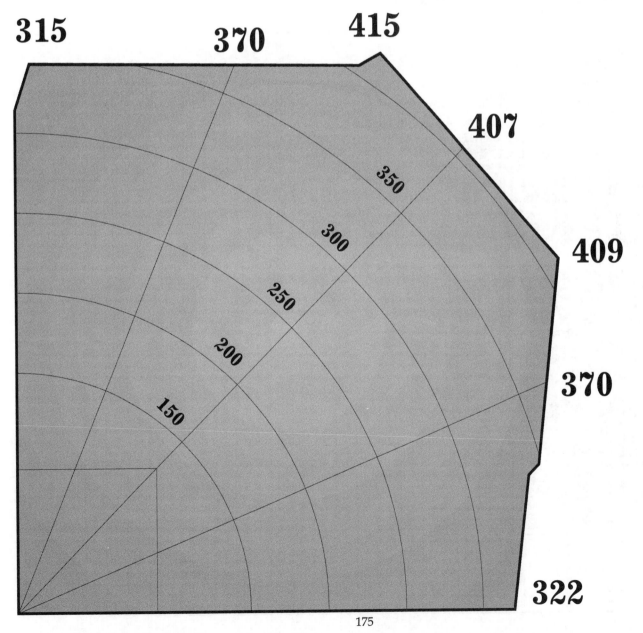

315 **370** **415**

407

409

350

300

250

200

370

150

322

THE BALLPARK IN ARLINGTON
HOME OF THE TEXAS RANGERS

The Ballpark in Arlington is a gem. The park blends tradition, intimacy and economics. The park's architecture celebrates granite, brick and structural steel. Unlike many new stadiums that are column-less, the Ballpark has columns, trading intimacy for a few seats with obstructed views. Instead of apologizing for the columns, the center-field home-run porch accentuates them, giving the park the feeling of Ebbets Field or South End Grounds.

The architecture is not the only element that makes this place a great baseball park. The field is asymmetrical with several corners and straight walls. These walls change the trajectory of many hits in unexpected ways. The Ballpark allows more triples than its contemporary American League fields. The park also favors left-handed power hitters while hurting righthanded power hitters. The righties' batting average at this park is slightly greater than their averages are at other parks. Lefties' batting average is basically the same here as in other parks. Because of the angled walls, outfielders make plenty of errors here. These errors, along with the higher batting average, higher triple and higher homer factors, make this park the third easiest in the American League in which to score runs.

Like Ebbets, Forbes and other classical parks before it, The Ballpark in Arlington was built in an underdeveloped area. The hope is that an economically powerful neighborhood will rise next to the park. To aid this process, two artificial lakes and several shops and restaurants were built next to the park on a riverwalk.

The Ballpark in Arlington, courtesy of the Texas Rangers.

Park Factors										
Year	Avg	R	H	2B	3B	HR	L-Avg	R-Avg	L-HR	R-HR
1994	99	89	97	92	136	71	101	98	88	62
1995	101	113	103	89	114	111	98	104	124	102
1996	105	114	105	94	164	105	103	107	140	89
1997	106	104	109	96	131	110	108	104	115	107

354

332

390

Opened for MLB in 1994

Fences: LF: 14 Feet

             CF & RF: 8 feet

Altitude: 551 feet

Capacity: 49,170

Area of fair

territory: 113,000 sq. ft.

Foul

territory: Average

404

400

407

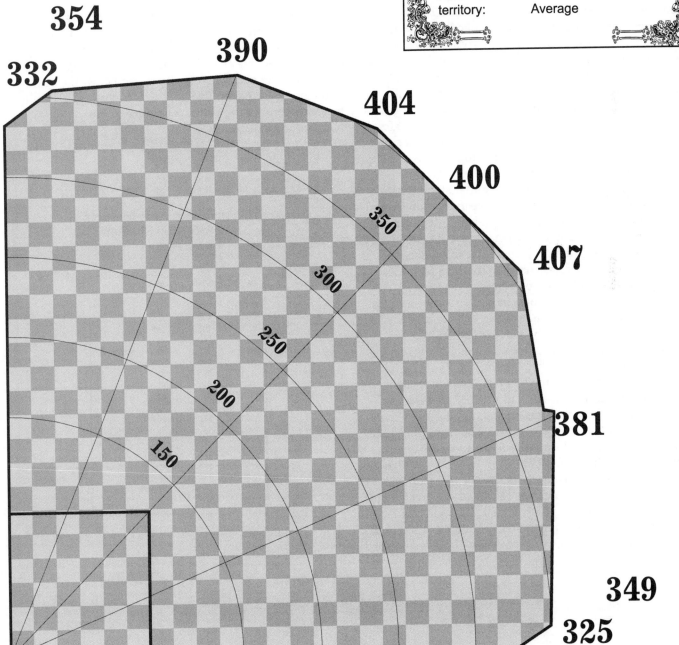

350

300

250

200

150

381

349

325

ARLINGTON STADIUM
HOME OF THE TEXAS RANGERS

Arlington Stadium was built in 1964 at an unbelievable cost of $7.47 million (1996 dollars). Officials chose a natural depression on the earth halfway between Dallas and Ft. Worth, in the centrally located suburb of Arlington. Not only was the price of the land cheap in Arlington, but the hole in the ground saved the team 90 percent of what the stadium would have cost if it had been built elsewhere. The only digging that had to be done was to connect the clubhouse with the dugouts.

Originally called Turnpike Stadium, its name was changed to Arlington Stadium when the Washington Senators announced they were moving to Texas and becoming the Texas Rangers. Arlington Stadium had the largest bleachers in the majors. It also had the most advertising. The heat at the park frequently rose to 100 degrees, requiring that most games be played at night. Most of the park was a single deck, not shielded from the elements. Before the second deck was added, people could walk from the street and find themselves at the top of the stadium. In its minor league days, the ballpark had beautiful grass slopes where people could sit down and watch the ball games. As more seats were added to increase capacity to major league levels, the park lost its minor league charm, becoming more like a cookie-cutter stadium.

As part of a deal reached between the Continental League (see page 49), the American League was to grant Texas an expansion team, but when it became evident that the AL was snubbing the deal, Texas officials went shopping for a team to relocate. The team that accepted the Texas offer was the Washington Senators. These were the second Senators. The first group moved to Minnesota and became the Twins for the 1961 season. Washington was granted an expansion team, which also called itself the Senators, that played in D.C. from 1962 to 1971. When the Senators arrived to Texas, they became the Rangers.

Unfortunately for the Rangers, their Texas opener was delayed from April 6, 1972, to April 22 because of a player strike. Perhaps this was an omen of things to come. The first Ranger team lost 100 games. The team closed the season with a 15-game losing streak. Horacio Piña led the team in saves with 15, and Rich Hand won a team high 10 games, both career highs for them. The next season was worse as the club lost 105 games. All there was to cheer for was the debut of Houston high school sensation and No.1 draft pick, David Clyde. But even Clyde could not help the team much with his 4-8 record that year. Clyde was rushed by the Rangers' management against the recommendation of scouts in order to help attendance and to justify a $125,000 signing bonus. Clyde languished for three seasons. He developed arm problems and was shipped to Cleveland.

By 1974, the team showed signs of improvement with a 79-83 record. In 1977 the Rangers won 94 games, but finished second in their division. The team would not make it to the playoffs until 1996, but by that time they were playing at the Ballpark in Arlington.

In spite of the constant heat and a wind that was always blowing out, Arlington Stadium was, for the most part, a pitchers' park. Lefthanded batters managed to hit home runs at an average pace, but righthanded hitters had a tougher time. Doubles were hard to come by, but triples came with relative ease. The chances for scoring runs in this park were about five to 10 percent below the average of the other AL parks. The park was friendly to strikeout pitchers, perhaps because of the number of night games.

More Arlington Stadium Park Factors		
Year	R	HR
1972	92	100
1973	99	69
1974	91	80
1975	100	93
1976	105	109
1977	107	109
1978	90	84
1979	98	92
1980	99	91
1981	79	55
1982	86	81
1983	99	62
1984	101	89
1985	121	145
1986	90	82
1987	109	108
1988	104	106
1989	105	134
1990	102	120
1991	96	91

Park Factors									
Year	Avg	R	H	2B	3B	HR	L-Avg	R-Avg	L-HR	R-HR
1992	98	93	98	98	92	96	96	99	104	91
1993	96	91	95	92	121	101	94	98	95	105

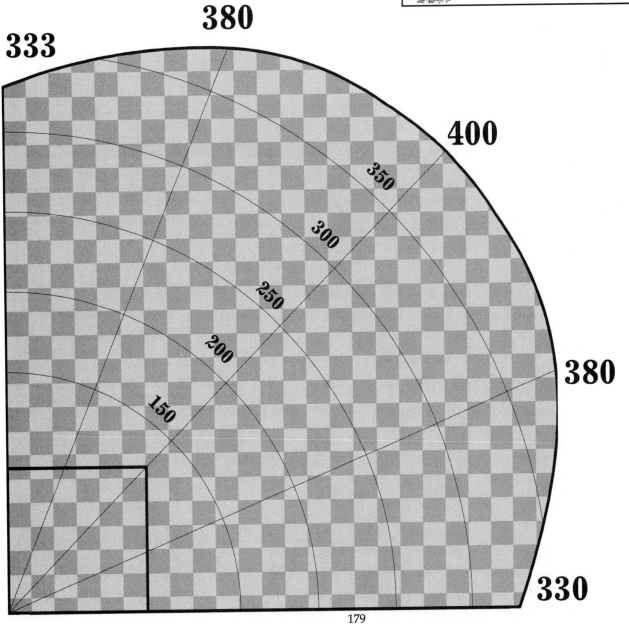

333   380   400   350   300   250   200   150   380   330

RFK STADIUM
HOME OF THE WASHINGTON SENATORS

RFK Stadium (originally known as D.C. Stadium) is the remnant of a time when order and symmetry were the desired aesthetic qualities in a baseball park. Its brightly-painted chalk lines shining against the green of the grass was a cleansing sight to behold. In contrast, the streets of Washington, D.C. were filled with wind-blown garbage and abandoned auto parts. Amidst a sea of chaos, RFK was an oasis. Its symmetric, round walls produced no unpredictable caroms. Fans were treated to a clean, new stadium every night. Other owners noticed that fans loved the stadium. As cities and county governments began to finance more stadiums, they saw in RFK an example of how to maximize their investment by accommodating two sports. In its time, the multi-purpose design of RFK was considered a stroke of genius.

RFK Memorial Stadium marked the beginning of the dark ages in ballpark construction. Originality went into hibernation. RFK was the first modern multi-purpose stadium, with retractable seats to accommodate football and baseball. This concept, combined with the Astrodome's artificial turf and skyboxes were the inspiration of the "cookie-cutter" stadiums. The RFK formula was copied over and over until it was perfected in Qualcomm Stadium at Jack Murphy Field. When Jack Murphy's seats are moved to play baseball, the fans are fairly close to the action, and it looks like a baseball field. When the seats are moved for football, it has the feeling of a football stadium.

The trend of multi-purpose stadiums first took a step back when Royals Stadium (now Ewing M. Kauffman) was built as a baseball-only facility in 1973. The baseball world would have to wait until 1991 for the next baseball-only major league stadium, New Comiskey Park, which still celebrated symmetry. It wasn't until Oriole Park at Camden Yards showed the general public the beauty of asymmetry that the architecture and field design of the old classic baseball stadiums began to be imitated. The growing wealth of football and major league baseball also allowed 1990s stadiums to be designed specifically for each sport.

The next generation of parks will combine the classic style with the modern technology of retractable

roofs. Bank One Ballpark in Phoenix is the first of this type to be opened.

When Michael Westbrook was a rookie with the Washington Redskins, he walked onto the field at RFK and said, "This stadium is beautiful. It doesn't look like a football stadium. It looks like a baseball field."

RFK Stadium Park Factors		
Year	R	HR
1963	102	88
1964	106	127
1965	104	100
1966	90	113
1967	107	96
1968	87	77
1969	93	97

RFK Stadium, courtesy of the United States Geological Survey.

335

381

410

378

335

350

300

250

200

150

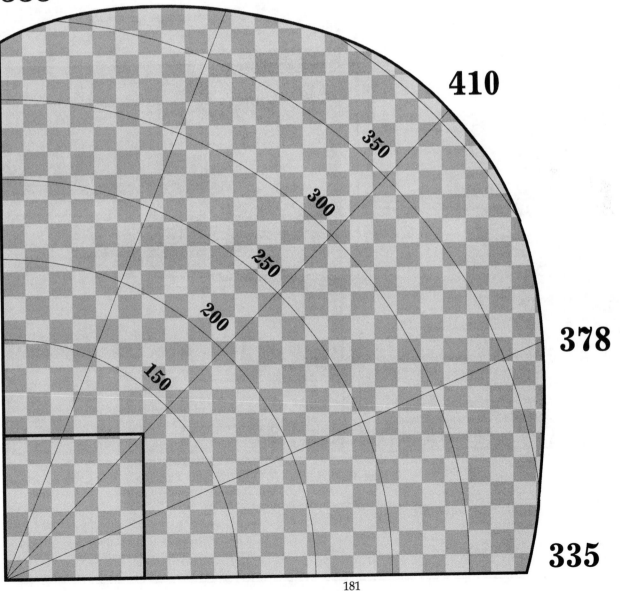

SKYDOME
HOME OF THE TORONTO BLUE JAYS

In 1989, SkyDome became the first successful retractable-roof stadium in major league baseball. Montreal's Olympic Stadium was originally conceived as a retractable dome in 1976; the dome itself wasn't completed until 1987, and it didn't become retractable until 1989. Now, structural problems prevent Montreal's roof from being retracted.

SkyDome, on the other hand, is an architectural triumph. The dome is left open during the baseball season (weather permitting) and in the winter, it is closed for both NBA games and Canadian Football League games.

The success of the retractable SkyDome has resulted in a new generation of domes, such as Bank One Ballpark and Miller Park. Unlike the symmetric, carpeted SkyDome, the two new parks are designed to please the more orthodox fans by including both asymmetrical dimensions and natural grass. If these two parks triumph in pleasing the fans, SkyDome's retractable dome may be copied into the next century.

In order to better prepare their youngsters for the big leagues, the Blue Jays opened a new stadium in Syracuse, New York with almost the exact same outfield dimensions. The P&C Stadium is beautiful--except that they had to give the park artificial turf to mimic the SkyDome. Without Astroturf, P&C would be one of the best parks in the minors. One thing that really looks silly is that they painted a white line showing where the warning track would start--if there was one. At least P&C is not a dome.

SkyDome photos courtesy of the Toronto Blue Jays.

Park Factors

Year	Avg	R	H	2B	3B	HR	L-Avg	R-Avg	L-HR	R-HR
1992	98	98	95	111	136	97	99	97	65	112
1993	103	109	105	114	201	138	98	107	92	182
1994	95	93	92	90	81	109	99	93	162	88
1995	95	100	98	102	112	112	91	101	77	146
1996	102	102	105	117	117	105	107	99	133	90
1997	97	93	96	103	142	79	98	97	70	85

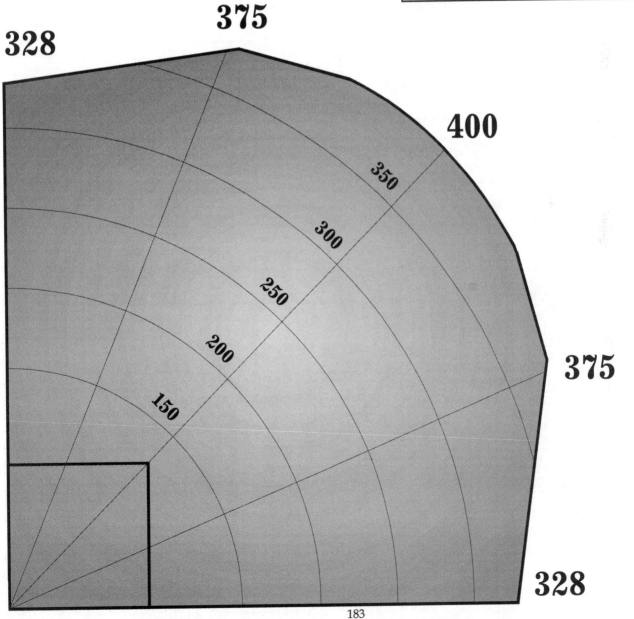

328

375

400

350

300

250

200

150

375

328

EXHIBITION STADIUM
HOME OF THE TORONTO BLUE JAYS

Exhibition Stadium originally was built for football, but somehow a baseball field was crammed into it. The result was a really goofy place to play ball. The grandstand behind home plate was uncovered, yet all of the outfield seats had a roof over them. The back of one end zone was the foul line between third base and the left field pole. The football field continued way beyond the right field power alley. The stadium also brought with it football weather. On April 7, 1977, the Blue Jays played their first game, and the field was covered by snow.

Between 1977 and 1982, Exhibition Stadium increased offensive production by about eight percent. The park favored line-drive hitters. The outfielders needed speed to cover the territory appropriately.

As an expansion team, hitting, defense and pitching were not the Blue Jays' strengths. The Jays had the second-worst record for an expansion team over their first five years of existence. If it weren't for the 1981 strike, Toronto would have won about 290 games in their first five years. The Mets won 261 games in their first five years, and the San Diego Padres were the third-worst five-year expansion team with 297 wins. Toronto tried to grow as much of its own talent as possible, and they eventually developed some tremendous baseball players. But on the other hand, they also gave extended playing time to some very, very bad players. One of those bad players who

received a generous chance to stick in the majors was someone who is now a pretty good NBA coach, Danny Ainge.

Getting out the gates fast doesn't necessarily lead to long-term success for an expansion franchise. The Mets ran in the wrong direction out of the gate, but they became the first expansion team to win a World Series. Colorado bettered Florida's yearly win total until 1997, when the Marlins brought the Championship home after just five years of existence. Toronto had a bad start, but they became the most successful expansion team overall, winning two World Series faster than any other expansion team. When they won their back-to-back titles in 1992 and 1993, the Blue Jays were playing at SkyDome, a stadium that celebrated the financial wherewithal of the city of Toronto and the Blue Jays.

Exhibition Stadium Park Factors		
Year	R	HR
1977	109	125
1978	104	101
1979	111	91
1980	101	101
1981	126	129
1982	118	109

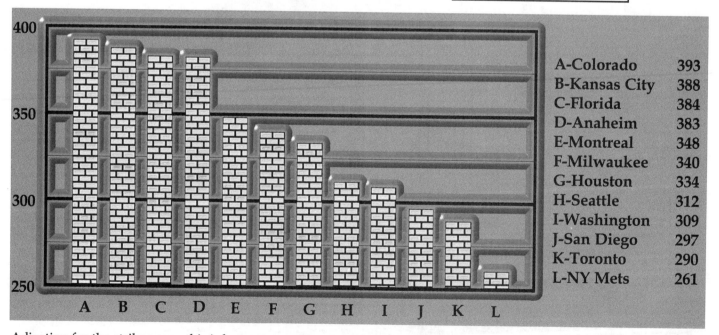

A-Colorado	393
B-Kansas City	388
C-Florida	384
D-Anaheim	383
E-Montreal	348
F-Milwaukee	340
G-Houston	334
H-Seattle	312
I-Washington	309
J-San Diego	297
K-Toronto	290
L-NY Mets	261

Adjusting for the strike years, this is how many games expansion teams won in their first five years of existence. Toronto and New York stumbled out of the gate, but they are the only two expansion teams to have won two World Series.

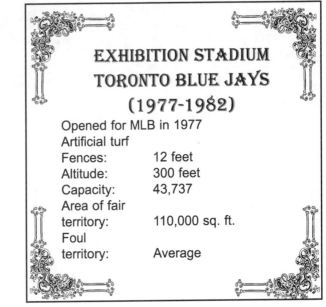

EXHIBITION STADIUM
TORONTO BLUE JAYS
(1977-1982)

Opened for MLB in 1977
Artificial turf
Fences: 12 feet
Altitude: 300 feet
Capacity: 43,737
Area of fair
territory: 110,000 sq. ft.
Foul
territory: Average

330   **375**

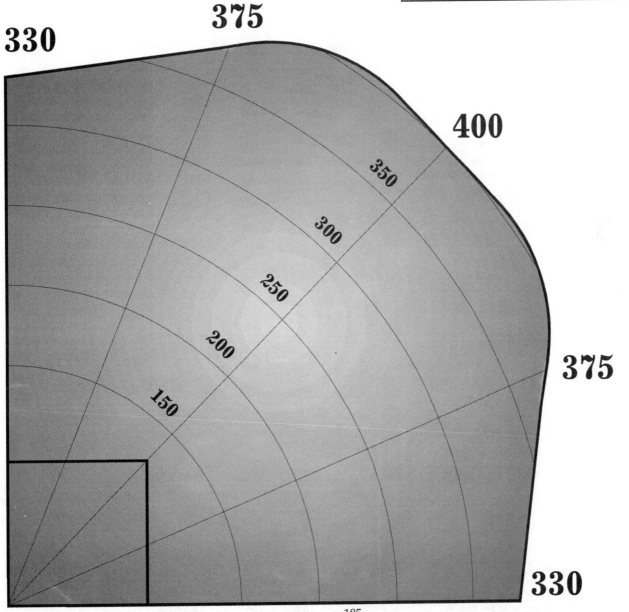

400

350

300

250

200

150

375

330

1998 MAJOR LEAGUE PARK FACTORS
ALL EXCLUDING INTERLEAGUE GAMES
BY JIM HENZLER

Edison International Field
Anaheim Angels

Average	94
Runs	95
Hits	92
Doubles	87
Triples	145
Home Runs	92
LHB-Average	96
LHB-Home runs	76
RHB-Average	93
RHB-Home runs	107

Fenway Park
Boston Red Sox

Average	108
Runs	104
Hits	109
Doubles	124
Triples	113
Home Runs	88
LHB-Average	106
LHB-Home Runs	74
RHB-Average	111
RHB-Home Runs	101

Jacobs Field
Cleveland Indians

Average	111
Runs	114
Hits	113
Doubles	108
Triples	95
Home Runs	97
LHB-Average	114
LHB-Home Runs	100
RHB-Average	109
RHB-Home Runs	94

The Astrodome
Houston Astros

Average	100
Runs	99
Hits	100
Doubles	125
Triples	75
Home Runs	97
LHB-Average	94
LHB-Home Runs	89
RHB-Average	102
RHB-Home Runs	101

Bank One Ballpark
Arizona Diamondbacks

Average	105
Runs	102
Hits	108
Doubles	96
Triples	146
Home Runs	91
LHB-Average	102
LHB-Home Runs	92
RHB-Average	107
RHB-Home Runs	91

Wrigley Field
Chicago Cubs

Average	103
Runs	99
Hits	101
Doubles	105
Triples	99
Home Runs	104
LHB-Average	103
LHB-Home Runs	111
RHB-Average	103
RHB-Home Runs	99

Coors Field
Colorado Rockies

Average	121
Runs	160
Hits	131
Doubles	108
Triples	137
Home Runs	138
LHB-Average	117
LHB-Home Runs	125
RHB-Average	124
RHB-Home Runs	149

Kauffman Stadium
Kansas City Royals

Average	100
Runs	107
Hits	101
Doubles	85
Triples	190
Home Runs	123
LHB-Average	100
LHB-Home Runs	119
RHB-Average	100
RHB-Home Runs	124

Turner Field
Atlanta Braves

Average	105
Runs	98
Hits	104
Doubles	106
Triples	136
Home Runs	94
LHB-Average	103
LHB-Home Runs	91
RHB-Average	106
RHB-Home Runs	96

New Comiskey Park
Chicago White Sox

Average	102
Runs	100
Hits	99
Doubles	109
Triples	106
Home Runs	98
LHB-Average	103
LHB-Home Runs	114
RHB-Average	102
RHB-Home Runs	90

Tiger Stadium
Detroit Tigers

Average	96
Runs	100
Hits	95
Doubles	81
Triples	67
Home Runs	138
LHB-Average	91
LHB-Home Runs	116
RHB-Average	99
RHB-Home Runs	162

Dodger Stadium
Los Angeles Dodgers

Average	96
Runs	83
Hits	94
Doubles	91
Triples	37
Home Runs	95
LHB-Average	94
LHB-Home Runs	100
RHB-Average	97
RHB-Home Runs	93

Oriole Park
at Camden Yards
Baltimore Orioles

Average	95
Runs	88
Hits	94
Doubles	86
Triples	80
Home Runs	98
LHB-Average	92
LHB-Home Runs	92
RHB-Average	99
RHB-Home Runs	102

Cinergy Field
Cincinnati Reds

Average	93
Runs	103
Hits	91
Doubles	111
Triples	89
Home Runs	97
LHB-Average	93
LHB-Home Runs	103
RHB-Average	94
RHB-Home Runs	93

Pro Player Stadium
Florida Marlins

Average	92
Runs	90
Hits	92
Doubles	92
Triples	103
Home Runs	93
LHB-Average	92
LHB-Home Runs	95
RHB-Average	93
RHB-Home Runs	92

County Stadium
Milwaukee Brewers

Average	104
Runs	107
Hits	106
Doubles	102
Triples	71
Home Runs	87
LHB-Average	106
LHB-Home Runs	86
RHB-Average	103
RHB-Home Runs	88

1998 MAJOR LEAGUE PARK FACTORS
ALL EXCLUDING INTERLEAGUE GAMES
BY JIM HENZLER

The Metrodome
Minnesota Twins

Average	103
Runs	100
Hits	105
Doubles	108
Triples	136
Home Runs	91
LHB-Average	102
LHB-Home Runs	119
RHB-Average	104
RHB-Home Runs	70

UMAX Coliseum
Oakland A's

Average	93
Runs	82
Hits	91
Doubles	86
Triples	90
Home Runs	88
LHB-Average	96
LHB-Home Runs	94
RHB-Average	90
RHB-Home Runs	81

Qualcomm Stadium
San Diego Padres

Average	86
Runs	75
Hits	83
Doubles	71
Triples	49
Home Runs	89
LHB-Average	86
LHB-Home Runs	86
RHB-Average	86
RHB-Home Runs	91

The Ballpark in Arlington
Texas Rangers

Average	108
Runs	114
Hits	110
Doubles	111
Triples	184
Home Runs	103
LHB-Average	110
LHB-Home Runs	115
RHB-Average	106
RHB-Home Runs	94

Olympic Stadium
Montreal Expos

Average	92
Runs	79
Hits	93
Doubles	86
Triples	88
Home Runs	73
LHB-Average	95
LHB-Home Runs	57
RHB-Average	91
RHB-Home Runs	81

Veterans Stadium
Philadelphia Phillies

Average	108
Runs	117
Hits	107
Doubles	110
Triples	178
Home Runs	116
LHB-Average	109
LHB-Home Runs	121
RHB-Average	106
RHB-Home Runs	114

3Com Park
San Francisco Giants

Average	99
Runs	91
Hits	93
Doubles	92
Triples	90
Home Runs	118
LHB-Average	104
LHB-Home Runs	127
RHB-Average	95
RHB-Home Runs	112

SkyDome
Toronto Blue Jays

Average	94
Runs	97
Hits	94
Doubles	109
Triples	61
Home Runs	90
LHB-Average	89
LHB-Home Runs	79
RHB-Average	98
RHB-Home Runs	101

Shea Stadium
New York Mets

Average	96
Runs	97
Hits	95
Doubles	96
Triples	143
Home Runs	96
LHB-Average	107
LHB-Home Runs	104
RHB-Average	90
RHB-Home Runs	91

Three Rivers Stadium
Pittsburgh Pirates

Average	102
Runs	106
Hits	102
Doubles	121
Triples	118
Home Runs	106
LHB-Average	94
LHB-Home Runs	78
RHB-Average	107
RHB-Home Runs	122

Kingdome
Seattle Mariners

Average	98
Runs	98
Hits	99
Doubles	102
Triples	66
Home Runs	102
LHB-Average	102
LHB-Home Runs	103
RHB-Average	96
RHB-Home Runs	101

Yankee Stadium
New York Yankees

Average	98
Runs	95
Hits	97
Doubles	109
Triples	63
Home Runs	84
LHB-Average	101
LHB-Home Runs	92
RHB-Average	96
RHB-Home Runs	78

Busch Stadium
St. Louis Cardinals

Average	98
Runs	107
Hits	103
Doubles	97
Triples	119
Home Runs	110
LHB-Average	98
LHB-Home Runs	136
RHB-Average	98
RHB-Home Runs	101

Tropicana Field
Tampa Bay Devil Rays

Average	100
Runs	108
Hits	103
Doubles	106
Triples	68
Home Runs	127
LHB-Average	99
LHB-Home Runs	152
RHB-Average	100
RHB-Home Runs	110

THE MINORS

Fun between innings: Flopper Soccer. Photo by Oscar Palacios.

INTRODUCTION

The farm system -- where did it all start from? Actually, it all began with the same man that changed the face of the major leagues: Branch Rickey. Yes, the minors were around before Rickey came into the picture, but he was the man who put the first "farm system" together. As the general manager of the St. Louis Cardinals, he figured out that a small-market club such as the Cardinals could not compete with the rich, large-market teams such as the New York Yankees in the bidding wars for minor-league talent. So Rickey, with the consent of the owner of the Cardinals, began purchasing minor league clubs around the country in 1921. Over the next 19 years, the St. Louis Cardinals obtained a controlling interest of about 10 percent of all the minor-league teams in the country. Soon the large-market teams began to grasp that if Rickey could achieve this with the Cardinals' limited budget, then they could do at least as well themselves.

Branch Rickey

The minor leagues of the 1990s bring us back to the good ol' days of baseball -- back to the time when a game was a family outing. Most minor league teams push the concept of "major league fun at minor league prices." Along with low-priced seats and parking, the players themselves offer an additional attraction. They often can be seen around town doing appearances for sponsors of the club. Most teams around the country have a program set up where the players are paired up with families from the community. This arrangement can provide the player with home cooking or even a place to live. All of this is just another way of gathering community spirit behind a local team along with helping some the players deal with being away from their families.

During a typical game you can look down toward left field and see a father bringing his son out for his first game. Look down toward right field and you might see a family reunion taking place in the picnic garden. Everywhere you look you see pure enjoyment on the faces of the fans, no matter how the home team is doing. In the minor leagues, the fans come out for the atmosphere as well as for the game. On the minor league level fans are the only constant. So the fans come out to see the "show" that the staff puts on every night. These shows include between-inning contests, pregame autograph sessions by the players and theme evenings. These evenings include nights such as the "shirt-off-the-back," where the players after the game give away their jerseys to the fans, and "dead head" night where a fan will receive free admission if they come in wearing the same outfit that Jerry Garcia was buried in. In the minors, the goal of the staff is to market the best "show," since they have little control over their players, whose movements are controlled by the parent club.

I would like to take a moment to thank a couple of people. First of all, thanks to Oscar Palacios, for letting me be a part of this great book. Thanks also goes out to Grant Blair for his terrific work on the essays about the PawSox and the Sea Dogs. A thank-you goes out to my brother, Brian, for being around for me to confide in about anything (I didn't forget you this time). And finally, thanks to my parents, Nadine and Robert, for their support throughout my adventures from Kansas to Wisconsin to Florida and back, along with everything else that I forgot about. Now, in the immortal words of the late Harry Caray, "Take Me Out to the Ballgame."

1997 Triple-A All-Star Game in Des Moines, Iowa. Photo by Dick Evans of DIX PIX.

CANAL PARK
HOME OF THE AKRON AEROS

The Aeros history started when Mike Agganis purchased the franchise, which began play in 1981 as the Lynn Sailors in Lynnfield, Massachusetts. He then moved the franchise to Burlington, Vermont, where it became affiliated with the Cincinnati Reds and later the Seattle Mariners.

In 1989, Agganis again moved the club to Canton, Ohio, where it became known as the Canton-Akron Indians, a Cleveland Indians Double-A affiliate. The Little Indians went on to win the Eastern League regular season championship in 1992, and continued to earn a berth in the EL playoffs for each of its first five seasons.

After eight seasons in Canton, Agganis again relocated the franchise, this time to Akron, Ohio, for the 1997 season. On October 10, 1996, Agganis, now team owner and CEO, officially dubbed the franchise the "Akron Blast," as a tribute to space science education and Ohio's aviation history. The team took on a completely different nickname, however. A month later, on November 7, "Akron Aeros" was selected from three nicknames published in the *Akron Beacon Journal.* "Spirit" and "Quest" were the other choices.

April 10, 1997 marked the unveiling of a new era in Akron, Ohio as the Akron Aeros, Double-A affiliate of the Cleveland Indians, began play at the sparkling new Canal Park. The ballpark's name comes from a canal behind the stadium that was used to transport goods in the late 1800s. Canal Park features 8,500 individual reserved seats and 25 luxury suites, as well as a large full-service restaurant and team merchandise store. One of the ballpark's main features is the largest freestanding scoreboard in minor league baseball. This huge structure (56 feet, 3 inches across and 68 feet high) is located behind the right field fence. 1998 will mark the franchise's 10th year in the Eastern League and 10th year as the Indians' Double-A partner.

Canal Park opened on April 10, 1997, with an Eastern League game between the Akron Aeros and the Harrisburg Senators. With 9,086 onlookers, Aeros starter Jaret Wright christened the facility with a swinging strike past Senators shortstop Hiram Bocachica. That topped off a $31 million project that had

League:	Eastern League
Level:	Double-A
Surface:	Grass
Affiliation:	Cleveland Indians
Affiliated since:	1989
Location:	300 South Main St.
	Akron, OH 44308
Phone:	330-253-5151
Email:	aaeros@neo.lrun.com
Website:	www.akronaeros.com
Altitude:	874 feet
LF:	331 feet
CF:	400 feet
RF:	337 feet
Capacity:	9,097
Park Opened In:	1997

broken ground just 15 months earlier. Although the Aeros finished last in the Eastern League with a 51-90 record during their first year in Akron, the fans' support for the new team was tremendous as the club drew a league-and Double-A-leading 473,272 fans to Canal Park.

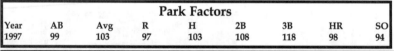

Park Factors

Year	AB	Avg	R	H	2B	3B	HR	SO
1997	99	103	97	103	108	118	98	94

Canal Park, courtesy of the Akron Aeros.

To a Midwesterner like myself, Albuquerque can be a shocking city -- not in a bad way, but just by how different it is. The Pueblo architecture is something else. I couldn't get enough of it -- that is until I got to Santa Fe, just 45 minutes from Albuquerque. There, everything is Pueblo style... too much Pueblo. But there's room in Albuquerque for some more, especially in Albuquerque's Sports Stadium. You really don't get a sense that the stadium blends with its city. This is a drawback for the stadium.

Another drawback is that the rounded outfield walls follow the "cookie-cutter" style. In a park where the ball carries, asymmetrical, angled walls would really add to the entertainment level of the games. However, there is already plenty of offense in the games.

Albuquerque is more than five thousand feet above sea level, meaning that the ball carries almost as well as it does in Denver. The park helps offense so much that it causes problems evaluating talent in the Dodger organization. In the past, the Dodgers have used this to their advantage. Before park effects were fully understood by the baseball lords, the Dodgers were able to make some sweet deals. Many of the Dodgers' offensive prospects have been over-rated by other teams. Their true abilities sometimes become painfully obvious when they leave friendly Albuquerque for less friendly pastures.

League:	Pacific Coast League
Level:	Triple-A
Surface:	Grass
Affiliation:	Los Angeles Dodgers
Affiliation Since:	1962
Location:	1601 Avenida Cesar Chavez Albuquerque, NM 87106
Phone:	505-243-1791
Email:	coastdukes@aol.com
Website:	www.dukes.fanlink.com
Altitude:	4945 feet
LF:	360 feet
CF:	410 feet
RF:	340 feet
Capacity:	10,510
Park Opened In:	1969

Park Factors

Year	Avg	AB	R	H	2B	3B	HR	SO
1994-7	107	102	117	109	95	98	103	102

Albuquerque Sports Stadium, courtesy of the Albuquerque Dukes.

Albuquerque offensive numbers can be deceiving because the park's elevation increases offensive production. Most major league parks are near sea-level. Below is a list of highly-touted hitters who went flat after leaving Albuquerque:

Karim Garcia:
Major League Numbers:

G	Avg.	Slg.
142	.211	.354

Albuquerque

	Avg.	Slg.
1995	.319	.542
1996	.297	.529
1997	.305	.645

Paul Konerko
Major League Numbers:

G	Avg.	Slg.
81	.214	.326

Albuquerque

	Avg.	Slg.
1996	.429	.643
1997	.323	.621
1998	.379	.701

Billy Ashley
Major League Numbers:

G	Avg.	Slg.
281	.233	.409

Albuquerque

	Avg.	Slg.
1993	.297	.539
1994	.345	.701
1996	.348	.522

Opposing general managers have caught on and now to take the Albuquerque offensive numbers with a grain of salt. Albuquerque made Karim Garcia, Paul Konerko and Billy Ashley look like can't-miss prospects.

If you see a prospect having a great season in Albuquerque, don't get overly excited right away. Wait until they make it to Dodger Stadium.

193

NORTH AMERICARE PARK
HOME OF THE BUFFALO BISONS

When people talk about the minor leagues, they often ask about attendance figures. Well, the Buffalo Bisons have written the book on how to put fans in the stands. They have drawn over one million fans for six consecutive seasons and have led the entire minor leagues in attendance over the past 10 years. This 10-year reign of minor league baseball started in 1988 with the opening of Pilot Field. The Bisons sold over 10,000 tickets within 84 minutes of putting them on sale for the opening of Pilot Field on April 14, 1988. The park opened with a sellout crowd of 19,500, something that the Bisons have since gotten used to. Within two months, they surpassed the franchise's attendance record for a single season. In August 1988, the Buffalo became only the second club in history to break the one million mark in attendance. Pilot Field was the location of the first Triple-A All-Star game, which was nationally televised in 1988. In January, 1990, Pilot Field underwent construction to add additional seating, a project that was completed in June of that year.

League:	International League
Level:	Triple-A
Surface:	Grass
Affiliation:	Cleveland Indians
Affiliation Since:	1995
Location:	275 Washington St. Buffalo, NY 14203
Phone:	716-846-2000
Email:	bisons@buffnet.net
Website:	www.bisons.com
Altitude:	585 feet
LF:	325 feet
CF:	404 feet
RF:	325 feet
Capacity:	21,050
Year built:	1988

Park Factors								
Year	AB	Avg	R	H	2B	3B	HR	SO
1996-7	92	93	83	86	82	38	103	96

The new addition brought the capacity from 19,500 to 21,050. The seating capacity is 20,900 with standing room for 150. Only days after the construction was finished, Pilot Field saw its largest crowd in history of 21,050.

In 1991, the National League considered Buffalo for an expansion team. The day after the National League Expansion Committee announced that Buffalo was not one of its cities of choice, the club was greeted by one of its customarily sellouts. The fans let the team know that they were still 100 percent behind baseball in Buffalo -- in whatever form of baseball that may be. Two major events occurred at Pilot Field during the 1995 season: *ESPN2* televised its first ever minor league baseball game on May 4, and Pilot Field was renamed North AmeriCare Park after a 13-year deal was struck with North American Health Plans.

The success in attendance has also carried over onto the field in the last couple of years, with the Herd winning the 1997 American Association championship over the Iowa Cubs.

North AmeriCare Park, courtesy of the Buffalo Bisons.

194

JOSEPH P. RILEY STADIUM
HOME OF THE CHARLESTON RIVERDOGS

Imagine an ownership group consisting of a comedian, a musician and the son of a baseball legend...what you get is the Charleston RiverDogs. That's right -- Bill Murray, Jimmy Buffet and Mike Veeck are all part-owners of the Charleston RiverDogs.

The RiverDogs debuted at Joseph P. Riley Jr. Park, "The Joe," at the beginning of the 1997 season with a 6-3 win over the Cape Fear Crocs. As an affiliate of the Tampa Bay Devil Rays, the RiverDogs should expect to put a young and exciting team on the field for years to come.

Charleston, South Carolina has a long tradition of minor league baseball dating back to 1886. The city's nicknames have included the Seagulls, Patriots, Rainbows, and finally, the RiverDogs.

Jimmy Buffet's concerts are always a party, Bill Murray is hilarious, and Mike Veeck is just as inventive as his father, Bill Veeck, had been. The senior Veeck put a midget into a game; Mike had a woman pitch for one of his minor league clubs. Mike also hired an announcing team to call the games for the St. Paul Saints. That doesn't sound to out of the ordinary, but this particular team consists of two men, Jim Lucas and Don Wardlow, and a dog named Gizmo. What makes this team even more interesting is that

League:	South Atlantic League
Level:	Class-A
Surface:	Grass
Affiliation:	Tampa Bay Devil Rays
Affiliation Since:	1997
Location:	360 Fishbourne St.
	Charleston, SC 29403
Phone:	803-723-7241
Altitude:	9 feet
LF:	306 feet
CF:	386 feet
RF:	336 feet
Capacity:	5,800
Park Opened In:	1997

Gizmo is a seeing-eye dog for Don, who was born with no eyes. Jim does the play-by-play and Don works in his color commentary throughout the game. Don keeps score

Park Factors								
Year	AB	Avg	R	H	2B	3B	HR	SO
1997	96	100	85	96	93	106	54	100

with his Braille typewriter and supplements his knowledge of the game by reading up on the history while spending as much time with the players as he can.

Besides baseball, "The Joe," is also the place for concerts. Last year about nine thousand fans tuned in for a six-hour show. There was a variety of music, so everyone found something they enjoyed. With that kind of success, the RiverDogs are sure to plan their next baseball season with post-game concerts in mind.

Joseph P. Riley Stadium, courtesy of Norman LoRusso.

ENGEL STADIUM
HOME OF THE CHATTANOOGA LOOKOUTS

Engel Stadium was built in 1929, making it one of the oldest minor league parks currently in use. In fact, it may be *the* oldest because the prior ballpark, Andrews Field, sat on the same site and was built in 1909. The Lookouts were an original charter member of the Southern League in 1885. Regardless of whether or not it is the oldest, Engel Stadium is definitely one of the best and most beautiful ballparks in the country. The park is named after Joe Engel, owner of the minor league Lookouts, who was famous for innovative promotions such as attracting 24,839 fans for a house giveaway during the Great Depression and trading a shortstop to the Charlotte franchise for a turkey. Engel also signed a 17-year-old female pitcher by the name of Jackie Mitchell, who struck out Lou Gehrig and Babe Ruth on April 2, 1931 (Whether Gehrig and Ruth were really trying is another story...).

Kiki Cuyler, Clark Griffith, Burleigh Grimes, Rogers Hornsby, Fergie Jenkins, Harmon Killebrew, Willie Mays and Satchel Paige -- all former Lookouts -- are enshrined in the National Baseball Hall of Fame. Both Satchel Paige and Willie Mays, ages 17 and 15 respectively, played their first Negro League games here.

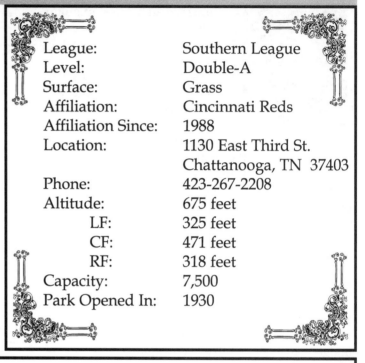

League:	Southern League
Level:	Double-A
Surface:	Grass
Affiliation:	Cincinnati Reds
Affiliation Since:	1988
Location:	1130 East Third St.
	Chattanooga, TN 37403
Phone:	423-267-2208
Altitude:	675 feet
LF:	325 feet
CF:	471 feet
RF:	318 feet
Capacity:	7,500
Park Opened In:	1930

Park Factors								
Year	AB	Avg	R	H	2B	3B	HR	SO
1996-7	103	98	96	101	90	100	82	94

A five-foot high incline in center field, with the word Lookouts written in huge white concrete letters (see photo at left), is the only incline in ballpark history with sharp sides rather than gradual slopes. It can be major hazard for a center fielder tracking a long fly ball.

Engel Stadium, courtesy of the Chattanooga Lookouts.

196

COOPER STADIUM
HOME OF THE COLUMBUS CLIPPERS

Which is the biggest city in Ohio? You may say Cleveland, Cincinnati, or maybe even Toledo, but you'd be wrong -- it is Columbus. That shows how having or not having a major league team can affect a city's image. For those who remain skeptical, here are the population figures: Columbus, 632,945; Cleveland, 505,616; Cincinnati, 364,114; Toledo, 332,943, and Akron, 223,019.

There was a time when Columbus was a major league city. The first team was the American Association Columbus Senators in 1883 and 1884. The next team was the American Association Columbus Solons, which played in the city from 1889 to 1891. Both of those teams played at Recreation Park. The next team to call Columbus home was the Negro National League Columbus Bluebirds in 1933. The Negro National League reformed in 1933 after it was dissolved because of the Great Depression and the death of Negro League founding father Rube Foster. The Bluebirds dissolved as a team after a miserable first half of the season. The Negro national League Columbus Elite Giants

League:	International League
Level:	Triple-A
Surface:	Grass
Affiliation:	New York Yankees
Affiliation Since:	1979
Location:	1155 West Mound St. Columbus, OH 43223
Phone:	614-462-5250
Email:	colclippers@earthlink.com
Website:	www.clippersbaseball.com
Altitude:	780 feet
LF:	355 feet
CF:	400 feet
RF:	330 feet
Capacity:	15,000
Park Opened In:	1977

called the city home in 1935. The team owner, Tom Wilson, moved his team from Nashville, where it originated in 1921, to Columbus for the 1935 season. The next year he moved his team to Washington, D.C., before finally settling in Baltimore in 1938. The years that followed were the glory years of the Elite Giants and the Negro Leagues. The team was dissolved after the 1951 season. (Please see p.28 for more on the Elite Giants.)

Cooper Stadium -- with artificial turf -- is depicted at the left. In 1999, the turf will be replaced with natural grass. With turf, there have been days when Cooper Stadium has been hotter than a car in the sun with its windows up.

Cooper Stadium, courtesy of the Columbus Clippers.

COHEN STADIUM
HOME OF EL PASO DIABLOS

The year was 1974, and Jim Paul had just purchased stock in a struggling baseball franchise that had drawn a mere 63,000 fans for the entire 1973 season. He changed the team's name from "Sun Kings" to "Diablos," lowered ticket prices, brought wacky acts and promotions to Dudley Field, and started putting people in the seats. The rest as, they say, is baseball history.

For the past 24 years, the Diablos have built a reputation throughout the world of professional sports as a leader in innovative promotion and marketing. That tradition continues today, as the franchise annually strives to eclipse the 300,000 mark in attendance. That barrier has been surpassed in four of the last five seasons.

Jim Paul and El Paso Diablos have won numerous awards for their ingenuity. They have been featured in *Sports Illustrated* and were on the April 1991 cover of *National Geographic*. The Diablos have won the MacPhail Trophy twice and were named the Double-A Organization of the Decade following the 1989 season. The Diablos played at Dudley Field until the middle of the 1990 season. On June 13, 1990, they moved to their present location, Cohen Stadium. The stadium is named after two brothers, Syd and Andy Cohen, who were key figures in El Paso's professional baseball past. The Diablos won the Texas League Championship in 1978, 1986 and 1994.

Another of Jim Paul's creations that has become synonymous with El Paso is El Paso Seminar, an annual event in which minor league staffs meet to exchange ideas with one another. This writer personally attended the 1996 and 1997 seminars and gathered information from other teams on different promotions and activities. This seminar is a vital way for the minor league clubs to see how their peers are doing from across the nation. The exchange of ideas makes this a very successful and productive weekend. Every year the seminar ends with a terrific barbecue dinner at Cohen Stadium. Although Jim Paul

League:	Texas League
Level:	Double-A
Surface:	Grass
Affiliation:	Milwaukee Brewers
Affiliated since:	1981
Location:	9700 Gateway North Blvd. El Paso, TX 79924
Phone:	915-755-2000
Email:	tickets@diablos.com
Altitude:	3695 feet
LF:	340 feet
CF:	410 feet
RF:	340 feet
Capacity:	9,765
Park Opened In:	1990

sold the team, he in turn sold El Paso Seminar to the National Association, the governing body of the affiliated minor league teams. The 1998 seminar will take place in Las Vegas in conjunction with the Triple-A World Series.

Park Factors								
Year	Avg	AB	R	H	2B	3B	HR	SO
1996-7	112	104	118	116	134	201	63	96

Photo: Roger Quiñones, April 1991

JERRY UHT PARK (1998)
HOME OF THE ERIE SEAWOLVES

Opened in 1995, Jerry Uht Park welcomed the SeaWolves as Erie's newest minor league baseball team. The franchise was welcomed with open arms, as evidenced by the New York-Penn League attendance record it established in its inaugural season.

The team went on to break its own attendance record the following two seasons, including a 1997 campaign that drew over 196,000 fans into "The Uht" for its 38 openings. In addition to its seasonal attendance mark, the team also set a single-game attendance record by stuffing over 7,300 fans into the park. The SeaWolves' 1997 per-game average of 5,136 is also a New York-Penn League all-time best.

The team tallied the best regular season record of any incarnation of Erie minor league baseball with a count of 50-26 in 1997. The record allowed them to coast into their first Stedler Division Championship.

Jose Guillen's rapid ascent to the big leagues began in spectacular fashion as a member of the Erie SeaWolves. It was the home opener of the 1995 season and the very first game played at Jerry Uht Park when the SeaWolves found themselves tied with the Jamestown Jammers in the bottom of the

League:	New York - Penn League
Level:	Short-Season Class-A
Surface:	Grass
Affiliation:	Pittsburgh Pirates
Affiliation Since:	1995
Location:	110 East 10th St. Erie, PA 16501
Phone:	814-456-1300
Email:	seawolve@erie.net
Website:	www.seawolves.com
Altitude:	685 feet
LF:	312 feet
CF:	400 feet
RF:	328 feet
Capacity:	6,000
Park Opened In:	1995

Park Factors

Year	AB	Avg	R	H	2B	3B	HR	SO
1995-7	104	103	113	107	120	81	121	92

ninth. Guillen stepped up to the plate and crushed the first pitch off of the Civic Center, which looms over the leftfield wall, to win the game.

The rampant success of the SeaWolves in Erie has enabled the city to be awarded a Double-A expansion franchise beginning with the 1999 season as a member of the Eastern League.

Jerry Uht Park, courtesy of Art Becker Photography.

199

VICTORY FIELD
HOME OF THE INDIANAPOLIS INDIANS

Not many things can overshadow basketball in the Hoosier State, but Victory Field is one of them. One of the most beautiful stadiums in the country, Victory Field is located in downtown Indianapolis, within walking distance of the RCA Dome. Victory Field opened on July 11, 1996, when -- ironically -- the Indians lost to the Oklahoma City 89ers. The loss, however, did not take away from the atmosphere, which was energetic to say the least. The park's predecessor, Bush Stadium (see Page 86), which was built in 1931, was a hard act to follow. There were a lot of great memories throughout its 65 years, but the $18 million Victory Field is well on its way to creating its own unforgettable legacy. But let's not forget about some of the players that made Bush Stadium a fun place to watch a game: Roger Maris (1956), Harmon Killebrew (1958), Moises Alou (1990) and "The Big Unit," Randy Johnson (1988-9) all got their start at Bush Stadium, just to name a few.

Most people who have been to Victory Field have only good things to say about it. Reggie Miller of the Indiana Pacers said, "It is awesome. Victory Field is a major league facility

League:	International League
Level:	Triple-A
Surface:	Grass
Affiliation:	Cincinnati Reds
Affiliation Since:	1993
Location:	501 West Maryland St.
	Indianapolis, IN 46225
Phone:	317-269-3542
Email:	indians@indyindians.com
Website:	www.indyindians.com
Altitude:	710 feet
LF:	320 feet
CF:	402 feet
RF:	320 feet
Capacity:	15,500
Park Opened In:	1996

Park Factors

Year	AB	Avg	R	H	2B	3B	HR	SO
1997	96	100	93	96	110	92	105	104

with a hometown feeling. The next time I go back, I want to sit on the grass in the outfield." The grassy area behind the outfield is a perfect place to lay back, relax and catch the game. Fans can bring all the food and drink they want, except alcohol (the line had to be drawn somewhere). If you sit behind home plate and look out past the outfield walls you can see the Indianapolis skyline -- a great view. Victory Field brings you as close to a major league-caliber park as you can get without actually being in one.

Victory Field is setting the standard for minor league parks. Photo courtesy of the Indianapolis Indians.

SEC TAYLOR STADIUM
HOME OF THE IOWA CUBS

It all began 51 years ago, in 1947 when the park was called Pioneer Park. In 1959, it was renamed Sec Taylor Stadium to honor former *Des Moines Register* and *Chicago Tribune* sports editor Garner W. "Sec" Taylor. The stadium that you see now was constructed in 1992, while the planning stages began in August 1988. This $12 million rebuilding of Sec Taylor began with the

League:	Pacific Coast League
Level:	Triple-A
Surface:	Grass
Affiliation:	Chicago Cubs
Affiliated since:	1981
Location:	350 SW 1st St. Des Moines, IA 50309
Phone:	515-243-6111
Website:	www.iowacubs.com
Altitude:	803 feet
LF:	335 feet
CF:	400 feet
RF:	335 feet
Capacity:	10,800
Park Opened In:	1992

Sec Taylor Stadium, courtesy of the Iowa Cubs.

demolition of the old stadium on September 10, 1991, and three months later on December 1, 1991 the first walls of the new and improved Sec went up. After three years, another new addition was added to the Sec.

In 1995 both clubhouses were remodeled to include new offices for the manager and the coaches, laundry and storage facilities, an expanded training room, an indoor batting cage, a new weight room and a family waiting lounge. The family lounge is a great idea, since it gives the players' wives, children and friends a place to wait after the game while the players shower and change. In addition to those improvements, 12 new skyboxes were added. The cost of the expansion was $2 million.

The 11,000-seat stadium features 44 skyboxes, expanded concession and restroom facilities, a picnic area and a mezzanine level. During the 1998 season Sec Taylor saw its three millionth fan walk through the gates. Sec Taylor Stadium has contributed to many of the awards that the Iowa Cubs have been able to claim. In 1992 the Cubs received the Bob Freitas Award as the top Triple-A organization in the country. Also in 1992, the Iowa Tourism Council named it the top tourist attraction in the state. In 1996, *Baseball America* ranked Sec Taylor Stadium the sixth-best minor-league ballpark in the country.

While attending a weekend series at the Sec, this writer sat all over the stadium, from the dining area in left field

to the box seats to the clubhouse, and I will say that Sec Taylor Stadium is one of the nicest parks that I have seen a game at. A good percentage of the fans I spoke with were either Chicago Cubs fans that made the trip to see Kerry Wood pitch or were Cubs fans that attended Drake University, located in Des Moines.

As Lee Eisner, an Alumnus of Drake University, told me, "As a lifetime, die-hard Cubs fan, going to school in the city of Des Moines, made it ideal to head over to Sec to see the Cubs of the future."

Sec Taylor Stadium, courtesy of the Iowa Cubs.

Park Factors								
Year	Avg	AB	R	H	2B	3B	HR	SO
1994-7	97	99	95	96	110	92	105	104

OLDSMOBILE PARK
HOME OF THE LANSING LUGNUTS

One of the most successful franchises, in terms of both fan support and merchandising, has been the Lansing Lugnuts. This team was formed when President and Managing Partner Tom Dickson bought the Waterloo, Iowa team in 1993 and moved it to Springfield, Illinois. The team then changed names from the Waterloo Diamonds to the Sultans of Springfield. The club played in Illinois for the 1994 and 1995 seasons while the ownership group was planning the franchise's next move to Lansing, Michigan.

This move, which is expected to be the franchise's last for quite some time, took place before the 1996 season, and the timing couldn't have been better. Lansing was the first Class-A team to sell 500,000 tickets for their opening season. When Oldsmobile Park opened in 1996 and the final attendance was calculated, the Lugnuts actually drew 538,326

League:	Midwest League						
Level:	Class-A						
Surface:	Grass						
Affiliation:	Kansas City Royals						
Affiliation Since:	1996						
Location:	505 East Michigan Ave.						
	Lansing, MI 48912						
Phone:	517-485-4500						
Email:	lugnuts@tcimet.net						
Website:	www.lansinglugnuts.com						
Altitude:	830 feet						
LF:	305 feet						
CF:	412 feet						
RF:	305 feet						
Capacity:	11,000						
Park Opened In:	1996						

Oldsmobile Park, courtesy of the Lansing Lugnuts.

enthusiastic fans while proudly displaying one of the nation's top logos. Which brings us to their next accomplishment: in 1997, the Lugnuts ranked No.1 in the minor leagues in merchandising sales. They have also been in the top 10 for merchandising each year of their existence. After their very successful inaugural season, the Lugnuts drew over 500,00 (523,443) for the second straight season in 1997 -- another top 10 record for the Lugnuts. In fact, their attendance ranked in the top 10 for *all* minor league teams. To make this accomplishment even more impressive, Lansing was one of only two teams below the Triple-A level to make the top 10. It only took Lansing until August 15, 1997 -- an amazing 135 games -- to have their one millionth fan walk through the gate.

As this writer personally witnessed, the fan's support during the 1997 Midwest League All-Star game was overwhelming. An open seat was virtually impossible to find, and in the general admission section, the grass wasn't even visible. The entire weekend was exciting. This new franchise has the support of the entire city in everything it does. From the name of the stadium -- Oldsmobile Park -- to the Nuthouse, a local bar & grill across the street, wherever you look in Lansing, Michigan, all you see now are nuts.

As they say in the state capital "Go Nuts!"

Park Factors								
Year	AB	Avg	R	H	2B	3B	HR	SO
1996-7	104	100	112	104	113	137	106	90

Oldsmobile Park, courtesy of the Lansing Lugnuts.

C.O. BROWN STADIUM
HOME OF THE MICHIGAN BATTLE CATS

The Michigan Battle Cats have had a hard time finding a home. First, the team moved from Springfield, Illinois, to Madison, Wisconsin for the 1994 season because the stadium in Illinois had deteriorated below the required league standards. In Madison, the team was known as the Hatters. The same story was repeated in Madison: the field wasn't good enough, so the team had to move again. This time the team moved to Battle Creek, Michigan. Seeing how successful the West Michigan Whitecaps had been in Grand Rapids (see pp. 213-214), the team decided to try the region as well.

The original name of the franchise was the Golden Kazoos. It was used to try and attract fans from Kalamazoo, an area that they thought was untapped by the West Michigan Whitecaps. But there were some legal problems dealing with the usage of the nickname, so the ownership renamed the team the Michigan Battle Cats. The Battle Cats' home, C.O. Brown Stadium, is a decent place to play. Although it is not in the same class as Old Kent Park in Grand Rapids, or on the same planet as Victory Field in Indianapolis, it is an above-average Class-A ballpark.

League:	Midwest League
Level:	Class-A
Surface:	Grass
Affiliation:	Boston Red Sox
Affiliation Since:	1995
Location:	1392 Capital Ave. NE Battle Creek, MI 49017
Phone:	616-660-2287
Altitude:	830 feet
LF:	323 feet
CF:	401 feet
RF:	366 feet
Capacity:	6,600
Park Opened In:	1990

C.O. Brown Stadium, courtesy of the Michigan Battle Cats.

Park Factors								
Year	AB	Avg	R	H	2B	3B	HR	SO
1997	97	101	97	98	97	129	109	90

ZEPHYR FIELD
HOME OF THE NEW ORLEANS ZEPHYRS

1998 was New Orleans' sophomore season at Zephyr Field. It all began on April 11, 1997, and its first year ended on August 25, 1997, after drawing 507,164 fans. This total brought the Zephyrs the honor of the biggest attendance increase in all of the minor leagues.

The stadium seats 10,000 people in the reserved section and another 2,000 fans on "The Levee, " a berm located in the outfield. The berm features a swimming pool and two hot tubs for the fan's enjoyment on the hot days down on the Bayou. The third level of the stands contains 16 VIP suites and two large party suites. An exclusive lounge and other amenities were added for the season ticket holders after the completion of the first season.

This facility is in use year-round. If the Zephyrs aren't playing ball you might catch the Storm Soccer team, the Louisiana Philharmonic Symphony, or a local college team (several use the field for their home games and occasional NCAA Baseball Regionals). An interesting fact about Zephyr Field is that a portion of the revenue that is generated from the events held there is put back into the stadium for possible upgrades. . . or just to keep Zephyr Field looking as great as it does today.

League:	Pacific Coast League
Level:	Triple-A
Surface:	Grass
Affiliation:	Houston Astros
Affiliation Since:	1997
Location:	6000 Airline Dr.
	Metairie, LA 70003
Phone:	504-734-5155
Email:	zephyrs@zephyrsbaseball.com
Website:	www. zephyrsbaseball.com
Altitude:	5 feet
LF:	333 feet
CF:	407 feet
RF:	332 feet
Capacity:	10,000
Park Opened In:	1997

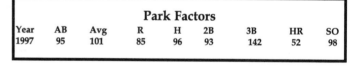

Park Factors								
Year	AB	Avg	R	H	2B	3B	HR	SO
1997	95	101	85	96	93	142	52	98

Zephyr Field, courtesy of the New Orleans Zephyrs.

LINQUIST FIELD
HOME OF THE OGDEN RAPTORS

Ogden, Utah, is about 35 miles north of Salt Lake City. The name "Ogden" may not ring bells in your head, but it had a wealth of meaning more than 100 years ago, and in 2002 its name will be beamed to the world.

Not far from Ogden, the United States became one nation in 1869, when the news of the "Golden Spike," the last spike of the transcontinental railroad, was relayed by telegraph. A simple word, "done," was communicated. The transcontinental railroad had the same impact uniting the East to the West as the Constitution had joining the first 13 states.

In 2002, the Ogden area will again be in the news when it hosts downhill and Super Gs races in the 2002 Salt Lake City Winter Olympics. Ogden balances on the spine of the Rockies. Its Alpine mountains are a perfect location for the Olympics.

These same mountains make Linquist Field a magical place to attend a ballgame. Having the majestic Rockies behind the outfield has the same effect as seeing a skyline: You definitely know which city you're in. You cannot separate Linquist Field from Ogden. The city feels like it is part of the park.

The field of play also has its own individual traits. The actual playing field's shape is somewhat similar to the Washington Senator's old Griffith Stadium. Linquist Field is much smaller than Griffith Stadium, though.

The Ogden Raptors came to town in 1994. This season was one of their most successful: winning the first-half title of the Pioneer League and drawing more than 100,000 fans for the entire season. The nickname "Raptors" is a catchy one, especially because this is dinosaur fossil country. However, it also makes for colorful headlines when you team loses: "Raptors' Playoff Hopes Extinct," the *Standard-Examiner* said when the home team was swept out of the playoffs in September of 1998.

League:	Pioneer League
Level:	Rookie Advanced Classification
Surface:	Grass
Affiliation:	Milwaukee Brewers
Affiliation Since:	1996
Location:	2330 Lincoln Ave.
	Ogden, UT 84401
Phone:	801-393-2400
Email:	homerun@OgdenRaptors.com
Website:	www.ogden-raptors.com
Altitude:	4295 feet
LF:	335 feet
CF:	399 feet
RF:	335 feet
Capacity:	4,800
Park Opened In:	1997

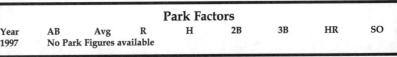

Park Factors								
Year	AB	Avg	R	H	2B	3B	HR	SO
1997	No Park Figures available							

Linquist Field, courtesy of the Ogden Raptors.

JOHNNY ROSENBLATT STADIUM
HOME OF THE OMAHA ROYALS (1998) & THE OMAHA GOLDEN SPIKES (1999)

New logo for 1999

Park Factors								
Year	AB	Avg	R	H	2B	3B	HR	SO
1994-7	107	102	114	108	97	78	148	84

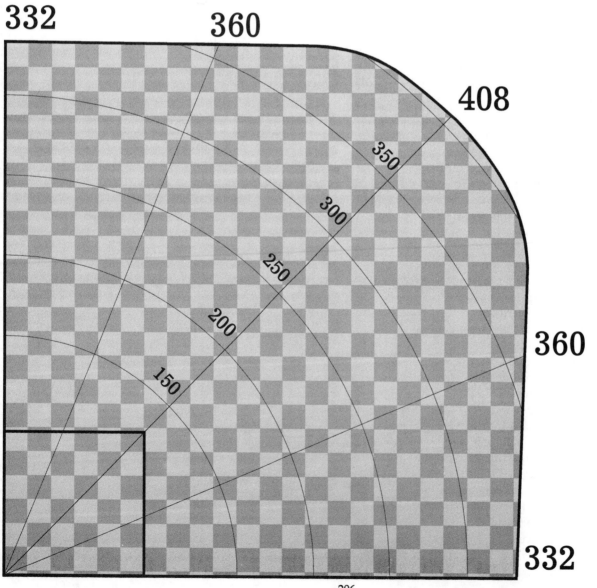

Minor league baseball first called Municipal Stadium home in 1949, as the Class A Omaha Cardinals began play in April of that year. Then in 1955, the parent club St. Louis Cardinals moved their top farm club to Omaha as the American Association's Triple-A Omaha Cardinals. The Cardinals left Omaha in 1959. For the next two years Omaha was baseballless. Then, due to a significant effort by local baseball fans -- led by former Omaha mayor Johnny Rosenblatt -- baseball returned to Omaha in the spring of 1961 with the Triple-A Omaha Dodgers. The Dodgers kept the team in Omaha for two seasons. On June 28, 1964, the stadium was renamed Johnny Rosenblatt Stadium in recognition of the mayor's efforts to bring back professional baseball to Omaha.

Omaha and Rosenblatt Stadium were again without a professional team until major league expansion created a new franchise in Kansas City, Missouri. The Kansas City Royals then hooked up with Omaha to form the Triple-A Omaha Royals in 1969. The two have now been connected for 30 consecutive seasons. Now in its 50th year, historic Rosenblatt Stadium begins its 30th season as the "home of the Omaha Royals." Over the past seven years, the City of Omaha has invested over $20 million dollars to make Rosenblatt the pride of Omaha -- and to ensure that it will continue to be the home of the College World Series, which it has hosted since 1950. Improvements have included new pavement and bleacher seating, a new scoreboard, the Stadium View Club restaurant and a state-of-the-art press box, constructed before the 1996 season. Additional

League:	Pacific Coast League
Level:	Triple-A
Surface:	Grass
Affiliation:	Kansas City Royals
Affiliation Since:	1969
Location:	Rosenblatt Stadium
	1202 Bert Murphy Dr.
	Omaha, NE 68103
Phone:	402-734-2550
Email:	mmashanic@earthlink.net
Website:	www.omaharoyals.com
Website (1999):	www.goldenspikes.com
Altitude:	1040 feet
LF:	332 feet
CF:	408 feet
RF:	332 feet
Capacity:	22,000
Park Opened In:	1948

Creighton University, University of Nebraska-Omaha and Nebraska-Lincoln collegiate baseball games. Rosenblatt Stadium was also the home of the former Omaha Dodgers and Cardinals professional baseball franchises.

construction completed the past two years includes a new batting cage, an auxiliary scoreboard, restroom renovations and new player clubhouses. These additions have made Omaha's Rosenblatt Stadium one of the foremost playing facilities in all of baseball.

Rosenblatt Stadium also has hosted numerous high school, college and professional football games, concerts, wrestling, boxing, and

Johnny Rosenblatt Stadium, courtesy of the Omaha Royals.

McCoy Stadium
Home of the Pawtucket Red Sox

It ended on July 23, 1981. Sixty-five days, 22 hours and 16 minutes after the Pawtucket Red Sox originally took the field for their contest with the Rochester Red Wings, Dave Koza dumped a single into left field with the bases loaded to score Marty Barrett and end the longest professional baseball game of all time. Pawtucket defeated Rochester 3-2 in 33 innings, and history had been made before the 19 diehard fans who remained at McCoy Stadium for all 33 frames. The Baseball Hall of Fame has immortalized the event with a display entitled, simply, "The Game."

Built in 1942, McCoy has been home to the PawSox since 1970. The team has been a Triple-A affiliate of the Boston Red Sox since it joined the International League in 1973. It is a no-frills concrete and steel structure shaped like a comma, with a grandstand that extends just past the first- and third-base bags. Unlike its big league counterpart up the expressway in Boston, with the triangle in center and the Green Monster in left, McCoy is a basic symmetrical park with a distance of 325 feet down each line and 380 feet to center. With only 7,000 seats, McCoy is currently the second-smallest Triple-A park in the country, but nevertheless more than five million fans have attended games there. A stadium renovation project will expand the capacity to 10,000 for Opening Day of 1999. One of the more interesting traditions at McCoy is "fishing" for autographs. Unlike most parks, the playing field is not level with the first row of seats, but rather 10 feet below. The dugouts are directly underneath the stands. To get autographs, kids must stand at the railing and lower balls, gloves, programs and pens over the side using string and cut-off milk containers. Then they wait for a "bite" from the players below. Fishing expeditions over the years could have netted autographs from future Red Sox stars such as Fred Lynn, Jim Rice, Roger Clemens and Nomar Garciaparra.

Over the years, McCoy has been home to some top offensive talents beyond those named above. At least in recent years, this is borne out by the fact that Pawtucket has either been at or near the top of the International League in total hits, home runs and runs scored at home. Its park indexes are quite revealing. According to data collected by Howe Sportsdata International, the PawSox have hit 783 home runs at McCoy between 1994-97 versus 473 on the road. The

League:	International League
Level:	Triple-A
Surface:	Grass
Affiliation:	Boston Red Sox
Affiliation Since:	1973
Location:	One Columbus Ave.
	Pawtucket, RI 02860
Phone:	401-724-7300
Email:	pawsox@worldnet.att.net
Website:	www.pawsox.com
Altitude:	73 feet
LF:	325 feet
CF:	380 feet
RF:	325 feet
Capacity:	7,002
Park Opened In:	1942

index of 166, when coupled with the fact that the team scores 10 percent more runs at home, indicates a real home-field offensive advantage for the PawSox. The downside: with all the hacking they've been doing at McCoy, the team is second only to the Toledo Mud Hens in strikeouts at home between 1994-97 with 3,732. Improved lighting has made the park much more hitter-friendly over the last 20 years than it had been previously.

Park Factors								
Year	AB	Avg	R	H	2B	3B	HR	SO
1994-7	103	100	110	102	10	30	166	101

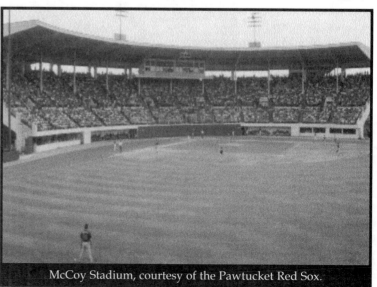

McCoy Stadium, courtesy of the Pawtucket Red Sox.

HADLOCK FIELD
HOME OF THE PORTLAND SEA DOGS

Back in 1949, the Portland Pilots won the New England League championship. Then the league folded. That sad occurence cost the city of Portland both a team and the national pastime in one fell swoop. Baseball flirted with the state briefly again in 1984 when The Ballpark in Old Orchard Beach was home to the Triple-A Maine Guides (1984-86) and Maine Phillies (1987-88), affiliates of the Cleveland Indians and Philadelphia Phillies, respectively. After a 45-year hiatus, professional baseball returned to the city of Portland in 1994 with the debut of the Double-A Sea Dogs, an affiliate of the then second-year Florida Marlins.

The crown jewel of what has been quite a love affair between the city and their ballclub, Hadlock Field has a definite old-time feel with a basic red brick and steel

exterior and a natural grass field. It is very much a neighborhood park -- a replica of Portland mascot Slugger the Sea Dog greets fans entering the park; a ball fouled straight back over the roof is likely to go bounding onto adjacent Park Avenue if a fan doesn't grab it first. To give the park a bit of a New England feel, a small lighthouse rises from behind the center field wall whenever a Sea Dog hits a home run. As far as the playing area is concerned, Hadlock is essentially a symmetrical ballpark, although the right field fence drops back ever so slightly in the corner. Further complicating matters for lefthanded hitters is the fact that the right side of the park is effectively wide open, allowing winds to blow in across the field from right to left. This is due to the fact that the grandstand portion of Hadlock extends only to the Sea Dogs' on-deck circle on the first-base side; a small section of box seats behind the dugout is the only other seating on this side of the park. Although the right side of the field features a large warehouse (a la Camden Yards) and a picnic area which abuts the field, the foul territory in right is slightly larger due to the absence of seating.

While it was at one time the haven of current major league pitcher and '97 World Series hero Livan Hernandez, it is the offensive numbers put up by the home team at Hadlock Field that are of particular interest. In 286 home games between 1994-97 Portland hit .271 as a team, eight points higher than its road average. As a consequence the Sea Dogs have scored 17 percent more runs at home over the last four years, which has helped translate into a home record of 161-125 (.563) during this peri-

League:	Eastern League
Level:	Double-A
Surface:	Grass
Affiliation:	Florida Marlins
Affiliated Since:	1994
Location:	271 Park Ave.
	Portland, ME 04102
Phone:	207-874-9300
Website:	portlandseadogs.com
Altitude:	25 feet
LF:	315 feet
CF:	400 feet
RF:	330 feet
Capacity:	6,860
Park Opened In:	1994

od. This home-field advantage for the Sea Dogs is bolstered by the fact that Portland also has been quite successful on the road, with an overall mark of 147-133 over the same four-year span.

Fans have been coming out to the ballpark in Portland in droves, with over 1.5 million in attendance at Hadlock through the 1997 season. Even those who can't make it to Hadlock Field are jumping on the Sea Dogs bandwagon, as the Sea Dogs logo has become one of the most popular in all of minor league baseball. The marriage of the Portland Sea Dogs and Hadlock Field is indeed a minor league success story, and one that should continue for some time to come.

Park Factors								
Year	AB	Avg	R	H	2B	3B	HR	SO
1994-7	103	103	117	106	108	125	151	109

Hadlock Field, courtesy of the Portland Sea Dogs.

THE EPICENTER
HOME OF THE RANCHO CUCAMONGA QUAKES

The Quakes may seem to be a fairly new operation, playing ball since 1993, but the franchise has been around for over 28 years. It started when a group of investors from Lodi, California got together $2,500 (pocket change compared to today's costs) and decided to start a new franchise in Lodi to begin play in 1966. They were known as the Lodi Crushers, and this eventually became the first "Quakes" team. Throughout California League history, franchises have frequently moved from city to city. However, during the 19 years that Lodi had a team, it was always the Quakes' franchise. The franchise was sold to a group of investors headed by current Quakes'

shareholder Roy Englebrecht and actor Mark Harmon. The current Quakes' majority owner Hank Stickney also became involved and purchased a large portion of the team. Stickney and his group of investors moved the team to San Bernardino in 1987 and stayed there, at 3,500-seat Fiscalini Field, through the 1992 season. When the city of Rancho Cucamonga told Stickney of its intention to build a brand-new, state-of-the-art ballpark to be ready for play in 1993, it was an offer he could not pass up. Fans were asked to select a name for the new team and on September 30, 1992, it was announced that six people had suggested the name "Quakes," which was chosen by the teams' management as the winner from over 200 different choices. The first game at the Epicenter was on April 8, 1993 and ended in a 7-3 victory over the High Desert Mavericks. Demand for tickets was so high that on May 22, 442 temporary bleacher seats were added (221 in left field and 221 in right field). On July 15, 1993, the Quakes broke the California League attendance record of 218,444, previously held by the Mavericks. The Quakes ended the season with a California League attendance record of 331,005. This was better than any Double-A team in the country and ranked fourth among Class-A teams. After the 1993 season the Quakes installed additional

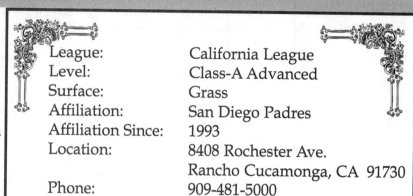

League:	California League
Level:	Class-A Advanced
Surface:	Grass
Affiliation:	San Diego Padres
Affiliation Since:	1993
Location:	8408 Rochester Ave.
	Rancho Cucamonga, CA 91730
Phone:	909-481-5000
Email:	rcquakes@aol.com
Website:	www.rcquakes.com
Altitude:	850 feet
LF:	330 feet
CF:	400 feet
RF:	330 feet
Capacity:	6,631
Park Opened In:	1993

seats in the outfield area, bringing Epicenter capacity to over 6,000. After the championship season of 1994, Quakes' attendance boomed in 1995. Total attendance was 446,146, easily the largest figure in California League history. Incredibly, the Quakes played to 97-percent capacity in 1995, with only 12,000 seats going unsold over 70 home games. In '96, the Quakes topped the league in attendance for the fourth straight season, attracting 410,214 visitors. For their five years of success, the Quakes were named by *Baseball America* magazine as the Class-A winner of the prestigious Bob Freitas award for franchise excellence.

Park Factors								
Year	AB	Avg	R	H	2B	3B	HR	SO
1994-7	100	101	99	101	95	120	95	97

Photos courtesy of the Rancho Cucamonga Quakes.

THE DIAMOND
HOME OF THE RICHMOND BRAVES

Every team may play on a diamond, but the Richmond Braves play at *The Diamond*. The Diamond has served as the home of the Braves since Opening Day, April 17, 1985. It replaced Parker Field on the same site after seven months of construction and expenditures of $8 million. Although the speed of construction was impressive, it was actually the cooperation of the cities of Richmond, Chesterfield and Henrico that was the most unique aspect of the construction process. The three cities pitched in a combined total of $4 million. Another $4 million was raised by the public and private sectors.

The Diamond's capacity includes regular seat-

League:	International League
Level:	Triple-A
Surface:	Grass
Affiliation:	Atlanta Braves
Affiliation Since:	1966
Location:	3001 North Boulevard Richmond, VA 23230
Phone:	804-359-4444
Email:	rbraves@bznet.com
Website:	www.rbraves.com
Altitude:	160 feet
LF:	330 feet
CF:	402 feet
RF:	330 feet
Capacity:	12,150
Park Opened In:	1985

The Diamond, courtesy of the Richmond Braves.

Park Factors								
Year	AB	Avg	R	H	2B	3B	HR	SO
1994-7	101	99	91	100	90	80	71	97

ing and luxury box seats, 11,978 and 156 respectively. In addition, The Diamond also has another 150 seats available in its restaurant. Located on the first-base side, the restaurant has a glass wall that provides an excellent view of the action.

During the 1997 season, the Richmond Braves added "Diamond Vision," which is a 77-foot high scoreboard and video screen. Another nice amenity for the fans in the concession lines or the people walking around the concourse are the monitors that allow everyone to follow the action on the field. The Braves achieved a milestone in 1997 as the six-millionth fan walked through The Diamond's gates.

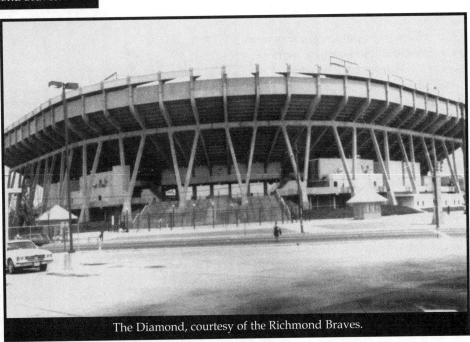

The Diamond, courtesy of the Richmond Braves.

FRONTIER FIELD
HOME OF THE ROCHESTER RED WINGS

Frontier Field is yet another new minor league stadium in the current construction boom we're experiencing. Just like many of the other new minor league stadiums, Frontier Field is minor only in name. The entrance is decorated like a shopping mall. I don't mean this in a bad way. On the contrary, minor league stadiums used to be treated like slum apartment buildings, but not anymore. Frontier Field shows that the minor league teams are proud of their homes. The money spent on decorations prove that management is treating minor league baseball like any business should be treated. Just like movie theaters had to appear more glamorous after the movie rental industry took off, minor league baseball is packaging itself better and is thriving at a time when cable T.V. brings plenty of baseball to homes across America.

Frontier Field invites you to watch a game. Its entrance is lined up with beautiful street lamps. Its concourse Walk of Fame is a beautiful celebration of bricks and iron. The bricks are for sale, of course. For $100 you can have your name engraved on a brick and placed near Rochester sports celebrities who didn't buy their way into the Walk of Fame. They have 25,000 bricks for sale! That's a revenue source my local mall is missing.

The premium box seats are a great place to watch a ballgame. However, the next section above them is as far as what I can normally afford at a major league stadium. The cheapest seat in the house is $5.00.

Being just one level away from the majors, the Rochester Redwings play solid, entertaining baseball. They usually have a few former major leaguer trying to make it back to the show. Unlike the lower minor league levels, you may recognize the names of some of the players. Among the 1998 Redwings players who had made it to the Show before were Steve Ontiveros, Ricky Otero, Bobby Muñoz, Jim Converse, Richie Lewis and Terry Burrows. None of these guys are future Hall-of-Famers, but they know how to play baseball. Bobby Muñoz and Richie Lewis played well enough to be recalled to the Baltimore Orioles.

League:	International League
Level:	Triple-A
Surface:	Grass
Affiliation:	Baltimore Orioles
Affiliation Since:	1961
Location:	One Morrie Silver Way
	Rochester, NY 14608
Phone:	716-454-1001
Email:	redwings@frontiernet.net
Website:	www.redwingsbaseball.com
Altitude:	515 feet
LF:	335 feet
CF:	402 feet
RF:	325 feet
Capacity:	10,868
Park Opened In:	1997

Park Factors								
Year	AB	Avg	R	H	2B	3B	HR	SO
1997	101	98	104	99	108	95	101	109

Frontier Field, courtesy of the Rochester Red Wings.

MUNICIPAL STADIUM
HOME OF THE SAN JOSE GIANTS

Baseball has a very storied history in the city of San Jose, California. As early as 1874, organized baseball was played in San Jose, and since the opening of Municipal Stadium in 1942, baseball has been a mainstay of the city, as minor league affiliates from nine different major league clubs have sent their finest prospects through "Muni." Past affiliations from 1942 to the present include the following teams: the Boston Red Sox, Pittsburgh Pirates, Los Angeles/California Angels, Kansas City Royals, Cleveland Indians, Seattle Mariners, Montreal Expos, Baltimore Orioles, and finally, the San Francisco Giants.

In 1940, the San Jose City Council unanimously approved plans to build a 2,900 seat baseball stadium at the corner of Alma Avenue and Senter road. The council hoped to bring a minor league team to San Jose and also induce a major league club to use Municipal Stadium as its spring training site.

Built as part of Franklin Roosevelt's Works Progress Administration (WPA), Municipal Stadium was erected for a total cost of $80,000 in 1942. The completion of the ballpark was delayed by one year due in large part to World War II and heavy rains and winds which drenched the South Bay area for 50 of 71 days at one point. By Opening Day 1942, the stadium was ready for play, except for the field that was to be used as a parking lot, which was covered with a grain crop that was not yet ready for harvest.

On March 8, 1942, San Jose Municipal Stadium seated 2,036 fans on Opening Day as the San Francisco Seals defeated the Portland Beavers 15-8. It marked the first time in over a decade that baseball teams of a Double-A caliber played within the city limits.

Since its erection, Municipal Stadium has received a few improvements. One of the biggest is Turkey Mike's Barbecue, located down the third-base line. With over 70 picnic tables and field seating, Turkey Mike's is a fan favorite for families, birthday parties and group outings. In addition to the availability of restaurant-style food, the Municipal Stadium "down-home" atmosphere is enhanced by murals painted around the entire stadium, portraying a timeline of baseball in San Jose and picturing every former San Jose alumnus to make it to the major leagues.

In 1988, the San Francisco Giants came to San Jose with their Class A affiliate, and the San Jose Giants were born. Over the last nine seasons the San

League:	California League
Level:	Class-A Advanced
Surface:	Grass
Affiliation:	San Francisco Giants
Affiliation Since:	1988
Location:	588 East Alma Ave. San Jose, CA 95112
Phone:	408-297-1435
Email:	sjgiants@ix.netcom.com
Website:	www.sjgiants.com
Altitude:	90 feet
LF:	320 feet
CF:	400 feet
RF:	320 feet
Capacity:	4,200
Park Opened In:	1942

Jose Giants have been literally the best team in minor league baseball. Since the team's conception nine years ago, 46 of their players have made it to "The Show" and the San Jose Giants rank first in winning percentage out of all the 116 full-season minor league teams, with a .588 mark. Of those 116 minor league teams, San Jose is the only team to post winning records in each of the last nine years.

Park Factors								
Year	AB	Avg	R	H	2B	3B	HR	SO
1996-7	90	97	75	87	85	111	45	111

Municipal Stadium, courtesy of Bernard Andre and the San Jose Giants.

LACKAWANNA COUNTY STADIUM
HOME OF THE SCRANTON/WILKES-BARRE RED BARONS

Lackawana County Stadium was built in the late '80s, an awkward time for stadium construction. The ballpark is symmetrical, and its dimensions are identical to Philadelphia Phillies' Veterans Stadium: 330 down the lines, 371 to the power alleys and 408 to dead center (Page 141). The dimensions were chosen to get future Phillies players used to them, and to better assess how they would perform at the Vet. However, these days the last thing minor league teams are doing is imitating the cookie-cutter stadiums. The stadium cost $22 million to build. If that stadium had been built today with the same money, Lackawana County would have a different stadium.

However, not everything is bad. After all, Lackawana County Stadium is in one of the prettiest areas of Pennsylvania. I remember the first time I ever saw the Scranton/Wilkes-Barre area. I was a college student doing an epic road trip to get to know the nation. I drove from Tucson, Arizona, to Boston, and stopped at every possible town. On my way back, I came up to Scranton/Wilkes-Barre. It was a late-December night. Dry, cold snow was beginning to blow on the road. After a highway turn in the hills, I saw a town that was the a perfect image for a holiday card. There were lights on the foothills. The area was Christmas white, and there were decorations everywhere. And out of all things, there was a statue of Casimir Pulaski.

The memory of the beautiful Scranton (and Wilkes-Barre, too) was so burned into my memory that years later I forced my wife to take a road trip back to the city. We were coming from Baltimore. We passed York, Harrisburg. We got into an argument because she wanted to go to HERSHEYPARK instead of Scranton (built by the same Chocolate magnate Milton Hershey). When we kept on driving to Scranton, my wife put a curse on me. Two days later, I was supposed to be in Buffalo's Pilot Field, but instead had to go for minor back procedure--the first of a string of six surgeries to come. Someday I'll take my wife to HERSHEYPARK, *"The Sweetest Place on Earth."* Then we'll drive three more hours and catch a Red Barons game.

League:	International League
Level:	Triple-A
Surface:	Turf
Affiliation:	Philadelphia Phillies
Affiliation Since:	1989
Location:	235 Montage Mountain Rd. Moosic, PA 18507
Phone:	717-963-6556
Email:	barons@epix.net
Website:	www.redbarons.com
Altitude:	640 feet
LF:	330 feet
CF:	408 feet
RF:	330 feet
Capacity:	10,982
Park Opened In:	1989

Park Factors

Year	AB	Avg	R	H	2B	3B	HR	SO
1994-7	101	100	102	101	112	183	77	96

Lacawanna County Stadium, courtesy of the Scranton/Wilkes-Barre Red Barons.

Ned Skeldon Stadium is one of the oldest minor league stadiums. In the recent construction explosion, it is a surprise it is still standing. The park is symmetrical, following the mold in which major league stadiums were being built in the 1960s. Very little effort was made to beautify the stadium when it was built. Actually, it wasn't even meant to be a baseball stadium. It was intended for horseracing. The stadium has too many obstructed seats. There is too much foul territory down the lines, keeping fans away from the action. It doesn't even have enough bathrooms.

It was a sad day in Mudhenville on May 7, 1998, when a 0.25-cent sales tax proposal was defeated. The tax would have funded a new, beautiful $68-million, lakefront stadium. When the fans in the stands of Ned Skeldon heard the news, they didn't even make the letters when the "YMCA" was played. The vote was 59.3 percent against to 40.7 percent in favor. With the recent construction boom, the Tigers may take their affiliation away from Toledo if the Mudhens don't get a new park. Considering the team is owned by the citizens of Lucas County, the locals should have passed the tax. Normally, I am against taxpayers subsidizing wealthy team owners, but in this case, the taxpayers own the team, and the ballpark is a disgrace for a Triple-A team.

Toledo, being one of the largest cities in Ohio, does have a major league history, but we have to go far in baseball history to find it. In 1884, the American Association Blue Stockings made their home at Toledo's League Park. The AA Black Pirates called Toledo home in 1890, playing at Speranza Park. The Detroit Tigers, the Mudhens parent club, played a regulation major league game in Toledo back in 1903. The Negro League Toledo Tigers and Toledo Crawfords played at Swayne Field, whose capacity was on the same level as Ned Skeldon's.

League:	International League
Level:	Triple-A
Surface:	Grass
Affiliation:	Detroit Tigers
Affiliation Since:	1987
Location:	2901 Key St.
	Maumee, OH 43537
Phone:	419-893-9483
Email:	mudhens@mudhens.com
Website:	www.mudhens.com
Altitude:	585 feet
LF:	325 feet
CF:	410 feet
RF:	325 feet
Capacity:	10,025
Park Opened In:	1965

Park Factors								
Year	AB	Avg	R	H	2B	3B	HR	SO
1994-7	97	98	96	95	87	78	124	103

Ned Skelton Stadium, courtesy of the Toledo Mud Hens.

215

OLD KENT PARK
HOME OF THE WEST MICHIGAN WHITECAPS

I remember the first time I walked up to Old Kent Park. I could not believe how beautiful it was. I remember thinking, "This is a Class-A park? What is going on?" Then it hit me. There's a remarkable boom of minor league stadium construction that is going unnoticed in the Major League Baseball world, of which Old Kent is a perfect example.

What makes Old Kent remarkable is not how many people it holds. It's capacity is only 10,900. Many minor league parks were built with huge capacities at times when people thought that bigger was better. Not Old Kent. They did a lot of things right when they built this stadium.

The first accomplishment is that Old Kent fits well with its surroundings. Grand Rapids is a very green city. Everywhere you look there are plants, hills and water. Old Kent has a little of all this. There is plenty of grass that slopes up to the entrance of the stadium. As you walk up to buy your ticket, the grass surrounds you. The green roof on the stadium matches the greenery around it. And what color matches green the best? Well, many homes in Michigan, especially in central and northern Michigan match green with white. And Old Kent does the same. Old Kent is not trying to be a slick cosmopolitan stadium. It knows what it is and it does a great job being what it is. Old Kent just looks like Michigan.

Another great attribute is that the moment you walk in, you're on top of the action. You can be hit by a foul ball as you're making your way through the turnstile. And once you take a seat, it makes you wonder if it might be better to watch a minor league game from this close up, or try to follow major league action from a distant seat.

League:	Midwest League
Level:	Class-A
Surface:	Grass
Affiliation:	Detroit Tigers
Affiliation Since:	1997
Location:	Old Kent Park
	4500 West River Dr.
	Comstock Park, MI 49321
Phone:	616-784-4131
Email:	white-cap@gr.cns.net
Website:	www.whitecaps-baseball.com
Altitude:	610 feet
LF:	327 feet
CF:	402 feet
RF:	327 feet
Capacity:	10,900
Park Opened In:	1994

Not all the seats are close to the action, though. The bleachers in right-center might as well be in Siberia. They could hold about a thousand people; about 30 brave souls sit there when the grandstand sells out More people might sit there if more home runs were hit into the bleachers, but the park has major league dimensions, and the Class-A kids have a hard time reaching those seats. Most still need a few more years to get strong enough to reach

Old Kent Park, courtesy of Aerial Impact Photography.

Old Kent Park, courtesy of Aerial Impact Photography.

Park Factors								
Year	AB	Avg	R	H	2B	3B	HR	SO
1994-7	91	98	85	89	89	69	60	100

No minor atmosphere is complete without the Chicken Dance. Grand Rapids does the Chicken with the best of them. Photo by Oscar Palacios.

those seats on a regular basis.

Along the left and right field lines are two grassy areas where families can sit with their kids and relax. The kids can run around without the adults having to worry that they are disturbing others.

Something scary did happen on the right field line area one day I was at Old Kent. There was a woman holding a newborn when a hard foul ball headed toward her. She didn't have time to get up, so she half turned away from the ball, but she didn't have time to turn and cover the baby completely. You could see the baby's bald, pink head completely exposed as the foul ball was screaming in that direction.

Fortunately, the ball sliced and hit in the grass, a mere five feet away. The moment the ball landed she wanted to get out of the stadium as fast as she could. She was crying uncontrollably. Her husband wanted no part of leaving, however. He consoled her for about 15 minutes, and they stayed for a few more innings. There's no moral to the story, except this: When you're close to the action, watch out.

The fences are a problem; they are symmetrical

Fun between innings.

Ballpark employee trying to make fans go buy food by eating a barbecued turkey leg in front of them. The author was not tempted. Photo by Oscar Palacios.

and boring. Oh, well. Not everything can be perfect. It would add so much more to the stadium if the fences were more challenging to outfielders.

Every inch of the fence is covered with ads, which is quite common for minor league parks. Why not? I read them all during pitching changes.

Old Kent is not near the downtown area of Grand Rapids, but Grand Rapids is not defined by its downtown (they are working on that with an impressive museum lineup, though). The stadium doesn't lose anything by not having a skyline fully visible beyond the outfield walls. What is visible beyond the outfield fences is trees. And what else could better represent Grand Rapids?

Between innings, Old Kent has the usual entertainment gimmicks: a battle of the mascots, contests for the fans, the Chicken Dance (they do a good one in Old Kent) and races. They also had a kid walking around eating a turkey leg to make the fans hungry, and two other kids in white tuxedos picking up garbage.

All in all, what Old Kent boils down to is that it is a very nice stadium with the typical minor league atmosphere that one would be disappointed not to find. Considering the night life in Grand Rapids, Old Kent is a must visit if you're in town searching for entertainment. Grand Rapids is among the leaders in attendance year in and year out, and Old Kent is the reason why. After spending rainy nights in stadiums in Rockford and other midwestern cities, I would rank Old Kent as one of the best Class-A parks.

Behind the left field foul line is a grassy area where people can bring blankets, sit down, and let their kids lose without worrying that they may bother other people. Many minor league stadiums feature these grassy areas. Photo by Oscar Palacios.

217

JUDY JOHNSON FIELD AT DANIEL S. FRAWLEY STADIUM
HOME OF THE WILMINGTON BLUE ROCKS

There are too many names in the stadium's title, so let's try to figure this out. First of all, it's not William Frawley Stadium or Fred Mertz Stadium. Daniel S. Frawley had nothing to do with "I Love Lucy."

The name Judy Johnson should be more familiar to baseball fans. Judy Johnson was elected to the Hall of Fame in 1974 after a fine career as a third baseman in the Negro Leagues. Johnson was one of the best Negro League players.

As a youngster, Johnson played football and baseball in Wilmington, Delaware. His father wanted to make him a boxer, but Johnson preferred baseball. He dropped out of high school and worked in Deep Water Point, New Jersey, loading docks. In 1918, he joined the first semipro team. In 1921, he joined the team of his destiny, the Hilldale Daisies, and played with them until 1929. Johnson played for the Homestead Grays in 1930. He returned to the Daisies for the 1931 and 1932 seasons. Johnson then joined the Pittsburgh Crawfords from 1932 to 1936 before returning to the Grays in 1937, his last playing season.

During his prime, not only did Johnson flash outstanding leather, but he hit .390 or higher in three seasons with the Daisies. He was a thin man, barely weighing 150 pounds, so he didn't have much power. As a manager, he broke Josh Gibson into the starting lineup.

Johnson returned to Wilmington after his retirement to run a small business, but came back to baseball as a scout for the Philadelphia Athletics, the Philadelphia Phillies and the Milwaukee Braves. Judy Johnson was elected into the National Baseball Hall of Fame in 1974.

Wilmington made a great move in naming their stadium after one of the greatest players in baseball history. The Blue Rocks have enjoyed a good run the last few years. Their General Manager, Chris Kemple, was recently named the Carolina League Executive of the Year--the second time he has received this award since 1993. It was a busy year for Kemple. His team won the league championship, Judy Johnson Field hosted the league's All-star Game, and the Blue Rocks led the league in attendance, drawing 320,540 fans in 1998.

League: Carolina League
Level: Class-A Advanced
Surface: Grass
Affiliation: Kansas City Royals
Affiliation Since: 1993
Location: 801 South Madison St. Wilmington, DE 19801
Phone: 302-888-2015
Email: info@bluerocks.com
Website: www.bluerocks.com
Altitude: 135 feet
LF: 325 feet
CF: 400 feet
RF: 325 feet
Capacity: 5,911
Park Opened In: 1993

Park Factors

Year	AB	Avg	R	H	2B	3B	HR	SO
1994-7	96	98	88	95	90	122	47	102

Judy Johnson Field at Daniel S. Frawley Stadium, courtesy of the Wilmington Blue Rocks.

THE MINOR LEAGUES

International League (AAA)
Buffalo Bisons
Charlotte Knights
Columbus Clippers
Durham Bulls
Indianapolis Indians
Louisville Redbirds
Norfolk Tides
Ottawa Lynx
Pawtucket Red Sox
Richmond Braves
Rochester Red Wings
Scranton/Wilkes-Barre Red Barons
Syracuse Skychiefs
Toledo Mud Hens

Pacific Coast League (AAA)
Albuquerque Dukes
Calgary Cannons
Colorado Springs Sky Sox
Edmonton Trappers
Fresno Grizzlies
Iowa Cubs
Las Vegas Stars
Memphis Redbirds
Nashville Sounds
New Orleans Zephyrs
Oklahoma City Redhawks
Omaha Royals
Salt Lake Buzz
Tacoma Rainiers
Tucson Sidewinders
Vancouver Canadians

Eastern League (AA)
Akron Aeros
Altoona (expansion team 1999)
Binghamton Mets
Bowie Baysox
Erie (expansion team 1999)
Harrisburg Senators
New Britain Rock Cats
New Haven Ravens
Norwich Navigators
Portland Sea Dogs
Reading Phillies
Trenton Thunder

Southern League (AA)
Birmingham Barons
Carolina Mudcats
Chattanooga Lookouts
Greenville Braves
Huntsville Stars
Jacksonville Suns
Knoxville Smokies
Mobile Baybears
Orlando Rays
West Jackson Diamond Jaxx

Texas League (AA)
Arkansas Travelers
El Paso Diablos
Jackson Generals
Midland Angels
San Antonio Missions
Shreveport Captains
Tulsa Drillers
Wichita Wranglers

California League (Advanced A)
Bakersfield Blaze
High Desert Mavericks
Lake Elsinore Storm
Lancaster Jethawks
Modesto A's
Rancho Cucamonga Quakes
San Bernardino Stampede
San Jose Giants
Stockton Ports
Visalia Oaks

Carolina League (Advanced A)
Danville 97's
Frederick Keys
Kinston Indians
Lynchberg Hillcats
Prince William Cannons
Salem Avalanche
Wilmington Blue Rocks
Winston-Salem Warthogs

Florida State League (Advanced A)

Brevard County Manatees
Charlotte Rangers
Clearwater Phillies
Daytona Cubs
Dunedin Blue Jays
Fort Myers Miracle
Jupiter Hammerheads
Kissimmee Cobras
Lakeland Tigers
St. Lucie Mets
St. Petersburg Devil Rays
Sarasota Red Sox
Tampa Yankees
Vero Beach Dodgers

New York - Penn League (Short-Season A)

Auburn Doubledays
Batavia Muckdogs
Erie SeaWolves
Hudson Valley Renegades
Jamestown Jammers
Lowell Spinners
New Jersey Cardinals
Oneonta Yankees
Pitsfield Mets
St. Catharines Stompers
Utica Blue Sox
Vermont Expos
Watertown Indians
Williamsport Cubs

Midwest League (A)

Beloit Snappers
Burlington Bees
Cedar Rapids Kernals
Clinton Lumberkings
Fort Wayne Wizards
Kane County Cougars
Lansing Lugnuts
Michigan Battle Cats
Peoria Chiefs
Quad City River Bandits
Rockford Cubbies
South Bend Silver Hawks
West Michigan Whitecaps
Wisconsin Timber Rattlers

Northwest League (Short-Season A)

Boise Hawks
Eugene Emeralds
Everett Aquasox
Portland Rockies
Salem-Keizer Volcanoes
Southern Oregon Timberjacks
Spokane Indians
Yakima Bears

Appalachian League (Advanced Rookie)

Bluefield Orioles
Bristol Sox
Burlington Indians
Danville Braves
Elizabethton Twins
Johnson City Cardinals
Kingsport Mets
Martinsville Phillies
Princeton Devil Rays
Pulaski Rangers

South Atlantic League League (A)

Ashville Tourists
Augusta Greenjackets
Cape Fear Crocs
Capital City Bombers
Charleston, S.C. Riverdogs
Charleston, W.V. Alley Cats
Columbus Redstixx
Delmarva Shorebirds
Greensboro Bats
Hagerstown Suns
Hickory Crawdads
Macon Braves
Piedmont Boll Weevils
Savannah Sand Gnats

Pioneer League (Advanced Rookie)

Billings Mustangs
Butte Copper Kings
Great Falls Dodgers
Helena Brewers
Idaho Falls Braves
Lethbridge Black Diamonds
Medicine Hat Blue Jays
Ogden Raptors

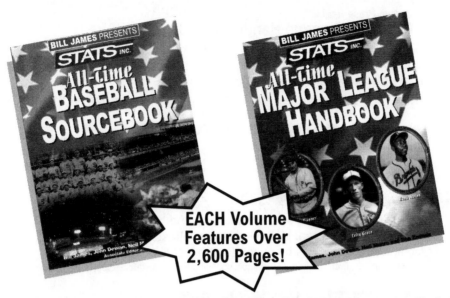

MEET THE WINNING LINEUP...

Bill James Presents:
STATS Major League Handbook 1999
- Bill James' and STATS' exclusive 1999 player projections
- Career data for every 1998 Major League Baseball player
- Leader boards, fielding stats and stadium data

"This book is better than your own personal statistician!" Rod Beaton, *Baseball Weekly*

Item #HB99, $19.95, Available NOW!

STATS Player Profiles 1999
- Exclusive 1998 breakdowns for pitchers and hitters, over 30 in all:
  lefty/righty, home/road, clutch situations, ahead/behind in the count, month-by-month, etc.
- Complete breakdowns by player for the last five seasons

"A must-have resource packed with unique statistics." Tom Verducci, *Sports Illustrated*

Item #PP99, $19.95, Available NOW!

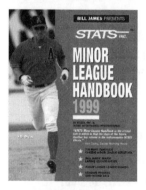

Bill James Presents:
STATS Minor League Handbook 1999
- Year-by-year career statistical data for AA and AAA players
- Bill James' exclusive Major League Equivalencies
- Complete 1998 Class-A and rookie statistics

"The place to check for info on up and coming players." Bill Koenig, *Baseball Weekly*

Item #MH99, $19.95, Available NOW!

Bill James Presents:
STATS Batter Versus Pitcher Match-Ups! 1999
- Career stats for pitchers vs. batters (5+ AB)
- Leader boards and stats for all 1998 major league players
- Batter and pitcher performances for each major league ballpark

"No other book delivers as much info that's so easy to use." Peter Gammons, ESPN

Item #BP99, $24.95, Available February!
Available only through STATS—not found in bookstores!

Order from  today!

SPORTS TEAM ANALYSIS & TRACKING SYSTEMS

Order form in Back of This Book

1-800-63-STATS   847-676-3383   www.stats.com

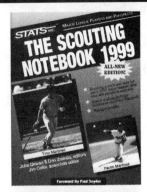
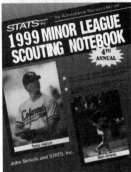
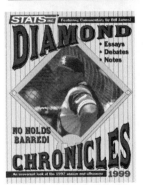

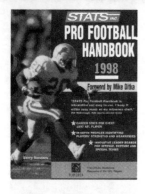

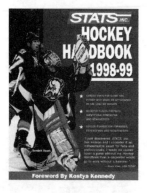 

STATS, Inc. Order Form

Name _____

Address _____

City _____ State _____ Zip _____

Phone _____ Fax _____ E-mail Address _____

Method of Payment (U.S. Funds Only):

☐ Check ☐ Money Order ☐ Visa ☐ MasterCard ☐ Discover ☐ AMEX

Credit Card Information:

Cardholder Name _____

Credit Card Number _____ Exp. Date _____

Signature _____

BOOKS (STATS Publications include free first class shipping)			
Qty.	Product Name	Item Number	Price	Total
	STATS Major League Handbook 1999	HB99	$19.95	
	STATS Major League Handbook 1999 (Comb-bound)	HC99	$24.95	
	*STATS Projections Update 1999	PJUP	$9.95	
	STATS ALL-TIME Major League Handbook	ATHA	$79.95	
	STATS ALL-TIME Baseball Sourcebook	ATSA	$79.95	
	STATS ALL-TIME Combo (BOTH ALL-TIMERS)	ATCA	$149.95	
	The Scouting Notebook 1999	SN99	$19.95	
	The Scouting Notebook 1999 (Comb-bound)	SC99	$24.95	
	STATS Minor League Scouting Notebook 1999	MN99	$19.95	
	STATS Minor League Handbook 1999	MH99	$19.95	
	STATS Minor League Handbook 1999 (Comb-bound)	MC99	$24.95	
	STATS Player Profiles 1999	PP99	$19.95	
	STATS Player Profiles 1999 (Comb-bound)	PC99	$24.95	
	STATS 1999 Batter Vs. Pitcher Match-Ups!	BP99	$24.95	
	Ballpark Sourcebook Diamond Diagrams	BSDD	$24.95	
	STATS Diamond Chronicles	CH99	$19.95	
	STATS Baseball Scoreboard 1999	SB99	$19.95	
	Pro Football Revealed: The 100 Yard War (1998 Edition)	PF98	$19.95	
	Pro Football Handbook 1998	FH98	$19.95	
	Pro Football Handbook 1998 (Comb-bound)	FC98	$21.95	
	STATS Pro Basketball Handbook 1998-1999	BH99	$19.95	
	STATS Hockey Handbook 1998-1999	HH99	$19.95	
	*STATS Fantasy Insider: 1998 Pro Football Edition	IF98	$5.95	
	Prior Editions (Please circle appropriate year)			
	STATS Major League Handbook '91 '92 '93 '94 '95 '96 '97 '98		$9.95	
	The Scouting Notebook/Report '94 '95 '96 '97 '98		$9.95	
	STATS Player Profiles '93 '94 '95 '96 '97 '98		$9.95	
	STATS Minor League Handbook '92 '93 '94 '95 '96 '97 '98		$9.95	
	STATS Minor League Scouting Notebook '95 '96 '97 '98		$9.95	
	STATS Batter Vs. Pitcher Match-Ups! '94 '95 '96 '97 '98		$9.95	
	STATS Diamond Chronicles '97 '98		$9.95	
	STATS Baseball Scoreboard '92 '93 '94 '95 '96 '97 '98		$9.95	
	Pro Football Revealed: The 100 Yard War '94 '95 '96 '97		$9.95	
	STATS Pro Football Handbook '95 '96 '97		$9.95	
	STATS Pro Basketball Handbook '93-94 '94-95 '95-96 '96-97 '97-98		$9.95	
	STATS Hockey Handbook '96-'97 '97-'98		$9.95	
	* Denotes Magazine			

Order from  today!

SPORTS TEAM ANALYSIS & TRACKING SYSTEMS

Order form in Back of This Book

1-800-63-STATS   847-676-3383   www.stats.com

FANTASY GAMES

Qty.	Product Name	Item Number	Price	Total
	Bill James Classic Baseball	BJCB	$129.00	
	STATS Fantasy Football	SFF	$49.00	
	Bill James Fantasy Baseball	BJFB	$89.00	

1st Fantasy Team Name (ex. Colt 45's):_____

    What Fantasy Game is this team for?_____

2nd Fantasy Team Name (ex. Colt 45's):_____

    What Fantasy Game is this team for?_____

    Note: $1.00/player is charged for all roster moves and transactions.

For Bill James Fantasy Baseball:

Would you like to play in a league drafted by Bill James?   ☐ Yes   ☐ No

---

STATSfax and e-STATS Services (*be SURE to include fax or e-mail address on form)

Game	Format (circle one)	Price/Service (circle one)	Total
Bill James Classic Baseball	Fax / e-mail	$5/week $20/month $60/season *all Classic Game services: 5 days/week*	
Bill James Fantasy Baseball	Fax / e-mail	$5/5 days a week $7/7 days a week $20/month (5 days) $25/month (7 days) $100/season (5 days) $125/season (7 days)	
STATS Fantasy Hoops	Fax / e-mail	$5/5 days a week $7/7 days a week $20/month (5 days) $25/month (7 days) $100/season (5 days) $125/season (7 days)	
STATS Fantasy Football	Fax / e-mail	$15/month $60/season *both: 3 days/week*	

For faster service, call:

1-800-63-STATS or
847-676-3383

or fax this form to STATS:

847-676-0821

STATS, Inc.
8131 Monticello Avenue
Skokie, IL 60076-3300

FANTASY GAMES	Price	Total
Product Total (excl. Fantasy Games)		
Canada—all orders—add:	$3.50/book	
Magazines—add: $2.00 S&H	$2.00/book	
Order 2 or more books—subtract:	$1.00/book	
IL residents add 8.5% sales tax		
Subtotal		
Fantasy Games Total		
STATSfax and 2-STATS Service Total		
(NO other discounts apply) **GRAND TOTAL**		

* orders subject to availability

All books include free 1st class shipping!
Thanks for ordering from STATS, Inc.

Order from  today!

SPORTS TEAM ANALYSIS & TRACKING SYSTEMS

Order form in Back of This Book

1-800-63-STATS   847-676-3383   www.stats.com